THE TEACHING OF MODERN LANGUAGES

A volume of studies deriving from the International Seminar organized by the Secretariat of Unesco at Nuwara Eliya, Ceylon, in August 1953.

GREENWOOD PRESS, PUBLISHERS
NEW YORK

Unesco has a deep regard for the diversity of languages, which are among the most subtle and the most individual instruments for the expression of genius.... Unesco has set itself to promote familiarity with the most widely spoken languages, so that larger sections of the world's population may communicate with one another. In so doing, the Organization is striving to make it easier for all the peoples to acquaint themselves with the world's civilization as a whole, while at the same time safeguarding and indeed developing the essential individuality of each one of them.

Luther H. Evans

(From the message of the Director-General of Unesco read at the opening session of the Ceylon seminar on 3 August 1953)

Copyright © UNESCO 1955

This reprint has been authorized by UNESCO

First Greenwood Reprinting 1969

Library of Congress Catalogue Card Number 73-88959

SBN 8371-2326-7

PRINTED IN UNITED STATES OF AMERICA

PREFACE

In August 1953 an International Seminar was held at Nuwara Eliya, in Ceylon, on 'The Contribution of the Teaching of Modern Languages towards Education for Living in a World Community'. Over a period of four weeks, participants from 18 countries not only discussed the relationship between modern language teaching and international understanding in general but also came to grips with a great many of the purely pedagogical aspects of the problem of the most effective teaching of languages of wide communication. It was the consensus that unless teachers of modern languages and educational authorities are constantly aware of the progress made and the experience gained in other parts of the world, the broader ultimate goal will remain largely unattainable.

To continue the work begun at Nuwara Eliya, the Unesco Secretariat undertook certain specific tasks. Among these was the publication of two companion studies, the present one and a bibliography on modern language teaching.

The present volume follows closely, in outline and in substance, the plan of the Ceylon seminar. The first six chapters correspond to the six general topics discussed at that seminar; the last six develop ancillary themes which the participants at the seminar considered to be of special importance. In each chapter a brief preliminary section introduces the topic, summarizes the views expressed at the seminar and presents selected documents. These documents were chosen from working-papers prepared for the seminar, from preparatory studies made by Unesco National Commissions in certain countries, and from communications made to the seminar by national delegations or individual participants. The volume includes also a few papers specially written after the seminar by participants or by members of the Unesco Secretariat.

The volume has been edited jointly by the Secretariat of Unesco and by Professor Theodore Andersson, of Yale University, who served as director of the Ceylon seminar.

It is hoped that the material here presented will be found helpful to those concerned with curriculum development as well as to educational administrators and practising teachers.

CONTENTS

INTRODUCTION. The Ceylon Seminar 11

CHAPTER I. The Humanistic Aspect of the Teaching of Modern Languages 16

    The Seminar Report 19
    The Basic Educational Assumptions, by the Committee on Language in the College (United States) 20
    Modern Languages and the Training of the Mind, by Emmanuel Handrich (France) 21

CHAPTER II. The Teaching of Modern Languages as a Key to the Understanding of Other Civilizations and Peoples . 29

    The Seminar Report 32
    The Study of the Civilization of Foreign Countries in Modern Language Classes in France, by Henri Kerst (France). . 33
    The Cultural Aim, by Fr. Closset (Belgium) 36

CHAPTER III. The Methodology of Language Teaching . 46

    The Seminar Report 49
    Teaching Spanish in Mexico to Students from the United States, by Elena Picazo de Murray (Mexico) . . . 51
    Teaching English as a Foreign Language, by P. Gurrey (United Kingdom) 61
    An Outline of General Principles as Applied to the Teaching of English as a Second Language (Report of an *ad hoc* Committee of the Ceylon Seminar) 78

CHAPTER IV. Audio-Visual Aids 82

    The Seminar Report 84
    A Report on Audio-Visual Aids, by Paul Féraud (France) . 87

CHAPTER V. The Psychological Aspects of Language Teaching 96

    The Seminar Report 98
    Psychological Pitfalls found in Classical Western Methods of
       Language Teaching, by Manich Jumsai (Thailand) . . 101
    Adolescents and Modern Languages, by Fr. Closset (Belgium) 106
    Tests and Examinations, by P. Gurrey (United Kingdom) . 110
    Tests and Measurements in Foreign Language Teaching, by
       W. D. Wall (Unesco). 116

CHAPTER VI. The Training of Modern Language Teachers 124

    The Seminar Report 125
    Notes on the Training of Language Teachers in Turkey, by
       E. V. Gatenby (United Kingdom) 128
    The Aims in Teacher Training, by Fr. Closset (Belgium) . 130
    Training Modern Language Teachers for Secondary Schools
       in Western Germany, by Elisabeth Winkelmann (German
       Federal Republic) 136

CHAPTER VII. Textbooks 150

    The Seminar Report 151
    Local Factors in Vocabulary Selection, by P. Gurrey (United
       Kingdom) 154
    English Textbooks and Teachers' Manuals for Thailand, by
       Manich Jumsai (Thailand) 157

CHAPTER VIII. The Teaching of Modern Languages by Radio and Television. 160

    Exporting a Language, by the English-by-Radio Department
       of the British Broadcasting Corporation (United Kingdom) 162
    Importing a Language, by the Swedish National Commission
       for Unesco (Sweden) 174

CHAPTER IX. Modern Language Teaching in Primary Schools 181

    Teaching Modern Languages to Young Children in the United
       States, by Theodore Andersson (United States) . . . 182

Chapter X. Special Aids to International Understanding   196

   International School Correspondence and the Teaching of
      Modern Languages, by Paul Barrier (France) . . . 199
   The Linking of Schools, by E. Audra (France) 209
   Foreign Language Assistants and the Teaching of Modern
      Languages, by E. Audra (France) 216

Chapter XI. Teaching Modern Languages to Adult
Migrants 226

   Israel, by the Israel National Commission for Unesco (Israel) 230
   Australia, by the Migrant Education Section of the Commonwealth Office of Education (Australia) 242
   Canada, by Watson Kirkconnell (Canada) 262

Chapter XII. Special Problems of Language . . . 267

   The Jigsaw Pattern of the World's Languages, by Felix Walter
      (Unesco) 267
   The Language Problem in Ceylon, by D. A. Wijayasingha
      (Ceylon) 273
   The Teaching of Arabic in Pakistan, by Serajul Haque
      (Pakistan) 275
   Teaching Spanish to Mexican Indians through the Vernacular,
      by Angélica Castro de la Fuente (Mexico) 281
   The Language Problem in the Trust Territory of Somaliland
      under Italian Administration, by Emilio Baglioni (Italy) . 287

Appendix. Members of the Seminar 294

INTRODUCTION
THE CEYLON SEMINAR[1]

The opinion is widely held that knowledge of a language is merely one of many possible roads leading to the understanding of a people. The social sciences, especially, are cited as giving direct access to international understanding. What more obvious way can there be of getting acquainted with a people than to study its history, its institutions, the political, social and economic forces in its contemporary society? There are many who consider that one can understand a people's essential personality through its art, its music, its literature—and they see no harm in reading the latter in translation.

To the modern-language teacher, however, a language seems the indispensable key to the understanding of a people. The person who has learned to be at ease in a second language—to feel at home with another people—takes for granted the role of language as an essential means of communication and understanding. The person who, on the other hand, has never lifted 'the language curtain'[2] behind which other people move and talk and think and feel in a way which is peculiar to them, may not even suspect that there *is* a way of living which is distinct from his own, let alone understand it. But there was no disposition on the part of the participants in Ceylon to call the language teacher's view into question. In addition to exploring, as they did quite thoroughly, ways and means of encouraging their students to deepen their understanding of other peoples and other cultures, the participants were perhaps also aware of their responsibility to those of their compatriots who might require explanations, and particularly examples, which would illuminate the relationship between knowledge of a language and improved understanding of the people speaking that language.

1. This introduction was written by Professor Theodore Andersson, co-editor of this volume and director of the Ceylon seminar.
2. Title of a challenging address delivered by William R. Parker, Executive Secretary of the Modern Language Association of America, at the Commencement Exercises for the Summer Language Schools at Middlebury College, Middlebury, Vermont, 11 August 1953, and published in *School and Society*, vol. LXXVIII, no. 2019 (31 October 1953), p. 129-33, New York.

In a book[1] which should do much to bridge the gulf separating those who speak a foreign language and those who do not, William R. Parker examines the place of foreign languages in the United States in a period of international tension. Recognizing that 'knowledge of a foreign language, whether slight or extensive, brings no automatic or certain sympathy with the people speaking that language', Professor Parker contends that 'foreign language study *speeds* and *increases* understanding when the desire to understand is there—speeds and increases sympathy when the germ is present'. He states further that 'foreign language study may, and often does (although there can be no guarantee), *create* the desire to understand, the germ of sympathy. It may, and often does, prevent *mis*-understanding. Given good will, foreign language study makes possible that ready and more nearly perfect communication between peoples upon which mutual understanding depends. Given indifference, foreign language study makes possible, through better communication, the discovery of good will.'

How can language teachers, without losing sight of the humanistic values in the traditional teaching of modern languages, best prepare their students for living in the world today? The results of the deliberations at Nuwara Eliya show that the first and most obvious answer is: by improving the teaching of language as a medium of communication. This involves a re-examination of such subjects as the psychological basis of language-learning, methods, materials, and the use of various mechanical and electronic aids, dependable ways of evaluating and testing the results of teaching, and, most important of all, the training of qualified teachers.

The shrinking of the world and the tension which characterizes the relations between nations today have given an increased importance to the concept of language as communication. The new emphasis on this aim will be noted many times in the course of the succeeding chapters. Those who favour this shift of values would of course not be willing to grant that communication with contemporaries in various fields is any less humanistic or cultural than is the communication with classical authors. From the very beginning, language teachers have been divided into two camps, which might be called the conservative or traditional or classical, on the one hand, and the progressive or modern, on the other. The seminar participants seemed to be of one mind in agreeing that this quarrel of the ancients and moderns has definitely been won by the latter in that almost no one now contends that the aims of modern-language study should not include the under-

---

1. Entitled *The National Interest and Foreign Languages*, a Discussion Guide and Work Paper for Citizen Consultations initiated by the U.S. National Commission for Unesco, Department of State. Preliminary edition, April 1954. U.S. Government Printing Office, Washington, D.C.

standing and the speaking of a foreign language or languages.

There were only two points on which some difference of opinion was registered. The conservatives were concerned lest the progressives content themselves with teaching mere conversational ability; the latter tried to reassure the former by contending that mastery of language skills is a necessary *beginning* to a humanistic education in the language field. Secondly, though nearly everyone aligned himself with the development which has included such methods as the natural, or direct, or living, or oral and which now in Europe bears the name of the active method and in America the rather confusing term of aural-oral approach, there remains a good deal of divergence of opinion as to what is really meant by these terms and what really constitutes the best practice in this kind of teaching.

The participants in the seminar showed a particular interest in the contribution made by Miss Panandikar in her analysis of the psychological aspects of the language-learning process. The basic concept of language as consisting primarily of speech sounds was not accepted without reservations by all members of the seminar. Nevertheless, in the opinion of most, this point of view fitted in closely with the ideas developed by Miss Panandikar in dealing with the subject of linguistic skills and their learning. It is appropriate in this connexion to mention the basic difference between the imitative and analytical learning of language. As Miss Panandikar suggested, the former proves most successful with younger children, a fact which has led some writers to advocate a much earlier start for language learning. This possibility, with an account of the extensive experimentation now going on in the United States, forms the subject of Chapter IX of this volume.

The subjects of method, materials, techniques and teacher training require no detailed comment here. The following chapters, written by many hands, deal with them all. It will suffice to record the gratification felt by the participants in the seminar over the large areas of agreement. They were unanimous in reaffirming a belief in the teaching of the four skills of hearing, speaking, reading and writing—in that order. All recognized the place of drill—though some would emphasize it more than others—in the acquisition of the basic linguistic skills. There was quite general recognition of the importance of analyzing a language carefully in advance of teaching it and of grading linguistic patterns as to usefulness and difficulty. Recognition was expressed of the important research done in such places as the Institute of Education of the University of London and the English Language Institute of the University of Michigan, where the theory and technique of teaching English as a foreign language are being carefully elaborated. More research still needs to be done in the fields of pedagogy and linguistics, sociology and cultural anthropology, and in the psychology of language learning; and there is a growing need to apply to language teaching the results of work done in these allied fields. Here as everywhere, progress demands the exploration of areas intermediate between two fields and of the possible application in a given field of discoveries made in another. Unesco is, of course, ideally suited to stimulate or sponsor such co-operative research.

In conclusion, how may we evaluate the seminar? All who took part, whether as participants or observers, were aware that the cause of modern-language teaching would be helped by it and that, as a result of it, language teachers would be better equipped to contribute to education for living in a world community. The seminar had been planned long in advance by Unesco. Although in many member nations language teachers are inadequately organized and complete preparation for the seminar could therefore not be made, yet the representatives at the seminar were well qualified and came resolved to contribute to the meeting and to derive from it information, ideas, insights and inspiration. The French delegation was uniquely prepared, for the French National Commission for Unesco had appointed a sub-committee to explore all aspects of language teaching and international understanding and published an admirable brochure on the subject.

One of the benefits derived by those in attendance and in turn by their colleagues at home was a perspective of what is happening in their field. The meeting in Ceylon gathered together 40 outstanding scholars from 18 nations, experienced in the teaching of modern languages and deeply concerned for its future, who were unanimous in condemning any restraints that traditional language teaching may still exert on the teaching of modern languages. They were resolved, instead, to consider language in all its aspects and to accept the challenge to teaching that this broad view implies. The battle of theory may therefore be said to have culminated in a victory for those who stress the active method of teaching the spoken tongue. Does this mean that languages will everywhere be taught with a primary emphasis on listening comprehension and speaking? Alas, we fear not. But as much has been done as can be done on an international level, with the encouragement of Unesco, to clarify this basic point. Now it only remains for language teachers in the various countries to try with a minimum of delay to convert sound theory into resourceful practice.

This meeting of minds in Nuwara Eliya does not mean that language teachers will now cease to re-examine fundamental

INTRODUCTION

matters of theory or discuss questions of method. The debate between the traditionalists and the progressives will go on—happily. The terms of the debate may change, but there will always be those who are impatient to move ahead and try new methods and techniques, and those who are loath to experiment with new points of view or approaches until time has proved beyond a doubt that they are sound.

The Ceylon seminar provided both perspective and stimulation. Participants from countries where there are no modern language teacher associations or where such organizations are inactive are now far more likely to undertake measures leading to the formation or activation of such organizations, and there was a definite need felt by the members of the seminar for an international organization of language teachers. An International Federation of Modern Language Teachers now exists, but its membership is confined to some of the countries of northern, western, and southern Europe. The hope was expressed that Unesco might explore the possibility of an enlargement of this federation or of the creation of a new organization of which this federation would constitute the European regional segment.

The Ceylon seminar may be considered as the culmination of a trend which goes back to the very beginning of language teaching. But the seminar was as much a threshold, a point of departure, as it was a culmination. We have made a mere beginning. Much work, research, experimentation remains to be done in a variety of fields. Unesco, in co-operation with other agencies engaged in this branch of study, can play an extremely useful role in this research. It can sponsor follow-up regional seminars which could continue to explore the subjects opened up in the Ceylon deliberations and could also give special attention to problems of particular urgency in their parts of the world. It can help under-privileged areas or countries which are desirous of undertaking research or education in the language field, and it can perhaps even help to supply basic materials. It can encourage the organization of an international association of foreign language teachers with regional sub-associations. Culmination? Yes. Point of departure? Yes. The Ceylon seminar marks an important turning point, for it recognizes a new orientation in the teaching of modern languages.

CHAPTER I
THE HUMANISTIC ASPECT OF THE TEACHING OF MODERN LANGUAGES

Any full discussion of the place of modern language teaching in the world today should properly begin with an attempt to evaluate aims. This is particularly the case if the link between modern language teaching and international understanding is going to be stressed from the outset, as was the case at the Ceylon seminar.

True, educational aims in the field of modern languages do vary enormously from country to country. In this respect, Western Continental Europe appears to be particularly privileged. A survey of their practices will show that many countries in this area can give pupils in their secondary schools five to seven years of a first foreign language, and often three to five years of a second foreign language. This means that in such countries pupils, at the age of 18 or 19, have generally (but alas! not invariably) acquired a sound practical knowledge of the language or languages they have studied. It means also that teachers can, at least from the third year of language study, concentrate increasingly on those broader aspects of cultural training to which more advanced language study lends itself. Language learning ceases to be merely the acquiring of a useful skill and becomes a part of education in the wider sense of the term.

In many other parts of the world, however, it is not usual to devote so many years to the teaching of one or more of the languages of world communication. This may be due to overriding economic considerations, or to the lack of trained teachers in sufficient numbers, or—and this is particularly true of many countries in south Asia which have recently recovered their independence—there may be a complex multilingual pattern within the nation and so many national and regional languages with legitimate claims to prior consideration that Western modern languages, even those which until recently were used as official languages and as languages of instruction, must now take third or fourth place.

It is to be presumed, however, that even those countries which are going through a painful process of linguistic reorganization —and they are by no means confined to Asia—would like to make the teaching of the world's link languages something more than the mere imparting of a linguistic skill to be used for practical purposes only. It is important that they should teach modern languages as part of a sound, well-integrated educational process and make this discipline serve as a vehicle of understanding as well as of communication. Whether in fact or in intention, then, this humanistic goal is an almost universal one in language teaching.

Whether the term 'humanistic aspect of language teaching', which was used to describe the first of the general topics discussed at the Ceylon seminar, is the aptest that could be found is another question. 'Culture' in its widest sense, or 'liberal education', might have served the purpose as well as humanism. But if the last-named concept is considered in its threefold classical aspect, then the term is perhaps as suitable as any other. According to this definition, humanism concerns itself with the nature of man in general, with the perfection of human nature through culture and, last but by no means least, with the sense of the brotherhood of all mankind, the *societas generis humani* of the ancients. Put in another way, the humanistic aims of modern language teaching concern themselves, or should concern themselves, with the development of self-knowledge, with the development of better knowledge of other men and particularly of their higher potentialities, and with the cultivation of a sense of human solidarity.

The presentation of the subject and the subsequent discussion ranged over a variety of topics; the historical development of the 'modern humanities' considered as an academic discipline; the uses of this discipline to develop the intellect; the development of the personality arising out of the mastery of a new idiom; the broadening of the cultural horizon leading to a more fully developed sense of humanity; the ways and means of emphasizing the humanistic aspect at appropriate stages in a modern language course; the development of physical control through learning to control the organs of speech and of mental control through the exercise of conscious accuracy; and, finally, the pitfalls that lie in wait for the unwary or ill-equipped teacher—general incoherence, platitude, exaggeration.

It was felt that when learning a language the adolescent underwent a species of therapeutic shock whose consequences were, in most cases, culturally beneficial. Asian teachers who took part in this particular discussion suggested, however, that if the new foreign language was extremely unlike the pupil's mother tongue this shock might need attenuating by some postponement of the study of the equally dissimilar culture connected with the new language. There is evidence that some contemporary textbook writers have taken this fact into account and deliberately select their background material in such a way as to tone down cultural differences.

The seminar report, which is the first of the documents reproduced in this chapter, is really little more than a brief statement of belief in the validity and paramount importance of the humanistic goal in language teaching. It also makes two additional points which require some explanation.

The first point that should be stressed, and that the seminar report refers to only obliquely, is that the non-Western boy or girl learning a Western modern language, and seeking to cope with the cultural aspects of that language, moves in an entirely alien cultural continuum. The whole Graeco-Roman-Hebraic-Christian heritage is something that has to be assimilated, at least in part, if the Western modern language is to make any sense culturally. Indeed certain aspects of this Western cultural heritage —the Renaissance for instance—may, because of their almost exclusively secular basis, appear not only strange and difficult to quite advanced Eastern pupils but even distasteful. Similarly, of course, the Western pupil who sets out to learn Arabic or Hindi or Chinese—and in the years immediately ahead increasing numbers will undoubtedly want to master these and other Eastern modern languages—must also make the extra effort to assimilate or at least to comprehend a wholly different world with its own set of cultural patterns and its own classical languages from which these Eastern modern languages are derived or have borrowed more or less extensively.

The other point concerns what may bluntly be called linguistic imperialism. Colonial powers and countries administering protectorates or trust territories traditionally impose their own national language as a language of administration and often as a language of instruction. There are often excellent reasons why this should be done and the benefits that this policy may confer on the colony or territory concerned may be considerable. Particularly if the language thus imposed is a language of wide diffusion, its imposition is likely to bring the colony or territory concerned out into the main stream of human intercourse and to foster contacts with the rest of the world. On the other hand, if this alien tongue is favoured, as it so often is, at the expense of a vernacular which may be every bit as rich and every bit as respectable, such policies are likely to cause resentment in the long run, and when the colony or territory has at length achieved its independence there will remain behind an animus against the former official language. Traces of this animus are discoverable in half a dozen Asian countries today and, for the time being at least, this feeling constitutes an additional obstacle to language learning. That is the problem that the Ceylon seminar had in mind when it adopted the last sentence in the report that follows.

As the report itself is so brief, it is followed by a somewhat more detailed statement taken from a report drawn up in the United States in connexion with the inquiry into the present position of foreign language studies in that country which is being conducted at present on an exhaustive scale by the Modern Language Association of America. Though the report in question deals with language teaching in the American college, it should be remembered that such teaching is, in that country, often initiated only during the last two years of high school, so that its basic assumptions are applicable to the secondary school systems of many other countries. In any case, the value of this document lies in its uncompromising statement of faith.

Lastly this chapter includes a paper by an eminent French teacher of German on one very important facet of the humanistic aspect of language teaching. The sub-committee of the French National Commission for Unesco, which met at regular intervals all through the winter of 1952–53 to prepare in advance the topics that were to be discussed at the Ceylon seminar, received and subsequently published no less than three reports on the humanistic aspect of language teaching. It is characteristic that French language teachers should show such interest in this part of the general problem. As Professor Louis Landré of the Sorbonne, the rapporteur for this general topic, has pointed out,[1] French preoccupation with the cultural aspect of language teaching has been constant and not unfruitful. It is a preoccupation that is fortunately shared by certain other countries, particularly in Continental Europe.

THE SEMINAR REPORT

The seminar discussed as its first main topic the educational aspects of the teaching of modern languages. There was general agreement that this study can and should rank with that of the classical languages, whether of East or West, and with the study of the arts and sciences, as an instrument of education capable of developing the highest cultural qualities: the mastery of the physical organs of speech; the intellectual qualities of mental discipline, receptivity to and critical appreciation of new ideas, and the power of self-expression; the emotional and spiritual potentialities afforded by access to the finest expressions of human experience and aspirations.

---

1. 'The Teaching of Languages and Culture in France', *Revue des langues vivantes*, vol. XIX, no. 2, Brussels.

The seminar was therefore of the opinion that, quite apart from utilitarian considerations, the study of one or more modern languages, in addition to that of the mother tongue, must find a place in any educational system aiming to preserve and develop the highest powers of the human mind and spirit. The seminar felt, however, that if the fullest benefit is to be derived from the learning of a modern language, in consonance with the aims just expressed, the choice of the language or languages to be studied should rest with each individual country.

THE BASIC EDUCATIONAL ASSUMPTIONS[1]

Every student in general education needs to receive training in one or more foreign languages and in the science of language.

Such training is needed because knowledge of and about languages lies close to the foundation of general education. Verbal skill, whether developed in learning a foreign language, or in learning scientifically established facts about one's own language, is an intellectual accomplishment. In studying a foreign language, for example, a student looks at a language objectively for the first time. His own language he has learned from the inside. The new one he has to approach from the outside, going in. This is in itself an experience and an intellectual awakening. Furthermore, seeing the thought, in however small segments, of another people through the language of that people is the beginning of the acquisition of culture in the true sense. There is probably no better way of sensing the spirit of another culture. To the extent that the man of liberal education should have a cosmopolitan outlook, this is an indispensable part of his training. Finally, in studying a foreign language, it is virtually impossible not to encounter situations which call attention to the concept of grammar, to the relationship of language to logic, to the problems of semantics, and to other problems involving the essential nature of language. It is here that the student sees the importance of taking an objective view of all language and of developing skill in the analysis of linguistic constructions.

In such a programme, it should be emphasized, the student achieves a competence in the critical handling of materials. He acquires, in the foreign language he learns, an ability that is important for his cultural improvement and in many cases for his

---

1. These paragraphs form the preamble to the Report of the Committee on Language in the College. Professor Norman A. McQuown of Chicago University, who was a member of the committee in question, represented the United States at the Ceylon seminar and presented this report to the seminar on behalf of the United States National Commission for Unesco.

future professional education. He develops especially in his study of a specific language the valuable habit of reflecting about language in general. This combination should enable the individual to think more accurately, to express himself more effectively, and to succeed better in a society where so many things are determined by the meeting of minds in verbal discourse.

To the extent that language training thus broadly defined contributes to the development of the individual's capacity, it is appropriate to liberal education. It provides him with skill in the use of a symbology which is pervasive throughout human activity —indeed, probably more pervasive than any other that could be named. For these reasons we repeat that the study of languages— of language—is nearer to the foundation than it is to the superstructure of liberal education, and that it cannot be omitted or slighted without serious ill effects upon the structure.

MODERN LANGUAGES AND THE TRAINING OF THE MIND[1]

'Training of the mind' is a wide and abstract notion which, however, very soon leads us back, when we begin to think about it, to the realm of practical action. This idea, and the importance we attribute to it, determines the value of our teaching of modern languages and the general lines we are to follow in that teaching, in full consciousness of the responsibilities we bear. The first necessity, therefore, is to define this idea and to distinguish it from other related ideas. Whether we are concerned with culture, humanism, instruction or education, the training of the mind is clearly a pre-requisite which cannot be neglected in any aspect of the teacher's work. This may give rise to a certain amount of confusion.

The first temptation to be avoided is that of regarding culture and the training of the mind as synonymous, since both aim at achieving that 'humanism'—in the most modern and 'humane' sense of the term—which Mr. Jean Jacob so accurately described, in speaking of Montaigne, when he said that the ultimate aim pursued was 'the acquisition of the capacities and virtues that give man full human stature'.[2] Cicero's *Studia Humaniora* no doubt were directed towards the same end. In a report I submitted to the recent conference of the International Federation of Modern

---

1. This paper is a slightly abridged version of the report presented by Emmanuel Handrich, Professor of German at the Lycée Henri IV and President of the French Modern Language Teachers Association, to the French sub-committee on language teaching and subsequently published by the French National Committee for Unesco in *L'enseignement des langues vivantes et la compréhension internationale*, Paris, 1953.
2. In 'La notion de l'humanisme moderne' published by the French National Commission for Unesco in the general report referred to in note 1 above.

Language Teachers,[1] I attempted to define culture in the following terms: the enrichment of the individuality by everything that the two dimensions of time and space can furnish—in other words, knowledge of the past and a sense of the universe. By which I meant that the 'classical humanities' were *primarily* responsible for handing on the heritage of the past while the *first* task of modern language teaching was to add the treasures of the world's varied civilizations. We may thus distinguish, as was then remarked, a vertical and a horizontal stream of culture. One of my German colleagues, however, pointed out that I had omitted any mention of *Bildung*, of general training. She was quite right; I was not supposed to deal with that topic. But she confirmed for me the fact that, in the eyes of the Germans, as in our own, there can be no confusion between *Kultur* and *Bildung*. While humanism is an ideal, and culture essentially disinterested, the training of the mind, which is the means of achieving culture, is also the means of equipping man for the struggle for life, for his trade or profession for earning his living, experiencing his joys to the full, and for what we might call the art of living.

We must likewise be careful not to confuse this training with the pursuit of scholarship, a more or less openly avowed aim in any form of instruction. I would draw attention in this connexion to the remark made by Mr. Jean Laporte, Professor of Philosophy at the Sorbonne: 'Many teachers make the mistake of proceeding as if a boy or girl should be able, immediately on obtaining the secondary school-leaving certificate, to close his or her books and subsist on what has already been learnt.' The reproach strikes home. For the new examinations which are being devised to take place at the end of secondary education, should we not gradually abandon the idea of discovering how much the pupil has learnt and pay increasing attention to the training of the mind? In view of the extraordinary expansion of the field of knowledge, it is surely our duty to consider the coming generations and the terrible danger threatening them if, in favour of scholarship, we thoughtlessly neglect the training of the mind.

There is one other distinction to be made: the training of the mind is not the same thing as education. It is not a question of ethics. It is not a question of religion. No doubt it contributes to the education and spiritual development of the man or woman; it is certainly the pre-requisite for that development, and it is extremely difficult to draw a line of demarcation between what concerns the intellect and what concerns the soul. Here, however, we intend to confine ourselves to the various aspects of the humble task the teacher has to fulfil.

---

1. Held at Sèvres at Easter 1953.

Having thus assigned ourselves limits, we may distinguish four essential stages in the training of the mind, in which we can then consider the part that the teaching of modern languages may play. These stages, of course, merge into one another and can be less clearly distinguished as successive in time than as levels of capacity in each of the minds to be trained. The first stage must be the *development of an open mind*, initiated by curiosity and itself developing curiosity further; the next, the *perfecting of the mechanism of thought*, that infinitely complex group of faculties popularly known as intelligence; the third, the *enrichment of the sphere of thought*, not indeed by scholarship but by the exercise of the miraculous faculty of memory; and the fourth and last, the *ennobling of the mind*, which links up with moral sense in the widest and most 'humane' acceptance of the term but does not involve a theory of ethics and is not to be confused with any such theory.

1. *The development of an open mind.* In a very interesting article on culture and education published in February 1939 in *Culture*, the review of the independent University of Neuilly, Miss Anne-Marie Guillemin, the well-known student of the classical humanities, speaks of the richness of a mind which nature has endowed with certain qualities. 'The quality of what we call open-mindedness— the necessary condition and very threshold of culture—is (she says) much less common than might be thought.' At the beginning, however, when the mind is in fact being trained, that quality can be acquired; it is the teacher's task to implant and develop it. Open-mindedness implies modesty, says Miss Guillemin : 'A mind too much occupied with its own concerns is closed to the offerings of the outer world and judges everything from its own egotistical standpoint.' After a certain age, it may perhaps be true that this is irremediable but if, through curiosity, a child's mind can be opened—and all children can always be won over by curiosity— what the writer calls the 'paralysis of pride' can soon be overcome.

There are few subjects so calculated to awaken curiosity and open the mind as modern languages. Where Latin is not included in the course, 'the modern languages have the task of showing the pupils something of ways of life which are different from their own'. So said Mr. Louis Landré, in the talk he gave in Brussels on The Teaching of Language and Culture in France. And without wishing for a moment to deny the peculiar virtue of the 'classical humanities', let us recognize that we possess a marvellous means of opening windows on the world, opening eyes, opening minds, I would even go so far as to say, by anticipation, opening hearts. The languages we teach are of the present day, the countries where they are spoken can be visited. Children love things which are of immediate interest and dream of exploration. We can all remember the joys of our first classes, when we saw the eyes of the beginners entrusted to our care light up with the pleasure of discovery and witnessed their pride in esoteric knowledge on the first reading of a newly learnt script such as that of German or Russian or of a passage of English pronounced differently from the way an uninitiated Frenchman might read it—a pride without conceit, however, quickly converted into modesty by the realization of the shortcomings of that first knowledge. And what a wealth of means there are at our disposal!—change of environment, by means of pictures, photographs, and films; change of environment by means of folklore and, above all, by songs, in which children will join with even more enthusiasm than wrong notes (which is saying something!), change of environment by the simple conversations of the first lessons, the first 'Guten Tag!' or the first 'How do you do?'; and finally change of environment through the first direct contacts with other countries—correspondence, exchanges and visits—launching out, wonder-struck from the coastal waters of school to the open sea. I shall not list all the means by which we may, almost effortlessly, promote the development of an open mind, i.e. the desire for knowledge, without which any form of instruction would be vain. I would simply ask the champions of the almost exclusive use of the direct method not to despise, at least in the early stages, even quite lengthy digressions in the mother tongue about the foreign country and 'different ways of life', about anything which may surprise or intrigue the children. We should probably not attempt to tell them everything from the beginning, but should try to say enough, in clear enough terms, to give the beginner some idea of the existence of a mystery which he will later have to solve for himself.

2. *The perfecting of the mechanism of thought*, i.e. of the intelligence. Great tomes could be written on this subject, and here we can do no more than indicate certain aspects of the problems. Rich as our own subject is and varied as are the means at our disposal, we must recognize that, so far as the development of the intelligence is concerned, we have to face great competition from other subjects; and that the struggle over the timetable is often desperate. We shall make no claim, incidentally, to substitute the development of a sense of accuracy by the study of grammar and exercises in translation for mathematics or any branch of scientific study. We do not believe that, by teaching about a civilization and a culture we can give as full a picture of man's activities as that given by our colleagues, the historians. But we should all agree that the study of modern languages usefully seconds almost all the other subjects

in the training of the mind and that, in this sphere, it has an outstanding value of its own. As early as 1895 the late Julien Rouge said: 'What is true of Greek and Latin is also true of English and German. No long course of study can store the mind with knowledge, irrespective of whether or not that knowledge is useful, without *affecting the character of the mind itself, through the labour and effort demanded*. Plato himself demonstrated what an undoubted influence is exercised upon the whole mind by every idea to which we give entry.'

The special functions of modern language teaching in the training of the intelligence—aside from its value as a supplement to the other branches of study and in particular to the classical humanities—can be summarized very simply as follows: to develop (a) an appreciation of words as such; (b) a grasp of the thought-structure of sentences; (c) the sense of having a part in a great human experience, full of lively and immediate interest.

A. Appreciation of words as such. The word, the *logos*, which suddenly, even from the first conversations in a foreign language, acquires a force of its own, independent of the object to which it is applied, the sort of magic power that Wilhelm von Humboldt long ago described by the term 'energeia'. At the conference of German modern language teachers held in Göttingen in June 1952 Dr. Hohn, of the Institute of Psychology of the University of Tübingen, developed the following argument: on the one hand, the object and, on the other, the name for the object are, at the outset (in children and in primitive peoples) very closely associated. To a child, the name of one object cannot be applied to others, it is a quality inseparable from the object itself. The discovery that the object may have another name results in the child's losing his simple picture of the world and shakes his mental security. This, however, marks the beginning of the process of intellectualization (*intellektualisierung*) which, according to Dr. Hohn, begins much earlier in a bilingual than in a unilingual child. It may be objected that Greek and Latin already serve to initiate this process. So far as my own recollection goes, nothing of the sort occurred. The Greek or Latin word remained a book word and sometimes got mislaid in my memory; it was never a living reality, scarcely even an intellectual concept. It became a part of an extremely interesting puzzle, corresponding to a French word but without referring back to the object it should have denoted. The very beginning of intellectual activity, however, consists in the process of attributing a definite and unambiguous symbolic value to words.

B. Grasp of the thought-structure of sentences. I can do no better, once more, than quote Julien Rouge. 'A child comes home crying from school and says "I lost my knife while I was playing with my friends in the playground". With the very first words we know the gist of what he is going to say: he has lost something again. With the next, we are re-assured: it is only his knife. And thereafter we listen less attentively to the rest of the explanation: while I was playing with my friends in the playground. A German child to whom such a mishap had occurred would report it to his father as follows—and he would not be using a childish artifice of style to postpone the confession—"I have, while I, in the playground, with my friends was playing, my knife—". At this point a French father would lose patience and interrupt his son and heir, hurrying him on with word and gesture: "Well, what have you done with your knife? Have you lent it, broken it, lost it, found it?" "Lost!" At last. The vital word, that gives the whole sentence its meaning and import, comes at the end.... It might be said without too great an exaggeration that the basic unit of speech in German is not the word but the sentence, while the structure of the sentence in English and other languages does not present such difficulties, it is probably true that the less strict the syntax, the commoner is the use of idioms. And foreign idiomatic expressions have the same liberating effect as what seems, at first sight, to be illogical construction. To avoid using philosophic terms, we may say that both develop the intelligence by compelling the mind to "think again", to break free of the symbol and the sound and go back to the source, the original intention of the thinker. The word, once separated from the object it describes, must be capable of free association with other words, without loss of significance (which is the pre-requisite for any true expression of thought).'

C. Lastly, although humanism (meaning true culture) is essentially disinterested, we must recognize also that the hope of one day using knowledge of a language not only to think better and more clearly but to form new friendships and interesting connexions, for travel, for business purposes or to obtain technical information from foreign works, is enough by itself for 'realistic' reasons to give wings to the developing intelligence. Someone has described the rats which, when forced repeatedly to cover the same ground, never remembered the course they had followed or took the same route from sheer habit, but which, immediately there was a piece of bacon at the far end of the course, showed marvellous ingenuity in making their way to their destination. Happily, our pupils are not rats, but the subjects which we teach have the great advantage of 'making the game worth while' and in this case the game is supremely worth while for it involves the most vital of human faculties.

3. The effort to develop open-mindedness and to perfect the mechanism of thought must not cause us to forget a third stage in training that, in our State educational system, we too often make the mistake of regarding as unimportant, if not indeed slightly contemptible. I have in mind the enrichment of the mind by the exercise of memory. I am not, of course, concerned with the thing learnt but with the faculty of learning and remembering—a miraculous faculty that sets thought free from reference books and all the labour of consultation which discourages and confounds it. Memory is not intelligence, just as money is not happiness, but memory, like money in some cases, may be a means of liberation. Admittedly there have been abuses in the past, in unsuccessful attempts at scholarship. The implicit motto was: 'Learn! You may possibly understand later or, at least, we shall imagine that you understand.' But the reaction went too far. Without digressing into the question of methods, we may say that, here again, it is vital to make the game worth while. A beautiful poem which is short and easy and which the teacher has brought his pupils to appreciate (without saying that it is beautiful but by showing that he himself loves it and has thought it worth while to learn it) can be taught in class because the children quickly grasp its interest. Intonation and sincerity of expression are then of great importance. And what subject offers greater scope than ours for the development of memory by oral communication? In *Les livres, les enfants et les hommes* Paul Hazard suggests the use of nursery rhymes for this purpose. 'If', he says, 'an impious hand attempted to put nursery rhymes into prose, we should be left with dead ashes. There is no better example of the magic power of rhyme and rhythm. English children learn them by heart; they recite them, sing them and dance them. They will never quite forget them when they are grown up. From the depths of the subconscious to which they are forced down by the weight of all the facts that have to be remembered ... these rhymes will rise to the surface and come to the tongue so that grave men, looking back to their childhood, repeat them with a smile.' Germans, Russians, the Scandinavian peoples and, no doubt, all the other nations possess a traditional children's or folk literature which may play the same part. What a gold mine for the exercise of memory!

4. These words of Paul Hazard lead us on directly to the fourth and final stage in the training of the mind under our somewhat arbitrary scheme—which incidentally, makes no claim to be exhaustive. The ennobling of the mind and its direction towards an ideal of beauty, goodness and human dignity is certainly not a matter of method or indeed of the subject taught; nor, strictly

speaking does it involve a faculty; it is a disposition of the mind that cannot be imposed but must be brought about by training. Since such training is primarily the responsibility of parents and of the church, how does it concern teaching in general and the teaching of modern languages in particular? The answer is easy. The person responsible for upbringing, father, mother or friend, is associated with only a part of a child's life and is often not at hand. Ethics and religion sometimes fall short in the achievement of their respective tasks because the minds to be trained are instinctively hostile to any form of sermonizing, secular or otherwise. Those sincerely concerned about the spiritual life of our young people will be the first to encourage the teachers instructing children to elevate their minds in their own particular fields. And it is here that we, as modern language teachers, can perhaps exercise the best and most direct influence. The teacher of the mother tongue no doubt has the better part, especially if he is also the class teacher, but his influence may be hindered by the fact that it is expected that the classics—in our case, Corneille, Racine, Bossuet and La Fontaine among others—are inevitably an occasion for moralizing. We have an infinitely less obvious part to play. It consists in showing, firstly, without preaching and without humiliating the child, how difficult it is for anyone to understand the thought of a foreigner, even when it is translated, and how difficult it is to express it in one's own language, even when it is understood. This demonstration will help to foster modesty in the individual—intellectual modesty, which is the rarest of all. To show what there is to admire in a foreign country is a means of inducing national modesty, which is perhaps the most necessary and the finest form of patriotism. Without ceasing to exercise political vigilance, to encourage young people to be tolerant in their attitude, to help them to understand why other people act as they do, to put themselves in their place, to forgive where necessary, and, above all, to abandon collective conceit and unjustified pride in the wrong things—surely all this is within the scope of the modern language teacher who takes seriously his responsibilities for the training of the minds committed to his care.

There is a phrase in which all teachers find inspiration, though they hesitate to pronounce it often—to pass on the torch. The modern language teacher is well aware that he has a torch to hand on. He must rid himself of the 'inferiority complex' which in the past has wreaked such havoc in our ranks, and seek a large part in the humble, sometimes thankless, but always intensely exciting task of training minds.

CHAPTER II

THE TEACHING OF MODERN LANGUAGES AS A KEY TO THE UNDERSTANDING OF OTHER CIVILIZATIONS AND PEOPLES

'What part can the learning of modern languages play in making people appreciative or at least tolerant of differing ideologies, customs and ways of living; making them realize the interdependence of nations, the varied contributions made by nations to world thought—in brief, how can languages lead people to a broadminded concept which would exclude narrow, conservative isolationism and nationalism and promote receptivity to a critical appreciation of new ideas?'[1]

It was in these words that an observer at the Ceylon seminar summed up the problem raised by the second general topic discussed. Though perhaps lower down the scale of *academic* values than the humanistic aspect of modern language teaching, or than the teaching of a foreign literature in the language classroom, teaching about foreign countries and the people who live in them must still be considered as a contributory factor, as something added to the mere teaching of a linguistic skill. If language teaching is to lead to greater understanding and is not to remain just an end in itself, then the pupil can and must at all stages be given some orientation in time and space to help him understand the complex 'personality' of that other nation or group of nations whose language he is attempting to master.

To achieve this end, as was pointed out by the rapporteur, Professor Louis Landré, the good language teacher should, without necessarily being a specialist, be able to digress into the fields of geography, history, folklore, art, philosophy and music, at least in so far as these disciplines concern the country he is teaching about. Of course, in a really well-integrated school, where teachers do not think of their subjects as being sealed off into watertight compartments, there is much to be said in favour of 'luring' one's colleagues into the language classroom from time to time and persuading them to teach the special aspects of the question that they are best qualified to deal with.

---
1. Miss Chitra Wickramasuriya, 'The International Seminar on the Contribution of the Teaching of Modern Languages Towards Education for Living in a World Community', *Journal of the National Education Society of Ceylon*, November 1953, vol. II, no. 3. Miss Wickramasuriya represented the New Education Fellowship at the Ceylon seminar.

It would be a mistake to imagine that there are no obstacles, administrative or pedagogical, to teaching about foreign civilizations and peoples in connexion with the teaching of modern languages. Particularly in Eastern countries, where opportunities to learn a language of world communication may be greatly restricted and where the competition to pass a set examination is very great, the teacher who attempts to depart from the purely linguistic study of a prescribed text in order to talk about the cultural background runs the risk of being pulled up sharply by an unsmiling student with the remark, 'Sir, that is not in the syllabus!'

The greatest enemies of this type of teaching are, however, the cliché, the generalization and the stereotype. The second-rate teacher will always find it easier to make sweeping statements about the country or the people he is discussing than to make the necessary subtle distinctions. The danger is increased by the fact that children themselves prefer generalizations; they like their heroes to be all white and their villains all black.

Stereotypes are usually half-truths that have become fossilized in the mind of the community and linger on until there is almost nothing of truth left in them. Teachers who are out of date and textbooks that are out of date contribute equally to the propagation of this evil. It is not always the teacher's fault. He may have visited the country of the language he teaches when he himself was a student. He may even have lived in it for some time and studied its people and its institutions with understanding and diligence. But he may never have been able to visit that country again to revise the old impressions. The educational authorities in his own country may think it unimportant or an extravagance to keep their language teachers supplied with the books and periodicals that could keep him up to date. For the first five or even ten years the information he imparts to his pupils is not perhaps seriously defective, but after fifteen or twenty years of this cultural isolation from which all too many language teachers suffer his portraits have become quaint, old-fashioned caricatures of the living present, and his information is misinformation.

Just as there are out-of-date teachers, so there are out-of-date textbooks which cause much harm. This important teaching aid forms the subject of a later chapter. Suffice it to say here that texts, and particularly 'civilization' texts, are responsible for much distorted teaching about foreign civilizations and people. Knowingly or unknowingly, their authors often traduce the country they describe. Broadly speaking, no textbook dealing with the 'civilization' of any foreign country which was written before the last war and which has not since been revised can safely be used in the language classroom.

The law of inertia prompts many teachers—and many schoolboards too—to use the same literary texts as they were brought up on themselves. And yet there have been British authors of some eminence since the death of Dickens, American authors since Hawthorne, French authors since Daudet, German authors since Kleist, Spanish authors since Galdós. Who shall say how much misinformation is imparted, how many stale stereotypes are fixed ineradicably in the minds of schoolchildren, by the slavish study of hopelessly dated and sometimes mediocre works.[1]

Yet, in spite of all these pitfalls and of the very delicate nature of this type of teaching, in which the teacher has to balance constantly like a tight-rope walker, avoiding that excessive and uncritical enthusiasm for the foreign country which would inevitably arouse scepticism among his pupils, and at the same time endeavouring to be fair and properly appreciative and to bear in mind the essential dichotomy of nations that are what they are and also what they aspire to be—in spite of all these difficulties, there seemed to the participants at the Ceylon seminar to be ample evidence that sound teaching along these lines is on the increase.

In the first place there is a growing awareness, particularly among younger teachers, of the mistakes of the past that need correcting. 'We trail along with us the stereotypes of a period that is past.... We must teach the young to mistrust undifferentiated judgments and false generalizations', said Dr. Koelle of Hamburg not long ago in a keynote address to the German modern language teachers.[2] In many countries of Western Europe the aim of the teacher is more and more to turn his modern language classroom into an enclave of foreign soil, rather like an embassy, with a distinctive atmosphere heightened by the use of *realia* of all kinds. In many French schools, the traditional *explication de texte* is made to serve increasingly as a jumping-off place for pertinent comment on the present-day life and manners of the country being studied rather than merely an academic exercise in philology. The United States, which for twenty years past has produced a varied collection of 'civilization' textbooks, was greatly stimulated in this particular direction by special needs that arose during the war years. One of the aspects of the well-known Army Special Training Programme was concentration on the production of appropriate 'area studies' and this technique and drive have been in part modified to serve normal scholastic needs.[3]

---

1. The reader interested in the general question of stereotypes is referred to the work published by Dr. Otto Klineberg now of the Social Science Department of Unesco, *Tensions Affecting International Understanding—A Survey of Research*, New York, Social Science Research Council, 1950, 227 p.
2. Göttingen, June 1952.
3. For area studies at the college level in the United States, see Wendell C. Bennett, *Area Studies in American Universities*, New York, Social Science Research Council, 1951, 82 p.

The seminar report on this section of the general discussion needs little comment. It presents a true picture, and the only thing it perhaps fails to reveal is the minority view of some Asian participants that the teaching about foreign civilizations and peoples should be postponed to a fairly late stage. The majority, however, did not feel that there was any real need to make this somewhat unnatural distinction between the teaching of a foreign language and the teaching of the mother tongue which, after all, from the beginning and at all subsequent stages is a constant unfolding of a way of life as well as of a means of communication.

The chief point of interest in Mr. Kerst's brief study which follows the seminar report is the suggestion that teaching 'civilization' has a proper place in time half way between elementary language study and the usual final stage which is the study of a foreign literature.

The longer extract taken from a working-paper prepared by the well-known Belgian author of *Didactique des langues vivantes* surveys the practical possibilities of this aspect of language teaching and establishes a useful parallel between methods and the mental equipment of the secondary school student.

THE SEMINAR REPORT

The seminar considered the place, in modern language teaching, of the study of the customs, institutions, way of life, thought, and history of the people whose language is being learned. It was generally agreed that information on such points and discussion of such topics should have a place in language teaching from the most elementary to the most advanced stages. The teaching given should include indications of the origin of the people and of the various elements from which its language has been formed. The geography of the country concerned should also be studied, along with its folklore, its religion, its economic, social and political problems and its achievements in all branches of the arts and sciences. Stress was laid upon the danger of prejudiced and stereotyped views. There should be no undue adulation of the foreign country; rather should the material be presented and used in such a manner as to train the pupil or student in objective appreciation of a civilization different from his own. In this way he can be brought, through the study of modern languages, to a fuller awareness of mankind, a richer knowledge of himself, and a clearer realization of the place in the world community of both his own and foreign countries.

In principle, such matters may well form the subject of the

material presented to the pupil with the primary object of progressively introducing him to the language. It was recognized that where the differences between the pupil's way of life and that of the country whose language he is studying are particularly marked it may be difficult to present the life of the foreign people in a manner that the pupil can understand. But the seminar considered that even in the most extreme cases it is possible to find some points of common interest.

It was stated during the discussions that in some countries the study of foreign civilizations might be considered of no immediate practical value to—or even inimical to—the best interests of the pupil's own country. The seminar was strongly of the opinion that knowledge of other countries cannot be anything but beneficial both to the individual and to the community to which he belongs.

It was further stated that the requirements of syllabuses and examinations might be so rigid as to preclude any study of institutions and civilizations. The seminar strongly deprecated any such system on the grounds that it may well hamper even the pupil's linguistic progress by depriving him of the stimulus provided by the broader approach, and that moreover it prevents him from deriving the fullest cultural benefit from his studies.

When, in the later stages of language learning, the linguistic material presented to the pupil takes the form of selected passages or works from the literature of the foreign country, the seminar considered that it was important that the choice of this material should be such as to include a true picture of contemporary life.

The seminar therefore considered that along with the learning of foreign languages there should be the fullest possible study of foreign civilizations. The linguistic material presented to the pupil, while avoiding all bias and prejudice, should be selected with this end in view. It should preferably be prepared by teachers or other persons having a thorough knowledge both of the country whose language is being studied and of the country of the pupil learning it.

THE STUDY OF THE CIVILIZATION OF FOREIGN COUNTRIES IN
MODERN LANGUAGE CLASSES IN FRANCE[1]

A nation may be likened to a real person, with its own heredity and traditions, all the complexities of daily life, and racial and linguistic 'relations' sometimes scattered throughout the world.

---

1. This text is a slightly abridged version of the paper presented to the French sub-committee on modern language teaching by Mr. Henri Kerst, Professor of English at the Lycée Henri IV, Paris, and published by the French National Commission for Unesco in *L'enseignement des langues vivantes et la compréhension internationale*, Paris, 1953.

The study of its physiognomy and character is what we understand by the term 'study of civilization'.

This subject therefore covers part of the same field as the syllabuses for which our history colleagues are responsible. The past helps us to understand the present; it is often, indeed, still present. What would Italy be without the Roman world? Or Spain without Arab civilization? Or Germany without the shades of the Hercynian Forest? The personality of each country has slowly developed through the centuries. Wars, often episodic and accidental in themselves, have marked important stages and must be taken into account. The United States of America today owe much of what they now are to the War of Independence and to the Civil War. Nor can political evolution and the institutions marking its successive stages be neglected; the soul of Russia has developed along a clearly marked line from the time of the Czars to the present-day regime.

Geography also explains many national characteristics. Even without reference to Taine's theories, it is tempting to consider that climate may have an effect on temperament, that the Italian landscape seems destined to be the home of the most brilliant schools of painting; that the harshness of the Spanish mountains, beneath a blazing sun, was bound to produce a literature of action and heroism, blended with passionate love; that England, because of her position, must eternally waver between Germanic austerity and the volatile charm of France; and that France herself, as Madame de Stael said, should be the meeting-place of the literature of north and south.

The modern language teacher must also be familiar with various current activities, which are largely determined by geographical factors. The characteristics of a country's economic life explain its customs, the standards of living of different social classes at different times, its every-day habits, and the blossoming according to the alternating seasons of tension and confidence produced by the cycle of struggle and success of those flowers of a richer life, science and religion, literature and art. The cultural life of a country depends on its physical life.

Going beyond the facts of history and geography, due account should be taken of certain more elusive factors, difficult to translate into statistics or dates. I have in mind the influences which seem to radiate naturally from certain countries at a given time, sometimes peaceful, as in the case of Italy at the time of the Renaissance, France under Louis XIV, or the United States of America at the present day, and sometimes taking the form of a 'racial dynamism' such as carried Philip II's Spain to the North Sea and the Pacific, nineteenth-century England all around the world, and Germany in the last fifty years from one end of Europe to the other.

To sum up, the traditional field of history and geography is the objective study of foreign countries, based on documentary materials, from the standpoint of an observer looking on from outside or above, a study for which some degree of detachment and systematic synthesis is necessary. The teacher responsible for the study of civilization will aim at making a subjective study of a nation's history by actual experience. He will delve into its subconscious and seek to depict its heart and soul. He will lay hold on what is vital and present, what represents the nation's potentialities and nature as a group. We do not get to know a person by reading his biography but by sharing his life.

We can see immediately where the study of civilization comes in relation to its two cousins, the study of language and the study of literature; its place is of the utmost importance. It is unthinkable that the language should be taught alone, in the 'pure' state, as it were. Language is a scheme, a mould, whose substance is either literature or civilization. Now literature is 'difficult' and can hardly be used in the early years of the study of a foreign language. Literature also presupposes a knowledge of the civilization if it is to be fully understood and explained. How, for instance, can Goethe be studied without reference to that decisive turn in human history between the eighteenth and the nineteenth centuries? Shakespeare and the Elizabethan court, Tolstoy and the Russia of the *barins*, Dickens and the poverty of the lower classes in England, provide other examples.

A country's civilization includes certain simple factors suitable for study even by beginners. When we talk about the 'home', the 'town' or the 'family', we are surely simply conjuring up for our pupils the English house in the little town where we ourselves once lived in a British family. Clothes, meals, motor drives or visits to the theatre are all features of civilization, *parallel* to, but *different* from, our own and those of our children, with which an increasingly complex picture can gradually be built up from the first year of secondary schooling to the last.

This is of the utmost importance from the educational point of view. So far as these features resemble those familiar to the pupils, they are bound to seem 'easy' to them and should be of interest to the whole class. Not all minds, it must be admitted, can appreciate literature; it is the prerogative of the more intelligent—the future specialists. In its higher forms, such as lyric poetry, relatively few are capable of truly 'feeling' it. A country's civilization, on the other hand, can to some extent be understood by everybody.

This leads to a second important consequence, this time

psychological. The difference between civilizations will arouse curiosity and thus produce a desire to know more about them, which is seldom the case with a purely literary text, the subject matter of which is already complete in itself and often above the standard of mental development normally attained by children.

More than ever in the modern world 'civilizations' must overstep political boundaries. We affect and are affected by the form of civilization found among other peoples, even when they are not our neighbours, so that this study, which is calculated to interest all pupils, will also be the most *useful* to them, leaving them—long after the literature or the language have been forgotten, for lack of the opportunity of continuing their study—a real, practical knowledge of the foreign country which may one day perhaps be our ally or our enemy but, in any case, must be our travelling companion on this small planet.

THE CULTURAL AIM[1]

Public opinion demands that the study of modern languages—unlike the study of 'dead languages'—should be directed in the first place to a practical end, though subsequently it should as far as possible, lead to the student's acquiring a literary training and an introduction to the other countries' culture.

In the study of modern languages, existing curricula have, generally speaking, three objectives: (a) a practical knowledge of the foreign language; (b) the formation of the student's character; (c) a general introduction to the civilization of a foreign people. It is with this third purpose—the cultural one—that we propose to deal.

The study of a foreign language is today concentrated not solely upon the language itself but also upon the foreign country and its culture. It is through its language that a nation expresses its conception of the world and hands down what it has to contribute in the way of spiritual values. By studying foreign civilizations and the psychology of other nations, young people not only expand their knowledge of mankind but are also led to a better appreciation of their own country and its values. Their minds are thus opened to other forms of life and they acquire that sense of the 'relative' which is basic to all true culture. For these reasons it

---

1. This section is condensed from the first part of a working-paper 'The Teaching of Modern Languages and International Understanding' prepared for the Ceylon seminar by Professor Fr. Closset of the University of Liège, former President of the International Federation of Modern Language Teachers. It will be seen from the second paragraph of this section that Professor Closset uses the term 'cultural' in a sense which is equally legitimate but different from the one used in the first chapter of this volume.

seems, in the view of the authorities in nearly all countries, that a thorough and objective study of the different modern civilizations is an indispensable part of the training of young people.

It is inevitable that practices should vary from one country to another; the essential thing is that there should be agreement as to the purpose of the efforts made. All should agree that the study of modern languages constitutes a substantial cultural discipline. All must be inspired by a determination to ensure in secondary education the necessary balance between purely practical tasks and broadly educational influences.

This educational influence in our teaching can be provided for in two ways. Either—this is the classical conception—modern language study is directed towards the cultivation of the intellect, that is to say towards training the pupils to concentrate, analyse and reflect; or—and this is the idea that has gained ground in recent years—its object is to bring the hearts and minds of the young, through an ever fuller and more direct study of modern civilizations, to understand other conceptions of life and action. Whether as a means to general culture or as an introduction to foreign civilizations, the study of modern languages aims to be at one and the same time a disciplining and broadening of the mind, a form of concentration and a form of liberation.

The 'classical' educators aimed primarily at inducing flexibility of the intellect, accuracy and mental alertness. But upon this theory of cultivating the mind as an objective in itself was later superimposed, not in order to combat it but to make the definition more specific, that of an introduction to foreign civilizations. Accordingly, culture, initially described as a general training of the mind, comes ultimately to mean, instruction in and a knowledge of civilizations.

While at the outset, by a natural process of trial and error, the 'direct method' concentrated rather on material facts and 'factual instruction' and won the day with its 'commonplace displays of geographical or technical knowledge', at a later stage, thanks to more thoroughgoing investigations born of experience, teaching came to range beyond concrete and purely external aspects and concerned itself increasingly with the 'inner realities' which constituted the true educational value of foreign civilizations.

It has been realized that apart from a knowledge of words and forms the mind must be given more varied, more substantial pabulum; pupils must be given 'something to bite on'. The 'active method' is not a mill that grinds out nothing; it must teach not merely words and forms of expression but also at the same time, make full use of *realia*. It should never be forgotten, moreover, that an essential objective is to preserve the 'taste for knowledge';

so that studying a modern language should resemble an encyclopaedic form of instruction having its part in the whole sum of human knowledge. It must, however, be circumscribed within the limits dictated by the pupils' age and development.

Through the teaching of foreign words, detailed and systematic instruction should be imparted about foreign things. Instead of being confined to generalities and commonplaces, the mind will be transported into the foreign sphere; subjects will be drawn from the foreign countries themselves, their aspects and their customs. These are the subjects that will provide the material for conversation and other exercises, and will supply inspiration for the authors of textbooks and readers.

The cultural purpose of the study of foreign languages is one that is finding ever-increasing favour. In many countries it is becoming ever more usual for modern language teaching to aim not merely at acquainting pupils with the pronunciation, grammar and syntax of another tongue but at giving them a precise understanding of the life and civilization of the country whose language they are studying. Though it is thus widely held today that the study of a foreign language should go hand in hand with the study of the civilization of the people speaking it, resistance to this opinion has not yet altogether disappeared. Cautious and conservative minds claim that 'teaching a civilization' to young people is a risky business. They maintain that the type of problem raised by such teaching and, in particular, the disconcerting measure of disagreement between the philosophies it sets out to compare are not suited to adolescent mentality.

In our view, well planned 'cultural' teaching must not only be a constant stimulus to the pupil but must provide an answer to the problems exercising him, must help him to develop harmoniously and completely, must introduce him to the questions he will have to face in life and must show him how other men react to them. Out of these elements—which are complementary but sometimes, naturally enough, contradictory—the pupil will compound a synthesis which will help him to build up his own character.

We have seen that those in favour of 'cultural' teaching are agreed in thinking that instruction in the language should be supplemented by instruction about the country concerned, and that this should not be confined to its external aspects (geographical features, habits and customs, institutions, history) but should also deal with the moral make-up of its people. While not perhaps without its dangers, such a process is incontestably in line with the 'humanist' character of this particular type of education.

Assuming that there is agreement as to the need for a study 'in depth' of the foreign country and its people, the question arises, what should be the basic spirit of this teaching? Two quite different views are met with here.

Some hold that the teaching should be, so to speak, 'impressionist', devoid of all dogmatism and pervaded, both in the oral and in the written work, by a spirit of free investigation. The advocates of this system contend that personal reflection should play a large part. They lay special stress on literature, which they regard as particularly valuable in any thorough study of foreign civilizations. The material for cultural teaching would be drawn from literary 'classics' and explanation of these texts is recommended. This analytical method, however, goes beyond a purely literary explanation of texts; it is also concerned with providing a psychological explanation of the passage under study, since the latter is inevitably an expression of the temperament or thought of a group of human beings. Therefore this method of dealing with texts, it is argued, gradually gives the pupil a personal idea of the true character of the foreign civilization under discussion.

Others favour a more 'systematic' method. This involves moving forward by a process of deduction. Greater stress is laid on *a priori* formulas. Order and unity are combined with the assimilation of knowledge. The matter studied comprises not merely books and literatures but life in all its manifestations. Features of this method are 'cultural anthologies', dealing 'systematically' with the foreign civilization involved and giving a clear and complete picture of the aspects of the country and the character of the people. This picture, when thoroughly analysed, permits a better grasp of what distinguishes the foreign country from the student's own homeland and of the characteristic traits of its inhabitants.

The second method seems to me better adjusted to the tendencies of modern teaching, always provided that it is free of dogmatism. There is no question, of course, of omitting the teaching of literature; instruction in literature will always be of profit to a gifted class. But in that case the teacher must be 'up to his task' and have sufficient keenness to develop his pupils' literary taste. This requirement is all too often not fulfilled.

These two views can be reconciled, provided that the anthology is not compiled solely to illustrate a lesson in the history of literature (however great the value of such lessons may be) but is also designed to give the cultural teaching a broad, solid and useful base. For this purpose, texts must be selected that combine in themselves undisputed cultural and literary value. This is not impossible, and, if it has not been done hitherto, the reason is that the 'literary history' factor has so far been predominant and has outweighed all other considerations.

The teacher can also use a literary anthology adapted in a certain measure to 'cultural' teaching. This anthology would also serve as a literary illustration to accompany a 'civilization textbook' used at the same time.

Aspects of foreign countries must be presented, both by the textbook and by the teacher, without any suggestion of chauvinism, without ever attacking them or making them appear ridiculous. The greatest objectivity must inform the choice and study of the texts, which should not provoke mental reservations or offend the pupils' sensibilities but introduce the foreign people with all its qualities and all its defects. History, art, literature, educational systems, scientific inventions and philosophy will be so presented as to indicate clearly the place that a given people or country occupies within the human family.

If the active method is applied, these texts will be a valuable help in training young people from a literary and linguistic standpoint, while enabling them to compare the characteristics of the different nations and distinguish their various ways of feeling and thinking. The time will come when the pupils realize that, despite all these differences, peoples have much in common with one another. This is the discovery to which everything else has led; it is the culmination of a truly 'classic' culture. All things considered, such a method as this, giving at it does a notion of international relationships that is at once concrete, direct and true, is perhaps of all methods the one best calculated to help realize the cultural goal of language teaching.

The greatest care is necessary when embarking on a study 'in depth' of other civilizations. Every culture partakes of elements that are by their nature universal. There is, therefore, a very broad field in which the basic elements underlying a given language will seem to be indistinguishable from those of other languages. But if the foreign language is re-examined in its own setting, on its own soil, so to speak, and even if too purely localized customs, or customs in process of disappearance, are left out of account, the universal or the general will inevitably be mingled with the particular or the individual. Here the teacher must be on his guard. In obedience to the principle that cultural teaching must always be based on seeing things in the 'concrete', he must know when to stop.

It is obvious that this type of instruction needs special preparation by the teacher, particularly from the linguistic standpoint. It also means that he must be personally well acquainted with foreign life and civilization. At the university level this involves his being able to engage in free research, without his having to give a series of official explanations as to why he is obliged to do so.

No restriction should be placed on teaching about any form of civilization, more especially as it is university practice to include in the syllabus an unspecified number of general or special courses. Institutions of higher learning are so organized as to enable them to flank the study of modern languages with chairs of history, social geography, philosophy and sociology, and universities include in their curricula or can establish courses in historical and comparative grammar and in descriptive or experimental phonetics, as well as courses specially devoted to foreign civilizations, literary history, the plastic arts, music and archaeology. Thus every facet of the life of ancient or modern peoples, taken at a particular moment of time or considered in respect to their historical evolution as a whole, can be the subject of specialized teaching. But the principle of correlation must be observed.

Progress in this direction seems to have been most marked in the Scandinavian countries and in certain others where importance is attached to foreign languages. Since the introduction of the 'direct method', especially in France, the tendency, in secondary education, has been towards a study of foreign civilizations *pari passu* with a study of modern languages.

It is natural that there should be clear differences of view as regards language teaching, since not all countries are similarly placed. In the case of smaller countries, where foreign relations play a predominant part, knowledge of one if not of two internationally used languages has become a social and economic necessity.

The same utilitarian need does not exist in countries where one of the main international languages is in current use. Only a very small minority of the children enrolled in the secondary schools each year will ultimately take jobs where it is essential to speak and write a foreign language with grammatical accuracy and a modicum of literary style. In the great majority of cases all that is required is an ability to understand the written and spoken word and to carry on a conversation. In these countries there is, therefore, no reason why greater stress should not be laid on a knowledge of foreign peoples, even at the expense of some of the time devoted to practical work. However, it seems that so far, while several of the smaller countries have developed their 'cultural teaching' usefully and without sacrificing the practical side, the countries whose language is one of the main international ones have not, except perhaps in the case of France, succeeded in carrying through a reform which they, of all nations, are in the best position to effect. Thus, paradoxically, modern language teaching conceived with a view to introducing the pupil to international problems has, on the whole, been much more developed in countries whose own language is not one of those in current international use.

In this, as in many other aspects of language teaching, we are, in fact, still at the stage of 'trial and error'. Cultural teaching is, in most countries, still in the process of gestation. The textbooks for the junior classes are mostly designed to give the pupils an idea of foreign countries in a simple and attractive form. In the case of the senior classes a fairly large number of books dealing with the life and customs of foreign countries can be drawn upon, but in practice they are not used so widely as they should be and in many instances are discarded in favour of texts that have an immediate linguistic or literary value. Admittedly, many of the books designed to impart a knowledge of foreign civilizations consist of a mere recital of facts and make dry reading which some teachers do little to relieve. Others whose texts bristle with difficulties are hardly such as to encourage a desire for learning, especially if they are adopted by teachers who are slavish adherents of the textbook and the curriculum. Others again are mere excuses for discoursing upon 'everything under the sun'.

How then are we to set about organizing the study of a foreign country, remembering that it must go hand in hand with the study of the language and be just as methodical and progressive?

The first two years of the first cycle should be devoted to the acquisition of the basic vocabulary and to the necessary automatic responses. That is already a considerable task. So far as is practicable, it is necessary—since the children are given strange objects to look at, such as pictures of life in the foreign country—to give a foreign savour to the acquisition of the current vocabulary. This whets the children's curiosity and also helps to keep them in the foreign atmosphere, in the environment that it is important to create and maintain. In this way they can be prepared for the kind of teaching that is to follow. It is only when this first indispensable acquisition of a vocabulary has been achieved and habits have been formed, that is to say at the beginning of the third year, that a methodical study of the foreign country can be contemplated. Besides it is just at this moment that the pupil is starting to read.

To begin with, it seems to us, the study of the foreign country must be linked with the exercises which have preceded it. Instruction should always be consecutive, from one end of the school cycle to the other, without breaks in continuity, the various sections dovetailing into one another with no sign of a break. From the fourth year onwards a fairly detailed and, above all, a graphic physical description of the country whose language is being studied should be given, a kind of bird's-eye view, to get the pupils accustomed to the country which they will later be called upon to understand in greater detail. If this procedure is followed, the teaching methods used during the first years need not be suddenly discarded; maps, pictures, views, panoramas, and particularly photographs, can still be used. It will then be natural to pass on gradually to a more complete geographical study. All this requires only a limited vocabulary and therefore provides an opportunity for simple but more interesting reading, especially if care is taken to make the teaching of geography both accurate and lively.

Once the country is known in its physical aspects, we must go a stage further and take the pupil inside those towns and cities of which he has been told, make him walk the streets, invite him to enter the houses and sit down as a guest at the foreign table. Little by little we can reveal to him the intimate life of the country and get him to know its particular manners and customs.

This is more difficult than what has gone before and requires a larger vocabulary, riper intelligence and more highly developed habits of thought. But there is no need to be too austere. We are still dealing with external details and concrete ideas. Instruction of this kind often attracts young people by awakening their curiosity and it can easily be assimilated into the general scheme.

A new stage must now be entered; the general organization of the foreign country has to be studied, but always by the same method. At this point it will be necessary to indicate in its main outlines the political and administrative constitution of the country, the way in which the laws governing it are drawn up, how justice is administered and education carried on and in what constitutional body the central power and authority are vested. One should even attempt, in order to show that nothing of interest in life itself is outside the scope of the teacher, to indicate in the same kind of way, without preconceived theories, the particular forms of social activity prevailing in the country concerned. This would fill one of the most serious gaps in the secondary education of many countries.

But institutions have their origins in the past. In studying institutions the pupil will already have been led to consider the historical reasons that have given rise to them. The teacher will therefore be induced naturally, in the course of his instruction, to specify these historical causes in a rapid general survey, in which he will point to the 'deciding factors' and place the accent on the dominant facts. He will teach as much of the past as is necessary to explain the present condition of things.

This parallel study of institutions and their origin is, in our opinion, suited only to thoughtful and mature minds. We should therefore place it logically at the beginning of the second cycle. It will be seen how, gradually and by a natural and steady progression, the level is raised, how instruction transforms itself and becomes more intellectual, appeals more and more to reason and judgment, yet without losing any of its vitality and practical value.

But if it is necessary for our pupils to know the geography of the foreign country, its manners and customs, its institutions and its history, it is no less essential for them to be taught about the way of life and thought of the people thus discovered. That means that the whole work should be crowned by teaching which will take into account individual and collective psychology and analyse proposed textual material from the human standpoint, that is to say, with a view to finding valuable information on a particular state of mind, on the psychology of a group, or on the significance of a religious, political or social movement.

Teaching about foreign civilization opens up unlimited possibilities for a keen and intelligent teacher. The whole object is to interest the pupil in the lesson, first through 'active' study of the language, through accustoming him to talk, and then through a form of teaching that is alive and encouraging for a young pupil. The latter must be given the impression that he has really acquired something, that he has mastered a new skill, that he has 'transported himself', profitably and interestingly, to a foreign environment. The teaching material used will be appropriate as well as attractive. The pupil will be interested in the foreign environment by being persuaded to want to know more about it, to collect books, newspapers, etc., and by being told of ways in which he can learn more, by having his attention drawn to broadcasts, films, theatrical performances, exhibitions and other cultural events. Pupils will be enthusiastic about cultural instruction if it is skilfully imparted, if it is not separated from the language study associated with reading, and if it is given in the foreign tongue.

To impart a knowledge of men, to develop a sense of human solidarity, and to create in young people an intelligent process of self-education—such are the objectives of the 'humanistic' teaching of modern languages. These objectives will be attained once our universities have produced a generation of 'humanist' teachers, scientifically trained and experienced in the technique of modern language teaching; once these teachers begin to teach modern languages with skill and enthusiasm, by the active method, rationally and patiently, in small classes equipped with a sound syllabus that takes account of physical limitations and of the requirements of progress; and once the authorities place the necessary teaching resources at the disposal of modern language teaching and do everything they should do to enable the teachers to improve themselves and the pupils to find their studies more rewarding, by giving teachers and pupils alike the material opportunities for direct contact with foreign countries and peoples. On that day, teaching will find itself in a new situation. The dust of prejudice will be blown away by a fresh wind and that will be all the better for the citizens of tomorrow.

CHAPTER III
THE METHODOLOGY OF LANGUAGE TEACHING

As Professor Gurrey observed in his valuable working-paper for the Ceylon seminar,[1] extracts from which are published later in this chapter, 'It is not until a pupil reaches a fairly high standard in his learning of the foreign language that he becomes interested in the people speaking that language, and begins to understand their thoughts, their way of life and their points of view. To promote international understanding, therefore, through the learning of languages, it is first necessary to promote the more efficient learning of languages themselves.'

This amounts to reaffirming the sound principle that the horse comes before the cart—in language teaching as in everything. By all means let modern language teaching be something more than the mere imparting of a skill, but the skill itself must be there as a solid foundation. Otherwise all the fine principles enunciated in the two earlier chapters will stand little chance of being translated into action.

Again to quote Professor Gurrey,[1] 'Although the learning of foreign languages has been going on for many centuries, the teaching of classes in schools, often large classes, to speak and to read and sometimes to write a foreign language is, comparatively, a new development. The formulation of theories of foreign language teaching and the working out of their principles are newer still . . . the scientific study of language learning is a young study. And it is only recently that the best known methods have received the full attention of thorough trial, experiment, testing, and the creative effort of devising for them special procedures and techniques.'

The participants at the Ceylon seminar were conscious, many of them, that the last fifteen to twenty years have indeed seen the dawn of what might be described as a new scientific era of language teaching. But even after a full week of lively discussion there was certainly no general agreement on the *infallible method*. What made agreement difficult, quite apart from the fact that no one really

---

1. *A Study of the Teaching of English as a Foreign Language in Countries in Asia, Africa and the Mediterranean.*

supposed that any one pedagogical device could possibly fit all cases, was the prolonged opposition between what one might call the traditionalists and the modernists. The former were supported by Continental European teachers accustomed to viewing modern language teaching as a closely integrated part of secondary education, a discipline whose methods have been evolved over a long period of time and in which general cultural goals have been given paramount importance. Their opponents, who were ever ready to quote Palmer or Bloomfield or their disciples, who swore by graded structures, descriptive linguistics and the importance of drill as a mnemonic technique, were teachers whose experience lay rather with the teaching of a European language as a second language in underdeveloped countries or who had done pioneer work in the new field of language teaching to adult migrants.

As a matter of fact, the division between the two camps was academic and temperamental rather than real. Both trends ultimately link language teaching to international understanding; both must be judged indispensable. It is quite evident that, in many countries outside Western Europe and North America, the problem of teaching modern languages is new and urgent and that the primary need is for devices for imparting a working knowledge of one or more foreign languages quickly and soundly. It is for the solution of these problems that the new techniques may prove most useful. On the other hand, the importance of study in depth must continue to be developed and broadened.

Though no single method was particularly in evidence, it appeared to many that the recent research in the so-called Anglo-Saxon countries and notably at the London Institute of Education and in certain universities in the United States such as Michigan, Cornell and Georgetown (to select only a representative sample) had already borne fruit and merited the closest attention. This research stemmed in the case of the United Kingdom from the earlier field work of teachers such as Faucett, Palmer, West and others, in the case of the United States from the investigations of linguists into the true nature of language, as exemplified by North American Indian languages, and on the experiments carried out in the emergency training of foreign language speakers in the armed forces during the last war. Similarly, practical techniques had been devised in countries such as Australia and Israel to deal with the language problems of migrants, but this is a subject that is discussed more fully in a later chapter.

In spite of the differences of attitude and of the not altogether surprising failure to support any one method, there was agreement at Ceylon on a general set of principles and these principles are stated in the seminar report. Nothing in this report will come as a surprise to a well-informed specialist in the contemporary field of language teaching. What is significant is not the revolutionary nature of the principles enunciated but rather that the report compresses into a relatively small compass almost all the essential aspects of present-day theory on the subject and that it was assented to by an international group whose members had widely different backgrounds and attitudes.

There is no need to list separately all the general recommendations made in this report—the emphasis on the oral-aural approach, on active methods, the condemnation of formal grammar taught for its own sake—they stand out clearly enough. One additional word might be said on the subject of graded structures. It was felt that in this field much remains to be done and that properly graded structures are probably as indispensable to the up-to-date language teacher as properly graded vocabularies are. Here again Professor Gurrey from the vast fund of his experience seems to have anticipated the conclusions of the seminar. In the working-paper already quoted from he wrote: 'Just as it is necessary to carry out a count of the simplest grammatical items in order to find out which are the most commonly used ones and the most needed, so a count of the simplest sentence patterns and subsidiary structures should be carried out in order to discover which structures and patterns should be taught first, and in what order. ... Research on the following points is badly needed: the usefulness of the commoner sentence patterns; the best order to teach them; the best intervals in a course to introduce them at different stages—beginners, middle, advanced, and for young pupils, for secondary school pupils and for adults.'[1]

Finally, before leaving the subject of the seminar report, it might be appropriate to mention certain recommendations regarding language teaching which came out in the general discussion on methodology even though they found no place in the report itself. These recommendations may properly be considered as minority reports but no less valuable for that. Firstly, though phonetics and the use of phonetic scripts may still play an important part in some language teaching systems, there was a strong feeling that phonetics have now been replaced in importance by phonemics. Secondly, it was urged by one group that it was as important to give proper attention to the teaching of intonational patterns as to grammatical or syntactical ones. A warning was issued against old-fashioned methods of teaching idioms. Listing them is not teaching them; they too probably require methodical grading. Another warning was issued against unprepared composition which simply amounts, as the speaker put it, to 'exercising

---

1. Gurrey, op. cit.

mistakes'. Lastly, on the general subject of the optimum period of time needed to teach a language properly in any normal school system, there was some solid support for the figures six hours a week for six school years. If these figures should indeed prove to be fairly sound, many school systems in the 'privileged' countries will have to reapprise their programmes.

The document that follows the seminar report has been included because it provides an interesting blueprint of a method that has actually been tested in an institution where language teaching is specifically directed towards the goal of enhanced international understanding. Some readers may disagree with the more dogmatic assertions it contains on the nature of language and of the learning process. The point is that this is a method designed to fit a certain set of circumstances, that it has been tried out and has proved satisfactory.

Professor Gurrey's observations selected from his working-paper need little introduction. They are the fruit of many years spent in teaching English as a second language and reveal their author as a shrewd practical teacher of wide experience.

Finally, it was decided to include another document produced at the Ceylon seminar itself. Its authors were in the main teachers who had, like Professor Gurrey, considerable experience in teaching a Western modern language outside Europe. The outline of general principles is presented by its authors in skeleton form with a maximum of economy. It is not without interest to compare or rather to contrast such a document with the recommendations issued by established teaching systems such as the *General Instructions for the Teaching of Modern Languages in French Secondary Schools*, the *General Directions Concerning Instruction in Modern Languages in Secondary Schools in North Rhine-Westphalia* or even with the American *Report of the Committee on Language in the College*, referred to in an earlier chapter.

THE SEMINAR REPORT

During the second week the delegates to the seminar devoted their attention to a thorough examination of various methods of teaching modern languages. It soon became apparent that where a more immediately practical objective is aimed at, methods may be different from those employed where aims are wider. Methods may also vary according to the size of classes.

In spite of these initial differences, certain general principles were subscribed to by the majority of the delegates. These were that:

1. The approach should be primarily oral.
2. Active methods of teaching should be used as far as possible.
3. The greatest possible use of the foreign tongue should be made in the classroom.
4. The difficulties of the foreign tongue in the matter of pronunciation, vocabulary and grammar should be carefully graded for presentation.
5. The teaching of a language should be considered more as the imparting of a skill than as the provision of information about the forms of the language.

The seminar agreed that the four fundamental skills to be taught are: understanding, speaking, reading and writing, in the order named. The teaching method may vary in the later stages according to the order of preference in which these skills are placed.

In the initial stage it is particularly important that the material should be graded in such a way as to give the pupil the maximum sense of achievement. The method of presentation should be so designed as to encourage mental activity on the part of the pupils. Because of the very special nature of language teaching, as well as on general educational grounds, it is vital that classes should be small.

It was agreed that from the very early stages an accurate pronunciation, including intonation, should be aimed at. In the achieving of this object, frequent repetition, speaking and singing in chorus have an important part to play and are vital adjuncts of the oral approach. The use of phonetic symbols can also be of great value, and is practised in many countries.

The effectiveness of reading exercises depends to a large extent on the choice of suitable texts. In this connexion one of the principal tasks of the teacher is the skilful preparation of the material in such a way as to enable the pupil to assimilate it more easily. It was agreed that reading is a frustrating exercise unless considerable oral ability has been previously acquired, and unless difficulties have been dealt with beforehand, and new words and expressions explained in different contexts. Unless this preparatory work is well done, reading becomes mere deciphering. Silent reading, followed by oral discussion, the division of large classes into smaller groups for reading, voluntary out-of-class reading, all were approved of as useful methods of encouraging pupils to read. Knowledge of the civilization of the foreign nation should be very gradually introduced in the early stages while, at the more advanced levels, this knowledge may be greatly increased by the use of texts chosen with this objective in mind. At these levels there is much to recommend the use of the method combining textual comment and appreciation. It was also agreed that classroom libraries of suitable texts were a necessary adjunct of modern language teaching.

In the discussion of written work, the general opinion was that in the early stages translation should not be used. At this level the use of copying exercises, dictation, substitution tables and story reproduction will lead on to the writing of simple descriptive passages based on familiar material.

Delegates were unanimous in their condemnation of the teaching of formal grammar in the early stages. Here methods should be used which convey the essential facts in such a way that they are absorbed with least difficulty. After the elementary stages of language study, there is room for a more formal approach to grammar, but even here it would be preferable to use inductive methods which encourage students to discover the rules of grammar for themselves. In this connexion the results of linguistic research should be carefully considered by the teaching profession in order that technique of presentation may be improved.

In the early stages, the acquisition of a basic vocabulary can be greatly assisted by the memorization of songs, rhymes and easy pieces of poetry. At all levels, vocabulary building should mean more than the mere accumulation of words and should be associated with the learning of the essential structural features, both formal and semantic, of the language. At more advanced levels, there should be opportunity for the study of the foreign language as a means of expression which can be compared with the mother tongue. This study will also be a valuable means of conveying to pupils ideas concerning the country under study other than purely linguistic ones.

TEACHING SPANISH IN MEXICO TO STUDENTS FROM THE UNITED STATES[1]

One of the main reasons why American students come to Mexico City College is their desire to learn to speak Spanish. In planning the organization of the Spanish courses described below, it was realized that teaching had to be really effective since the students would necessarily test their progress day by day by trying to make immediate use of their classroom Spanish. In short, they had to be provided with the proper language tools if they were to enjoy themselves and enter into the life of the city.

A careful study was made of the existing textbooks and methods of approach. Two extremes were in evidence: one type of material

---

1. This note on the evolution of a method is condensed from the working-paper prepared for the Ceylon seminar at the request of Unesco by Sra. Elena Picazo de Murray, Department of Hispanic Languages and Literatures, Mexico City College.

was based on the written language, with a much too formal and theoretical approach to grammar; the other, the conversational method, lacked a systematic progressive plan for developing a true mastery of the language. Such mastery cannot be achieved solely by the memorization of set dialogues or phrases, or by the accumulation of grammatical facts. Therefore, special materials and a special system had to be devised.

At first, lessons were mimeographed and tried out in the classroom. Quite often, student reactions suggested new subjects, necessary simplifications or pertinent additions. Eventually, two textbooks were evolved from this co-operative effort. Later on teachers were directed in the formation of a student work book that facilitated the tiresome task of correcting homework and aided in unifying work done in the classroom.

It was decided to adopt what might be called an idiomatic approach, because during the trial period it was found that students who had had previous courses in the language showed a knowledge of grammar rules that ranged from fair to excellent but that they knew practically nothing of the spoken language. Sometimes these students were teachers or prospective teachers whose written language was faultless but perhaps a little stiff. Their spoken language was hesitant, stilted and, in spite of their relatively sound basic knowledge, they could not understand even the simplest phrases when these were delivered naturally. Obviously, there was at least one big fact that had been ignored: the spoken language differs greatly from the written. The spoken language can be carefree, colourful, picturesque, full of expressions which, broken up into their component parts, often mean nothing at all in translation. If these expressions or these constructions are taken away, all too often what we have left is a cold, colourless, stilted perfection of sentence and phrase that reflects neither the spoken language of the people nor the purity and elegance of good or great writing.

This awkward type of speech does not create the current of sympathy, understanding and friendliness that is one of the chief aims in learning a language. I have observed that it inhibits the native listener. He will unconsciously change his own natural phraseology for a more laboured, grammatical form; he will carefully avoid all idioms when he senses that the person he is talking to does not understand them. Writers possessed of the most exquisite style use a colloquial form of language when they are not delivering a speech. Therefore, why not teach a language the idiomatic way when spoken language is the aim, and the literary way when mastery of the written language is sought? When the student advances beyond the strictly functional level he can, if need be, pursue his studies in public speaking and essay writing, just as he does in his own language. Concentration on the spoken language would not handicap his more advanced studies, but an over-prolonged concentration on the reading of a language, especially if it is based on too formal or too literary styles, does not result in a transfer of knowledge to the spoken language.

In developing a system, efforts were made to apply the scientific in a practical way and the practical in a scientific way. The first trials were not quite so successful as had been anticipated. As a result, the Spanish curriculum was modified several times until it was felt that a method had at last been devised that constituted a step forward in language teaching.

The final plan was evolved from the careful study of the following postulates in the field of language teaching:

If language is a skill and skill is the result of habit, the logical conclusion is that in order to secure the ultimate objective, i.e. the development of skill, then efforts must be made to develop habits. To develop skill, the plan and the work of each class should have as its objective the development of certain sets of habits; and the overall plan should bring these separate sets of habits into a unified whole.

Full mastery of a language means having the receptive ability to understand what one hears and what one reads; and the productive ability to make oneself understood orally and in writing. There are, then, four sets of habits to cultivate in order to achieve these abilities.

The ability to understand what one hears. When language functions naturally, as it does in normal life, we do not hear words, but series of sounds that, according to their grouping, we interpret as words. These words, also according to their grouping, convey ideas. Therefore, ability to understand what one hears presupposes the identification of sounds with words, words with construction (grammar), construction with idea.

Conclusion: A language class should include exercises that integrate sound, vocabulary and grammar, and that convey an idea. These should be designed to develop receptive powers in the student and be followed up methodically so that habits are formed.

The ability to understand what one reads. In reading, the eye encounters letters which, according to their grouping, we recognize as words. These words, also according to their grouping, convey ideas. The process, therefore, is: integration of spelling with words; words with grammatical or idiomatic construction; construction with idea. Two of these elements we found functioning together before: words and construction. Spelling is added and sound is eliminated. However, since there is evidence of mental pronouncing when one is thinking or reading silently, sound is not eliminated altogether.

Conclusion: A language class should include practices that integrate spelling, vocabulary and construction, and that convey an idea. These should be designed to develop receptive powers in the student and followed up methodically so that habits are formed.

The ability to make oneself understood orally. This implies the easy and spontaneous production of series of sounds that mean words; words are to be properly grouped so as to convey the idea desired. Again we find three elements of language functioning together, the same ones that function when we understand what we hear. This time, however, there must be easy production.

Conclusion: A language class should include practices that tend to stimulate the production of correct sounds and word grouping which is adequate to convey a desired idea. They should develop productive powers in the student and be followed up methodically so that habits are formed.

The ability to make oneself understood in writing. This means the production of proper spelling to be interpreted as words and the adequate grouping of words so as to convey the desired ideas. The same three elements of language function here that function when one reads. But if it is true that one pronounces mentally when thinking or reading silently, there must be some silent pronouncing in writing as well. Sound—even when not heard or produced—is not altogether eliminated.

Conclusion: A language class should include practices which tend to stimulate the integrated production of spelling, words and constructions. These practices should be designed to develop the productive powers in the student and be followed up methodically so that habits are formed.

It is obvious, then, that: the elements that make up a language are sound, words, construction and spelling; of these four elements, words and construction function in all phases of language; sound functions prominently in two phases and less prominently in two; spelling functions in two; three and sometimes four of these elements combine together when language functions. Therefore, all component parts of a language are equally important, with the possible exception of spelling.

Having taken these things into consideration and knowing what type of exercises should be followed, it was possible to set the goals. But in order to plan details of procedure the student's learning process could not be ignored. It is widely accepted that this learning process follows four well-defined steps:

METHODOLOGY

1. Recognition with conscious effort. If well-planned exercises accomplish this, the student is led to
2. Recognition without effort. This is sufficient for the receptive skills mentioned before but, for the productive phases enough practices should lead the student to
3. Production with conscious effort. Enough exercises of this nature carry the student to
4. Production without effort, which naturally leads to automatic response.

Exercises had to be devised that: follow the student's learning process; integrate the elements of language as they function in hearing, reading, speaking, writing; train separately in each phase of language; bring together the result of each separate training into a unified whole.

It was decided then to distribute the work among three instructors in the following way:

One teacher would train in grammar and vocabulary since:

1. Grammar cannot function without vocabulary, nor can vocabulary function without grammar.
2. Most points of grammar, e.g. verb tenses, adjectives and adverbs, have to be treated both as words to be learned and with regard to their function, usage and position in the sentence.
3. By the well-graded planning of exercises that follow the student's learning process it might be possible to achieve mechanization of words and their proper grouping in a number of speech patterns to be determined as experience dictated.
4. If the student could learn to produce the determined speech patterns automatically and to use them properly he would have begun to think in the new language (imitative and controlled speaking).

A second teacher would train in pronunciation because:

1. The study of pronunciation implies both recognition and production of sound.
2. The instructor needed to have a thorough knowledge of the differences in pronunciation between the two languages. He had to be able to diagnose the error in order to correct it.
3. By the use of well-planned exercises that followed the student's learning process it might be possible to develop rapid comprehension.
4. By the use of well-planned exercises that followed the student's learning process it might be possible to achieve immediate integration between spelling and correct sound.
5. By carrying these exercises a little further it might be possible to accomplish the automatic production of sound without the

55

written symbol, thus achieving correct pronunciation in speaking (imitative and controlled speaking).

A third teacher would bring together the work of the other two in class periods devoted to oral practices in construction because:

1. By the use of well-graded exercises that follow the student's learning process, while integrating the separate types of training he has received, he might acquire ease in the proper use of vocabulary, grammatical constructions, good pronunciation and adequate intonation.
2. The exercises in this class would try to carry the student from 'producing with conscious effort' to 'producing without conscious effort'.
3. The exercises in this class would apply vocabulary and grammar in the most varied way possible but always within the limits of the student's knowledge (from controlled to free speaking).

With this latest decision about the distribution of labour, there was only one other thing left to decide: *What* to teach. It is immaterial whether this was decided first or whether it was evolved from early experience. At any rate, these factors had to be considered: where does a language class start from? Other academic subjects have had some foundation in the early classes. A foreign language seldom has. The teacher and the textbooks often proceed without establishing a reasonable basis for their teaching. This makes the work not only much more difficult for both the teacher and the student but also less effective. Why not, then, base instruction on the student's previous language experience? Since a student naturally carries into the new language the habits he has formed in his own, why not take advantage of the habits that are common to both languages and use them as a rational basis for the new? By eliminating the similarities in the two languages, the content of the course would be made up of the differences between the native and the foreign tongue. Comparisons would be drawn more effectively if the student's language were accepted as the point of departure. Obviously then the course of study cannot be the same for students of different language backgrounds: Spanish for French-speaking students has to be planned differently from Spanish for English-speaking students. The same book would not do for both. Therefore, it was decided that the course of study for English-speaking students would be based on the differences between the two languages. The textbook should start at a point of similarity in sound and in construction and work gradually to increase the student's experience until no reference to English need be made. Course content developed around these ideas:

1. In vocabulary not too much time was spent on cognates but deceptive cognates were emphasized.
2. Spanish sounds that do not exist in English were taught.
3. In grammar, the constructions that do not coincide in the two languages were taught, as were the idiomatic equivalents of verb tenses not usually found in grammar texts.
4. In spelling, emphasis was placed on the sounds that each letter or combination of letters represents.
5. Idioms selected for emphasis were: (a) words that when combined lose their individual meaning and jointly acquire a different one; (b) expressions of exactly the same thought in both languages that use a completely different set of words; (c) expressions of exactly the same thought in both languages that use the same set of words but in a different order.

Elementary Spanish was spread over five quarters, each quarter being of ten or eleven weeks' duration during which the student received two hours of instruction five days a week. These ten weekly hours were under the guidance of three teachers during the first four quarters; and under two during the fifth. Each teacher trained the group in the phase of language in which he was particularly efficient. However, the material used by these three teachers was the same, though handled with a different objective in view. Each class complemented the other and all three had a common goal. The work and materials were distributed as follows:

FIRST QUARTER

Grammar and vocabulary (Teacher no. 1. Daily during all five quarters).
Purpose: Securing automatic response in the joint use of vocabulary and verb forms.
Content: (1) Vocabulary that had been selected by taking into account the needs of the college student who faces life in Mexico for the first time. (2) Grammatical constructions that had been selected according to: (a) frequency of use; (b) similarity to English. (3) Idioms and idiomatic constructions that had been selected according to: (a) frequency of use; (b) the possibility of their arising from a combination of vocabulary and constructions that are being studied in the daily work.
Practices: (1) Memorizing of vocabulary with emphasis on correct pronunciation. (2) Understanding of grammatical rules. (3) Reading of examples (recognition). (4) Translation into English (recognition of vocabulary and word groupings). (5) Quick oral verb drills (for the achievement of production without conscious effort). (6) Objective exercises of graded difficulty (producing with effort). (7) Changing sentences to various forms and tenses (producing with effort).

(8) Dictation of vocabulary to be written in Spanish and translated into English (elementary exercises in ear training; integration of sound with words and with meaning; training in spelling). (9) Translation of sentences from English to Spanish (integrated production of vocabulary, idioms and construction. The idea is furnished, the student concentrates on the mechanics).

General: (1) English was not forbidden in this class. (2) No memorizing of rules was demanded. (3) Grammar was strictly functional and was applied orally and in writing until each particular problem was mastered. (4) Grammar rules had been simplified, avoiding explanations that were too technical, and even at times disregarding traditional forms, in an effort to make them practical and understandable. (5) Conjugation in the traditional manner was avoided. Verb drills that follow synopses, rather than conjugations, were preferred. (6) Oral work, individually and in unison, was practised constantly. (7) Every type of exercise was repeated until good pronunciation, adequate intonation and normal speed were acquired.

Pronunciation (Teacher no. 2. Three times a week during the first quarter, twice a week during the second).

Purpose: (1) Recognizing and producing unfamiliar sounds. (2) Training in the comprehension of the spoken language. (3) Developing good habits of pronunciation, and of spelling.

Content: Careful study of the physical production of Spanish sounds, aided by diagrams, with special emphasis on how they differ from English ones.

Practices: (1) Detecting unfamiliar as opposed to familiar sounds (recognition in its simplest form). (2) Imitating isolated sounds, syllables, words (producing with conscious effort). (3) Oral repetition of invariable idiomatic expressions (the student concentrates on pronunciation, sound assimilation and intonation. This may carry him to production without effort). (4) Listening to connected speech delivered normally (the teacher reads a portion of the reading lesson while the student listens with his book closed. This is done after the corresponding vocabulary and constructions have been studied in the grammar class. The purpose is recognition or the identification of series of sounds with words, words with construction, construction with idea). (5) Reading aloud: (a) repeating in unison after the teacher, word by word for precision; phrase by phrase for assimilation; sentence by sentence for intonation and speed; (b) individually, for correction of personal errors. (6) Taking dictation of sentences: (a) using normal delivery, the sentence is dictated freely and completely; it is never broken up into individual words; (b) students listen until they understand the idea; (c) when the dictation is finished, students read and translate what they have written.

General: The obvious purpose of this dictation practice is ear training, as well as the integration of sound with spelling. If done intelligently, this type of exercise makes the student reconstruct the sentence mentally, thus turning this exercise into a productive as well as a receptive means of learning.

Conversation (Teacher no. 3. Twice a week during the first quarter; three times a week during the second and third; twice a week during the fourth. Oral composition is the substitute for conversation in the fifth quarter).

Purpose: (1) Furnishing practice of integrated skills. (2) Encouraging spontaneous expression.

Content: The use of speech patterns (this is correlated with the content of the grammar course).

Practices: (1) Construction of sentences based on verb drills practised in the grammar class. A wide variety of verbs is used here in all the forms that have been studied in the grammar class. (2) Adding elements to suggested sentence beginnings or endings. (3) Following speech patterns in the construction of original sentences. (4) Memorization; reproduction and variation of dialogues that deal with everyday situations. (5) Answering questions based on the reading. (6) Short oral and written compositions on an assigned topic.

General: Though for lack of a better name this class is called 'conversation', it must be stressed that true conversation in a language class cannot but be artificial. Probably the closest one can come to normal conversation is the question and answer type of practices, whose weaknesses are obvious. It might be better to call this class 'Practice in oral construction', since the student is led from partial to complete construction of sentences. An effort is made to enable him to make up the type of sentences he might have to use in actual life with, of course, variations of vocabulary. In this class, too, a great deal of choral work is done. Choral work is extremely valuable in doing away with self-consciousness and poor attention by the student. If it does nothing else, it certainly furnishes abundant oral practice that cannot be provided in classes where choral work is not performed.

SECOND QUARTER

Grammar and vocabulary (Daily as before. Teacher no. 1).
Content: Progressive increase in grammatical constructions.

Pronunciation. Decreased to twice a week. (Teacher no. 2). Pronunciation treated incidentally; concentration on ear training and oral training as to intonation and speed.

Conversation (Teacher no. 3). Increased to three times a week. The student is now presented with a broader vocabulary and more varied constructions. This makes the construction class easier to handle. The purpose and the practices are very much the same as in the first quarter. Extensive reading is introduced, followed by discussions of the subject.

A minimum of English is used in all three classes during this second quarter.

THIRD QUARTER

Grammar and vocabulary (Daily as before. Teacher no. 1). Purpose, content and practices, the same as in the previous quarter, though proportionately more advanced. Special attention given to deceptive cognates.

Conversation (Three times a week. Teacher no. 2). Purpose, content and practices very much a continuation of previous quarters. Dialogues are improvised around suggested situations.

Extensive reading. (Formally introduced here for the first time. Twice a week. Teacher no. 3).
Purpose: (1) Broadening of passive vocabulary. (2) Training the student to understand the written and more formal language of the essay. (3) Developing a feeling for words.
Content: Prefixes, suffixes, related terms; cognates.
Practices: Rapid reading; finding the subject of each sentence; deducing meaning through word formation.
General: The readings were prepared by faculty members of the college, though not necessarily by instructors in the Spanish Department. The brief essays deal with general cultural subjects and are written simply but naturally.

Oral translation, though not demanded, is used when necessary to clarify students' grasp of the material. From this level onwards, the classes are conducted exclusively in Spanish.

FOURTH QUARTER

Grammar and vocabulary (Daily as before. Teacher no. 1). Purpose, content and practices progressing on the same plan as outlined above.

Conversation (Decreased to twice a week. Teacher no. 2). Purpose, content and practices progressing on the same plan as before.

Extensive reading (Increased to three times a week. Teacher no. 3). Purpose, content and practices progressing on the same plan.
General: Conversation is decreased because at this level the student is able to get along by himself. He has made the acquaintance of Mexicans and does not need as much directed practice as formerly. Extensive reading is increased.

FIFTH QUARTER

Grammar and vocabulary (Daily. Teacher no. 1).
Purpose: Mastering of construction and filling in of any gaps that might have escaped attention.
Content: (1) Complete grammar review. Each problem is thoroughly studied. (2) Abundant idioms; vocabulary expansion.

Practices: (1) Translation from English into Spanish. (2) Original construction of sentences integrating grammar and vocabulary.
General: More attention to individual deficiencies is given at this time.

Composition (Daily. Teacher no. 2).
Purpose: The developing of facility in the spoken and written expression of the language.
Content: Sentence structure; phrases and clauses.
Practices: (1) Translating from English into Spanish. (2) Paraphrasing. (3) Oral and written composition.

From this plan of work, it may be seen that:
1. An effort has been made to consider all phases of language.
2. Techniques include all types of exercises and none is barred.
3. Rather than an entirely new method a systematic and scientific approach has been evolved.
4. There is marked emphasis on Peter Hagboldt's theory that 'effectiveness does not depend so much on the appeal to one sense or another as it depends on the intensity of impressions and the frequency with which impressions are repeated'.
5. Each phase of language needs a separate training, but all should be brought together into a unified whole.
6. It is hardly possible to fail if all the elements treated here are given due consideration; and enough time is allowed for the development of each separate skill. The student's learning process should never be lost sight of because it is of fundamental importance for the success of any method.

TEACHING ENGLISH AS A FOREIGN LANGUAGE[1]

General

The four language learning skills of listening and understanding, reading and understanding, speaking and writing, have been discussed fully by several writers, particularly by Dr. H. E. Palmer, who has made such a great contribution to the theory and practice of teaching foreign languages, notably English. Palmer always emphasized the need for the teacher to know precisely what skill he was attempting to teach. It is true that an understanding of the subject matter followed by a clear explanation is almost always a guarantee of *some* success, and a strong drive to bring one or two of the four language learning skills into lively activity is another

---
1. This section has been abstracted from the working-paper prepared for the Ceylon seminar by Professor P. Gurrey and entitled 'A Study of the Teaching of English as a Foreign Language in Countries in Asia, Africa and the Mediterranean'.

guarantee; but it would be well to comment briefly on these four skills, as they are not of equal importance in each stage of language learning. Listening is an activity of adult life, when muscular control, interest and concentration have been developed, and when rest and repose are pleasant. But, in childhood, movement and a constant shifting of attention is habitual and largely unconscious. It follows that in teaching young children, if not all children, and perhaps many adult classes too, listening must be followed by action, by action that reveals whether understanding or misunderstanding has taken place. The action need not necessarily be actual bodily action, though for the youngest pupils that is best. It may merely be putting a pencil tick or dash opposite a picture, pointing to or holding up a small picture, but it should never be omitted in teaching young children.

Differentiating in language learning between the four main skills—listening, reading, writing, speaking—was a useful analysis,[1] and marked a step forward in understanding the complex process of language learning. It brought to the fore the difference between *responding* to language and *using* language. The difference is that in responding the learner puts meanings to symbols, spoken or written, but in using language the speaker or writer has to produce both meanings and symbols to express them, unless he is reproducing a story, translating, or in some other way recasting ideas that are 'given'. The differentiation of the four skills leads to a better grading of exercises, in which the easier tasks of listening and reading can predominate at first over the more complex tasks of speaking and writing. Also, and a very important point in language learning, what has to be 'expressed' can be 'given' first, so that both meanings *and* symbols need not be produced by the learner. Consequently, stories, information, the content of a passage in a reader, can be the best material for the early stage of speaking and writing, and can be 'given' and then discussed and explained before the learner attempts to 'express' it in the new symbols.

We come now to the expression in a foreign language of ideas and facts that are not 'given', but that have to be produced by the speaker or writer. Anything that the learner 'has in mind' that has to be 'expressed' in the new language has to be clothed in new symbols. So the learner has to carry out two processes, two different mental activities, to think the thoughts and to clothe the thoughts in symbols that will cause the hearer (or reader) to think approximatively the same thoughts. But, and here is the point, the learner may not have those thoughts clearly enough in his

---

1. See also: 'A Survey of Abilities Needed in Learning English', by D. F. Anderson in *English Language Teaching*, London, British Council, August 1951, p. 171-93.

mind for expression at all, much less in a new language. He therefore stumbles in speaking, or hesitates, and his teacher thinks his language learning is at fault, whereas it may be his thinking that is confused. We have to remember here that ideas and other forms of thought are very often less completely and less clearly formulated than is normally believed. The deduction to be drawn from this is that before demanding 'free' expression in speech or writing from our language-learning pupils, we ought to prepare them for this free expression by questioning them, by getting them to discuss their ideas, to explain them and 'work over' them in such a way that, when they come to make their statement of speech, or to write their ideas, these will have been *developed*, clarified and completed by the oral preparation, or by jotting down notes, outlines and rough drafts in the way of written preparation. The fifth skill, then, that is used in language learning is this producing of ideas. It is a specialized skill because the ideas have to be produced immediately clothed in the new language; they must not be 'translated'. So our pupils have to be *trained* to think in the new language, and this can be helped by such preparation as questioning and by other ways of helping the learner to clarify his mental content. Finally we come to the sixth skill: the forming of judgments of value: 'That is a car' *can* be a judgment, but 'That is a good car' is a judgment of value. Such sentences demand the exercise of mental comparisons in which estimating and evaluating quality is most often involved. This skill may be brought into activity early if it is directed towards concrete things and obvious likes and dislikes, but where there are questions of policy, theory, complex motive or other background influences or conditions, only advanced pupils should be asked to speak or write in 'free' composition. To sum up: obviously the linguistic activity calling for 'composing', that is, producing some thoughts or ideas without the teacher's help, and framing them in words, should not be called into play until the learner is well into (or well out of) the imitative-repetitive and automatic-response stage of learning the language, otherwise mistakes are bound to increase.

There is no long tradition of teaching languages with conscious use and reliance on linguistic theory and on the teachings of psychology. Consequently there is still no complete acceptance or understanding, and in many countries no widespread knowledge, of the body of experience and experimental results that has been accumulating during the last fifty years or so. A similar development has taken place in the production of the textbooks written as instruments for carrying out the procedures of modern methods of teaching language. Unfortunately a curious thing has happened: the best textbooks published today fit so satisfactorily into classroom conditions, and carry out so satisfactorily the procedures of these modern methods that teachers in many lands merely 'follow the book'; indeed, they are often instructed to keep to it, and thus deprive themselves of initiative, of the opportunity of mastering the finer points of the best modern methods, and of developing their own skill, interest and creative ability as craftsmen. The reason for this is not only that teachers are so often trained to follow the book; but because so many of them are not confident enough to rely on their own skill and understanding of modern methods. Another reason is that many of them have not had a long enough training—or one that develops their language teaching skill—for them to master those skills and procedures, and the theories too, that good modern language teaching demands. Again, the textbooks published so far are unfortunately not *quite* good enough, they dictate, but do not point the way to better procedures, and they do not always dictate the best procedures. The consequence of this regrettable state of affairs is that teachers, in following the book, teach in a half-hearted way, and carry out the instructions in the book inefficiently. So that those teachers who follow the book and who are led to believe that that is all that is required of them, are not really using those modern methods that have proved their worth by their effectiveness, but only a diluted form of them.

It would be difficult to say exactly how many of those methods that have been condemned by language-teaching experts are still in common use. There can be no doubt that many are used in schools, and widely too, as anyone with first-hand knowledge will know, but the facts are not normally made public or freely discussed. Also there appear to be few attempts in some countries either to discover and examine the exact state of language teaching in their schools, or to remedy an unsatisfactory situation if one exists. The reports that have been furnished by knowledgeable persons in authority make statements such as the following: 'the old-fashioned methods of drill in formal grammar are widely in use'; 'formal grammar and translation are the popular methods'; 'the textbook plays the tune and pupils and teacher dance to it'; 'a complete shift from the direct method to the grammatical method takes place in the secondary school'; 'the chief method is just coaching for the stereotyped examination'; 'in the secondary schools the direct method is neither popular nor successful'; 'translation is the commonest method, though not officially approved'; 'most lessons are reading with "explanations"—usually in the mother tongue'; 'the mother tongue is freely used, and translation encouraged'; 'not much attention is usually paid to pronunciation or conversation'; 'formal grammar is much beloved of the older generation of teachers'; 'the learning of words, rules of grammar, and translation into English are the usual methods'; 'the main effort is given to spelling, vocabulary and "idiom" (that is, to clichés!)'. Statements such as these as to the prevalence of old-fashioned methods are disheartening.

Speaking

The consensus is that either 'the direct method' or 'the oral method' is the proper method for teaching a foreign language *to beginners*. Naturally there will always be a difference between the best practice and the worst, but it must be evident that teachers everywhere either have not learnt or have not accepted the teaching and advice of the experts, the best teachers. It may be that reformed methods of teaching language require more skill and intelligence than the old grammar-translation method. Nevertheless, these modern methods do not require highly skilled craftsmanship or special teaching gifts to be fairly competently used; they *do* call for more energy, more mental alertness and some inventiveness. It is however strikingly evident that there is a great need for clearer thought about these methods, for more exact exposition of principle and procedure, and especially for more expert and enlightened training of teachers.

It will have been noted that no distinction has been made here between the direct method and the oral method, as if they were identical. It is true that when the direct method is mentioned, some form of the oral method is often referred to, because the use of the direct method is best exemplified in oral work; although of course grammar and translation also are usually dealt with orally at first. And no doubt we shall continue to call good conversation and other oral work in the foreign language 'the direct method', and shall continue to think of it as an oral method. But essentially it is a principle, not a teaching method; a system that operates through many methods; a way of handling the new language, and of presenting it to the class. It demands a direct bond, that is, a direct association, between word and thing, and between sentence and idea—instead of an indirect one through the mother tongue. This is well understood everywhere, and everywhere educationists impress on teachers that the mother tongue shall not be used, but everything must be expressed in the new language. Looking at it simply, we might say that the direct method is a teaching habit, avoiding the use of the mother tongue when teaching new languages. Dialogue or almost any kind of speech in the new language carries out the precepts of the direct methodists. The main issue therefore is simple: Is the mother tongue to be used or not? And those in authority with experience of this issue in every country have said, in effect, it is not only unnecessary to use the mother tongue, but it is far better not to do so *when teaching beginners*.

A principle, put forward by Palmer for teachers in Japan brings to the fore an issue of the greatest importance. Is speech to be the main aim or activity or 'method' in the learning of English? Palmer was the great exponent of this principle, and West was the great exponent of the 'English for reading' aim. Obviously this question should receive a definite and final answer, for teachers should know what the specialists and the best practitioners advise.[1] To present fairly clear issues, it would be best to answer the question for each stage separately. This series of answers secures some agreement among specialists and that is all that can be hoped for, although it is insufficient:

Up to 10 years of age. Speaking first, and for several years. There is no real need to begin reading immediately or to do very much at this stage. It would be better to establish firm habits of correct speech than to try to teach an extensive vocabulary or to develop fluent reading—valuable as that is.

In the lowest secondary school classes. Speaking first, and the first year mainly spoken when teaching pupils with poor reading habits or without plenty of reading material. With pupils who have good reading habits, reading might start after six or eight weeks of oral work only, but it should always be subsidiary to the teaching and the practising of the spoken language.

In middle and upper school classes. The use of the spoken language should nearly always begin with new work, and should usually complete the study of passages read—silently *or* aloud. Much silent reading at this stage ensures progress in learning if earlier work has been thorough, but speaking must continue. It is often best to include short periods of intensive questioning in almost every lesson, in order to ensure that the pupils in these upper classes continue to improve their command of the *living* language.

For adults. It is essential for adults to have some careful and precise ear training, because their hearing of new sounds, especially those near to the sounds of their mother tongue, is rarely acute, and their minds are unaccustomed to detecting slight differences. For these reasons a few lessons on the sound would be best to begin with. Otherwise speaking and reading can go on together, with some writing, for it is essential to make use of ear, eye and hand in teaching adults, because their linguistic abilities are usually not a

---

1. See: 'Reading or Speaking First?' by David F. Anderson, an account of research in China, which showed that reading should be first. *Overseas Education*, vol. XVIII, no. 2, London, HMSO, January 1947.

flexible and sensitive as a child's. Consequently they should start reading and writing much sooner after an oral start than classes of young pupils.

But there is no real rivalry in these two aims, for the emphasis on the one or on the other depends on the needs of the country concerned, not on which is the better. The emphasis that Palmer put on the order of the four language operations, listening, speaking, reading, writing, was of the greatest value at the time, and still points to that important distinction: speech or language, which is the subject of Sir Alan Gardiner's notable contribution to linguistics.[1] But it is not always easy for practising teachers or even for writers of textbooks to keep firmly in mind the concept that language is what is spoken, and that the written symbols are but a reflection of the spoken word. For adults, moreover, the written word often comes first, and in learning a new language, for those with long experience of books and the printed word, it may be better so. But fortunately we have at last discovered that children can learn a foreign language by first learning to speak it.

With the introduction of the oral method there came a decisive shift of emphasis. Instead of the beginner first meeting the new language in print, with its apparent need of translation and therefore of grammar, the beginner now had to listen to sounds and to imitate them. Teachers quickly found out that they could not teach grammar because the pupils had no objective symbols to examine, and no grammar of, for example, *spoken* English has yet been written. So, too, translation could not be used because the pupils could not hold the new sentence or paragraph in their heads. But fortunately most of those who began to use the new methods completely abandoned the old. A complete change of attitude about language was made—by most teachers. Now pupils were to learn to *use* the language from the beginning, even before they 'knew' it; they were to learn to speak the new language by speaking it! The change was tremendous, and many of the old teachers were aghast. How could they speak the language when they did not know it? But the 'reformed' methods in the hands of an intelligent and lively teacher had indisputable success. But what it inevitably entailed was not always perceived—it required the learning of correct pronunciation. It forced attention to pronunciation and so to a study of the speech mechanisms and to phonetics.

A feeling for language involves a quickened facility and acuteness in seizing the meanings of words and an acuteness of hearing involving not only the exact sounds of words and subtle variations of sound but more especially subtle differences of tone, rhythm and stress. Now the great majority of pupils are lacking

---

1. *The Theory of Speech and Language*, Oxford, Clarendon Press, 1932, 372 p.

in a high degree of sensitiveness in these specialized intellectual and sense abilities, and their lower degree of sensitiveness prevents them from learning the new language quickly and really correctly. It can be proved quite easily by any observant person that the majority of pupils do not *hear* the exact sounds of the new language: they hear the sounds they are accustomed to hear, sounds that are near or overlapping or similar to the new sounds. And when they try to make the new sounds, they imagine they make them correctly. This needs no proof, because every person who has had his voice recorded and played back hears for the first time his own voice as others hear it. But for proof we have only to go to the phoneticians, and hear how urgently they insist on adequate ear-training at an early stage, for they have discovered by experiment how inaccurately we hear the sounds of spoken languages—even our own mother tongue. Further evidence is to be noted in the immediate understanding of English by Africans when it is spoken by Africans, but often their complete lack of understanding when they come to the United Kingdom; or the understanding of Africans speaking English by Englishmen living in Africa, whereas the newcomer has to learn the African dialectical pronunciations of English.

English-speaking people who live in countries where English is the medium of communication but not the mother tongue usually soon learn to accept a great variety of 'near' pronunciations. They rely, of course, a great deal more on 'context' than they normally would and they often do not actually *hear* the non-English sounds and pronunciations. In examining the subject of the pronunciation of foreign languages we have to remember that the intellect plays a very important part in listening, and its pressing urge to grasp the meaning of what is being expressed in sound or, as often happens at first, *some* meaning gives very little scope for attention to individual sounds. Furthermore, the amount of time and care given to pronunciation in teaching rarely approaches the amount given to vocabulary and grammar—or even half the amount. Whereas in the teaching of French in African schools in French territories great care is always taken to teach only the pronunciation that would be acceptable and immediately intelligible to a Frenchman, it must be acknowledged that the English that is spoken by pupils leaving school is in many countries intelligible only to those English-speaking people who are accustomed to making the necessary allowances when listening. The causes of this poor level of pronunciation are evident: too few teachers have English as their mother tongue, and too little well-informed teaching of pronunciation and of methods of teaching correct pronunciation goes on in training colleges.

Reading

The ideal is that all young pupils should have had a sound training in reading their mother tongue before they start reading the foreign language. If they have had that they do not have to face two major difficulties when they begin to read the new language: the difficulty of trying to read and the difficulty of trying to understand the new language. Unfortunately, in many countries, pupils are not taught to read their mother tongue with ease and immediate understanding, nor with due attention to precise meaning. This is because there are not enough books in their mother tongue for it to be worth while, or the books that are available are not suitable for young children, or because the mother tongue is considered unimportant. Or is it because teachers do not know the more highly specialized techniques for teaching the finer skills of reading? To neglect the mother tongue because some other language will be of more value to the pupil is to make a great mistake. The teacher who teaches a pupil to read his mother tongue fluently, attentively and with enjoyment or interest is rendering him a great service; for otherwise he may never acquire those skills and aptitudes in the learning of his second language which is the medium of his instruction in general subjects. Or he may not acquire them for very many years, and in those years his learning and progress in education will be held back by his inability to read quickly and attentively, with accuracy in noting relevant points, and intelligently. It has been found by research in Africa that pupils usually read so slowly that they cannot cover half the ground that they should and the majority read so inattentively that they do not usually perceive with any exactness what the writer has said. In order to make the progress that they are capable of, they need intensive training in *exact* comprehension for several years before they go to a secondary school. But unfortunately this is not generally recognized. One consequence is that failure to reach a good examination standard is usually attributed to poor linguistic ability instead of to poor reading habits. The pupils with quicker intelligence often overcome this disadvantage but the others, feeling that they are not mastering their general subjects, often wander into the country or along the seashore learning the book *by heart*—and their examination answers suffer accordingly. This incredible waste of time might be saved if those pupils had been taught to read quickly and accurately in their mother tongue.

The first point in an improved programme would be for the teacher of reading in the vernacular to go on with his task after his pupils have begun reading the second language; and he should go on for several years at least, until his pupils can read their mother tongue with fluency and exact comprehension. The second change in plan would be for the best teachers to take charge of this work of teaching the youngest pupils to read, for it is the field for the specialist teacher, and the most incompetent teachers should not be relegated to the lowest classes to do this highly skilled work. This would entail specialized training in the training college and preferably the appointment of specially qualified trainers on the staff. The third change should be in the textbooks. The first reading books in the new language—readers and supplementary readers—should contain only the stories and passages that have been told orally to the class or have been read in the mother tongue or are otherwise well known to the children—so that in the first book the children are reading only what they have met before. The idea that novelty and story-interest are necessary in this first task is a mistaken one, there is quite enough novelty involved for the children in making out what is in the book. To be able to read the new language at all is completely satisfying—especially as the progress they make is astonishing to them.

To many teachers 'reading' means only reading aloud. This was the result of early methods of teaching reading. To begin, during the first years of learning, with the reading aloud of the new language cannot teach a pupil to read it aloud with correct tone and rhythm, *together with* intelligent expression of the meaning. *That* should be left until the pupil has acquired a really good command of the language, and knows precisely what he is reading. Reading aloud as a method intended to develop the skill of reading the new language must, in the first few years of learning the language, be condemned as an impossible task, and a misguided objective. Pupils are ready for it when they can read the language silently with ease and when they have learnt a good pronunciation and, even then, only when they have studied the passage to be read aloud and understand it fully.

Very often pupils are called upon to read aloud the sentences that they are going to study when they have not the necessary speech equipment to do so adequately. Their pronunciation is poor, their understanding of the sentences poorer, and their use of stress and tone misplaced. Correct language habits are not being acquired by them and, what is often worse, all the other pupils are constantly hearing the new language mispronounced and spoken with the wrong rhythms and tones. A more enlightened procedure is urgently needed in many schools. In the first few months, or for the first year—and with slow learners for the first two years—new sentences should always be read aloud first by the teacher, followed by the pupils imitating the teacher as closely as he can persuade them to do so. He should do this and call for further repetitions to improve the speaking by single pupils, or by a small number of the pupils in chorus, but he should never make large groups of pupils speak in chorus, and certainly not have the whole class shouting out the sentences, or droning them out mechanically. The reason for this is that when large groups speak in chorus they always lower the standard of pronunciation, tone and rhythm, and also of expression, unless they are especially trained by a teacher who always demands a high standard.

Experts have sometimes failed to place enough emphasis on the exceptional value of copious reading for all learners. Almost everyone can be a reader, and the interest of a story provides the natural stimulus. Voracious reading gives the reader such familiarity with the language that eventually he barely realizes that he is reading a foreign language. It gives him that facility by building up for him an enormous passive vocabulary, and by training him to respond to meaning that is expressed in a very varied assortment of structures and collocations of words. The importance of wide and enjoyable reading for the learning of foreign languages can hardly be overemphasized. All those in authority need to be aware of that importance, for the teaching of foreign languages usually falls short of promoting international understanding because the older pupils have not acquired enough facility in it.

'Comprehension exercises' have not yet become popular in the teaching of second languages even though the *lecture expliquée*, that has been so fully developed in France and in French schools in Africa and Asia, is well known. The reason why teachers may not have perceived its usefulness for the earlier stages of language teaching is perhaps that they assume it is a method applied only to literature. In the classroom, therefore, in the reading lesson, the emphasis is merely on understanding: 'Do they understand what they are reading?' asks the visitor; 'Do you understand that, children?' asks the teacher. But it is not realized that there are many degrees of understanding. Anyone who reads widely in the language he is learning 'understands' the general drift of the thought or 'what is happening' long before he clearly grasps its exact meaning; and he will often go on reading without making sure he knows the exact meaning of every sentence. The child in school 'understands' in the same way, and so answers yes to the question, for he feels that he grasps enough meaning to enable him to go on reading. Moreover he is unwilling to expose his ignorance to the rest of the class. But the value and purpose of comprehension questions are quite different. They are asked in order to direct his attention to exact meanings and to the complete purport of each sentence, to train him to be more fully aware of what the writer has said and to be mentally alert when he reads and quick to seize the meaning of what he reads. The value of comprehension questions is that the pupils can answer them, and answer them correctly, for the text is always in front of them. Thus, with eyes fixed on the text, they can answer a large number of questions correctly. Then, new linguistic habits and associations become established, instead of incorrect ones, as so often happens. The questions at first should be strictly limited to details actually mentioned in the words of the text; later, when the pupils have noted precisely what the writer has said, they can go further afield and ask for inferences and so on. Two purposes are served by this close questioning: the pupils have excellent practice in using the language correctly (the beginnings of the 'free' use of the language), and they also gradually acquire the valuable skill of exact reading. It must be emphasized that to develop this skill of exact reading the teacher needs to ask dozens of questions at first on every paragraph read.

In the third year of learning the new language, or perhaps a little earlier, questions to promote thinking about what has been read and a freer use of the language can begin. The reading then is followed first by questions on the text and then by others aimed at making the pupils think about the ideas and facts they have read about. These will mostly be inference questions: 'Why?' 'What is it like?' 'How did they do that?' 'How does it work?' Here again, we have some good language practice, and practice that is not so far removed from the text. But the best exercise for those who have made good progress in the language is that of getting the gist of passages and articles they have read.

It is possible that in every country there are a number of senior pupils who are able to read a second language for enjoyment and who, in spite of unfavourable conditions for reading, often manage to read at least a few books in it every year. There is one factor, however, that prevents the complete and often even partial success of any plans for 'reading for enjoyment' among pupils at the top of a secondary school, when they are most capable and most desirous of reading widely; it is the school examination. This becomes almost an obsession for the pupils; they fear that their failure will ruin their chances of succeeding in their chosen career. They usually therefore dread this examination and work hard and long even though their work is often misguided and misdirected.

Writing

Much of the written work during the first years of learning a new language will be writing answers to questions, completing sentences and other types of sentence work. The effectiveness of many of the exercises commonly in use urgently needs scrutiny and assessment. There is no exercise which provides such an incentive to 'correctness' as writing and which, in the advanced stages, provides such a discipline in thinking in the new language, for external compulsion to write stimulates the mind to make use solely of the new language. But in the past the teacher usually forced his class to write 'free compositions' long before the pupils were capable of doing so, so that, for the beginner, the task became a struggle with grammar and not with the expression of ideas in a foreign language. The first point to be noted is that the writing of 'free' compositions should come later—only when a *good* command of the language has been acquired. But when pupils have not had copious practice in free expression in their mother tongue, free expression should not be started until the seventh or eighth year of foreign language teaching, though with a later commencement of learning it might be started in the fifth or sixth. But it is rash to lay down exact years because a long and carefully planned preparatory course of writing which leads up gradually and continuously to 'free' expression would enable an early start to be made. And this is the second important point: that as the task is a difficult one for most pupils there should be a long period of preparatory exercises planned in graded steps, each step taking the pupils from controlled, imitative work towards longer and more independent expression. Suitable exercises, gradually demanding longer and more complete answers, and the use of more continuous constructions, should be given over a period of several months and, with backward classes, a whole year at least.

Grammar

The teaching of grammar has for a long time been a vexed question. The reforms brought about by the introduction of the direct method have split the opponents of formal grammar teaching into groups—such as those who advocate no grammar specifically, those who advocate grammar only by inductive methods, and those who are for functional grammar only. In another camp there are those who teach 'informal grammar', those who teach 'only the grammar that is met with in the learning of the new language', and those who still retain 'some grammar' (which may mean: the principal parts of verbs learned by heart, simple explanations of the commoner terms, etc.). This leads to much disagreement and confusion. Not only that but, in many countries, the teaching of grammar on roughly the old formal lines goes on. And so the children are set to learn 'the rules of grammar' (so-called), the parts of speech, the grammatical categories, parsing and analysis, instead of getting on with the learning of the language by using it, learning to speak it by speaking it, to read it by reading and to write by writing. This fact should be faced. A more critical study of their pupils' knowledge and understanding of the functions and relationships of words might lead them to defer the teaching of formal grammar until their pupils had reached the top classes of the secondary school, when the language had been mastered, and when the study of 'the anatomy of the language'—the structural fibres that knit together the bones—can be more objective, and perhaps more profitable.

There are the widest differences in various countries, but there need not be such disagreement or such confusion. At present the old tradition of learning grammar instead of learning language lies heavily on the primary school syllabus. If only everyone wedded to the old-fashioned grammar syllabus could think out the problem afresh, and could fix his mental eye firmly on what the teacher is trying to do and on the needs of the pupils, these old-style syllabuses would not appear in the official school recommendations. We have to see quite simply that the teacher is teaching his pupils to understand, to speak, to read and to write language—to use language and to respond to it. No full grammar programme is needed to help the child to do that. At first he can use and understand a new language without knowing any grammar at all, for he learns to make use of sentences that are grammatically correct. We know now that a great deal of a new language can be learnt without knowing any grammar. There is therefore no need for the skilful teacher to use grammatical terms or for his pupils to learn any. For the first four or five years, if the foreign language is begun in the first year of school, no grammatical terms and ideas are needed. If it is begun in the third or fourth year of school, no grammar for the first three years and, if it is begun later, there should always be at least one year (better, two years) for thorough oral practice before any objective study of the language is begun. But there comes a time when some grammatical terms will save the teacher from making up circumlocutions, and some grammatical ideas may help learners to avoid mistakes. The teacher can begin to use grammatical terms without giving grammar lessons on them. When the children have made up numerous sentences about their actions at the moment and those of their comrades, who carry out these actions in front of the class, there is then no harm in the teacher using the term 'present continuous', and explaining why the tense is called 'continuous'. There is no need at this stage to explain what a tense is, or to call for the present tenses of other verbs. If the teacher wants to do that, he must ask for actions to be carried out and for sentences to describe what the pupil is doing. The children soon get used to the new name, and need no further study of the point at that stage. This example gives the clue to the teaching of almost every point of grammar that the class will meet with during their first and second year of study, and it can be applied in nearly all of their course until they reach the top of the secondary school, when some more exacting work may be done in the grammatical relationships of words and clauses. What is necessary, however, is the constant and thorough practice on sentences containing new inflexions and grammatical items that the pupils normally have difficulty with, such as the use of the article or of 'he, she, it' when these are not used in the pupils' mother tongue. The proper slogan should therefore be, not 'less grammar'; but 'more grammar' —meaning more practice in using inflexions and tenses, more oral drill, and a more copious use of sentences containing the grammatical items that the pupils find difficult to learn.

In secondary schools, the use of parsing and full analysis is a waste of time compared to the effectiveness of many other exercises. Parsing does not help a pupil to use the language more effectively, nor to understand it more accurately. It is a relic of the old methods of teaching Latin, and more justifiable there because so many of the inflexions in Latin express, in the verb, more than one idea. Just as parsing is useless, so analysis can only be of value when it is habitually supplemented by sentence construction, sentence building and other types of exercises calling for synthesis in expression.

Activity Methods

Teachers often report that there is much veneration of the direct method without clear ideas of what it entails. This 'veneration without understanding' is to be found everywhere, although there has been such a revolution in teaching the meanings of new words by the use of pictures and the presentation of the things themselves that the understanding of these procedures is very widespread, and they are to be found in use by even the poorest of teachers. Consequently, in view of this understanding and the experience that teachers have now had, it should be possible for other procedures and techniques to be learnt, and another step forward to be made. But, unfortunately, the teaching world has not grasped one important element in the method which that great pioneer Gouin devised and used. The Gouin method was the foundation of the direct method; but many of the exponents of the direct method missed this part of the Gouin method, or did not favour its use. It can be described quite simply in language learning: 'Sentences are recited *and acted out* at the same time.' It is astonishing that one half of the method has suffered almost complete neglect and obscurity. It is not only the spoken language but the action with it that, according to Gouin, is the secret of learning language. And biologically and psychologically he was right. Speech being a physical activity—the result of a subtle play of muscles—which reveals (or 'expresses') the more prominent content (or 'interest') of consciousness, the expression of this content, or 'meaning', by action drives home the exact meaning of the sentence, making it a reality—something belonging to real life and everyday living, instead of its being an isolated verbal formula. So much early language learning is mere juggling with words, verbal symbols without purpose or power to produce any result—words in their most vague and empty aspect, mere verbal schemata, hollow shells bereft of their sociological and teleological life, and of any role at all, however simple, in the lives of those who utter them. But they need not be mere hollow shells. From the very beginning language with action can be meaningful and purposeful. And it is this co-operation of action with thought and its expression in language that is such a force in the learning of language. For everyone uses action to reinforce meaning—gesture with hand, head, eye, arm, shoulder, body—because we feel that it requires this emphasis, and this movement to make the meaning clear to a companion. For we think with our bodies, not with 'grey matter in a thinking box'. So when learning a language we ought to use action and gesture to reinforce meaning and intention —it is only natural that we should do so. And with young beginners nearly all the sentences should be about action, and they themselves should express this action by their action. Learning then would be more deeply established than it usually is at present. The harnessing of action to speech can easily be graded for the different ages of the pupils: at first mime without speech, then mime and speech, and action with speech, then brief dialogues, three-corner chats (e.g. 'a mother takes her little boy to the barber's'), then four-square discussions (e.g. 'Father and Mother take their son and daughter to buy Christmas presents'), and so on until the week's lessons become centred on little one-act plays, full of action and the simplest language about it, and then later a series of lessons to cover a longer play. One great advantage is that there is none of the 'book' language that is found so frequently in textbooks, even in some of the best ones; the whole time the pupils are working on, and becoming familiar with, the natural everyday language of real people. A further value in using action, plays and other dramatic material (e.g. puppet plays) is that the interest and activity of the pupils is greater than with any other kind of material, consequently these effective incentives to learning are continuously in operation without the teacher's having to whip up an artificial or transient interest—nor can the teacher monopolize the talk! Thus learning is more complete and thorough. And not only those values are secured but the further one that pronunciation becomes of major importance to the pupils, old or young, who otherwise might neglect it, or think they need not trouble about it.

Because it promotes the use of more natural and everyday language, stimulates greater pupil activity and greater interest, the dramatic method is a most effective one. Another virtue of this method is that the action and the situation, as well as past happenings, bring so much more meaning to each sentence than even a story would. Furthermore, this method can be used almost from the beginning of the new language learning, though of course at first only in a very simple way. But this very effective and easy method has not been made sufficient use of in many countries. Nor have its possibilities been explored. For instance, the regular use of short dialogues with action for the teaching of the tenses must be the best way for dealing with this difficult item in the grammar programme. Similarly, the use and practice of the interrogative forms of sentences, and the use of interrogative pronouns and adverbs, can all be learnt easily with simple action and impersonations of policemen, bus-drivers, shoppers, and so on. A further criticism may be advanced: in some countries the reading of plays is part of the course. This is admirable, but reading a play without the action is not drama. With adults it may be very effective—with the stimulus of an expert who is enthusiastic—but usually it is merely reading, and the dramatic quality is often missing or toned down. But with action, even if awkward or hesitant, language learning becomes much more alive and real, and its incentives to learning and its impressions on memory and language learning habits are immediate and strong. Dialogue with action, however simple, and all kinds of movement with speech, gesture and character impersonation, and acting little plays, enables the children to consolidate what they have been trying to learn, and to practise the language that they have been reading and hearing so that they are most at home with it.

Very many nursery rhymes are set to music, and many of the folk and traditional songs and 'rounds' are simple in language and easy to learn. Where quite young children are taught a foreign language songs and musical rhymes are a great help, for nearly all children learn them with pleasure and remember them with ease. In some European countries, for instance Finland, most young schoolchildren can sing many English songs with delightful accuracy and tunefulness. But in Africa and Asia this useful aid for teaching young children (and adults too) is often neglected. Experience has proved that the different traditions in music and the different note-interval and scales in various countries are no bar to learning and enjoyment.

The use of nursery rhymes and traditional songs for the younger children can help considerably in learning pronunciation and rhythm, especially in pronouncing consonants. The teacher needs a quick ear, however, to make sure that difficult or unusual sounds are properly pronounced; the *l* sound in English, for instance, is not used by the Ewes in West Africa, and special care is needed to teach it. The use of stress too in singing marching songs and other tunes would be beneficial to those peoples who, except in moments of strong emotion, do not use stress in speaking their mother tongues. The older pupils also should learn some songs, not only for the enjoyment but for the training they give in the speaking of poetry—especially those pupils whose mother tongue uses 'tone' and not stress. These need training if they are to speak foreign poetry with appropriate rhythm.

AN OUTLINE OF GENERAL PRINCIPLES AS APPLIED TO THE TEACHING OF ENGLISH AS A SECOND LANGUAGE[1]

Aims

First to Third Year

1. The ability to understand very simple English spoken at normal speed within the vocabulary and structures laid down in the syllabus.
2. The ability to speak very simple English with an internationally comprehensible pronunciation and intonation, as far as the environment permits, within the vocabulary and structures laid down in the syllabus.
3. (a) The ability to read aloud fluently within the vocabulary and structural range of the syllabus; (b) the ability to read similar material silently with reasonable speed and to show

---

[1]. An informal group was set up by the director of the Ceylon seminar to study the problem of the teaching of foreign languages in South Asia, particularly in those countries where the Western foreign language has ceased to be the medium of instruction but has remained as a second language. The report of the group refers specifically to English but the general recommendations could apply to the teaching of any language.

evidence of comprehension by answering questions either in the foreign language or in the mother tongue.
4. The ability to build simple sentences and paragraphs within the range of the syllabus without having to provide the ideas themselves.

Fourth to Sixth Year

1. The ability to understand simple English, spoken at normal speed, within the vocabulary and structures laid down in the syllabus.
2. The ability to speak English with an internationally comprehensible pronunciation and intonation within the vocabulary and structures laid down in the syllabus.
3. (a) The ability to read aloud and silently, at a good speed and with comprehension, material within the vocabulary and structures laid down in the syllabus; (b) the ability to read and understand, with the help of a dictionary, a straightforward piece of full[1] English on a non-specialized subject.
4. The ability to write a simple letter of description or express a personal opinion on a simple topic in correct English.
5. (a) The ability to translate into the mother tongue a piece written in the foreign language within the vocabulary and structures of the syllabus; (b) the ability to translate simple, carefully chosen material from the mother tongue into the foreign language.

Seventh to Eighth Year

1. Ability to understand simple full English spoken at normal speed.
2. The ability to speak English with an internationally comprehensible pronunciation and intonation.
3. The ability to read aloud expressively material in full English at a more advanced level and to read similar material silently with comprehension.
4. The ability to make summaries of narrative, descriptive or informative material in full English.
5. The ability to write letters, reports and accounts of incidents and to give in correct and concise English a personal opinion on a simple topic.
6. (a) The ability to translate into the mother tongue a piece written in the foreign language; (b) the ability to translate simple, carefully chosen material from the mother tongue into the foreign language.

---

1. i.e. English that is not written within any vocabulary count or scale of graded structures.

Notes

1. In the earliest stages concepts strange to the pupil should be excluded. The material should be based on the child's environment. But in the intermediate stage the content of the course must begin to provide a window on the world, without limiting itself to the countries whose language is being learned.
2. In the eighth year pupils should be introduced to the reading of literature in currently acceptable English. The literature should not be used as a basis for linguistic exercises.
3. A detailed statement of aims must be issued to teachers, and examinations must be based on these aims.
4. Examining bodies should bear in mind that the types of syllabus and examination used have a profound effect on the nature and qualities of the teaching in schools.

Carrying Out of Aims

A syllabus should be built up in accordance with the aims. A course and a series of readers should be produced, specifically intended for the country concerned and following the principles enunciated in the report of the textbook panel.

For vocabulary selection the *General Service List of English Words* (West-Longmans), supplemented by an additional local list, could profitably be used.

For sentence pattern selection, such publications as the Australian course 'Listen & Speak' and the Madras syllabus might be consulted, but further research would be useful.

In grading words, it should be remembered that a new meaning of a word may be a new learning effort.

In grading words, the needs of the structures introduced at each stage, and the need for interesting reading material should be taken into consideration.

Testing Whether Aims have been Achieved

The following types of tests are suggested.

First to Third Year

Oral test: including reading aloud, questions and answers, and possibly the description of a simple picture. It is advisable to test pupils' command of question patterns by asking them to put some questions to the examiner.

Dictation.

METHODOLOGY

Written comprehension test: written reproduction of a passage read aloud two or three times by the examiner.

Written paper, including the description of a picture, the answering of questions framed in such a way as to test command of vocabulary or sentence patterns, completion tests, etc.

Fourth to Sixth Year

As for first to third year but at a higher level and with the addition of a translation paper from and into the foreign language; and a composition and letter.

Seventh to Eighth Year

As for fourth to sixth year but at a higher level and with the addition of a précis test.

CHAPTER IV
AUDIO-VISUAL AIDS

The very portentousness of the term 'audio-visual aids' may be in part responsible for the suspicion with which all the various contraptions and devices—some undoubtedly complicated and some quite simple, some expensive and some cheap—that are available to help the language teacher do his job more effectively, are still regarded by many members of the profession and by educational authorities as well.

There are other reasons too for this latent hostility, some of them ones which teachers would be reluctant to admit even to themselves. On the part of some older teachers, for instance, there is a consciousness of mechanical inaptitude, the fear that they would make fools of themselves if they attempted to operate even so simple a device as a tape-recorder before young people considerably more familiar with such things. The solution for such teachers, as Mr. Feraud suggests in the article which appears later in this chapter (A Report on Audio-visual Aids) is to put a bright pupil in charge of all such gadgets.

More widespread and less openly avowed is the fear of teachers, whose own pronunciation of the foreign language they teach is less than perfect, that the language-teaching film or the tape-recording will 'show them up'. It then becomes a question of deciding which is more important, the personal pride of the individual teacher or the educational progress of the pupils in his charge.

Finally, there are exaggerated fears of the expense involved in providing mechanical aids. True, few countries today could afford to equip many of their schools with the 'language laboratories' of the kind that are being set up in many high schools and colleges in the United States, but filmstrip projectors, tape-recorders and the like are cheaper now that they are being produced in larger quantities. Also, one such device can with proper planning often do duty for a whole school or even for a group of schools.

In any case—again as Mr. Feraud has pointed out—the term 'audio-visual aids' properly includes such widely diffused and generally accepted paraphernalia as the blackboard, the textbook and those miscellaneous objects of foreign origin which language teachers collect and display to arouse the interest of their pupils and to which the somewhat pedantic term of *realia* has been applied. All these are visual aids and many teachers have still plenty to learn about their effective use in the language classroom.

It is unfortunate that all the commoner cheaper devices should be visual aids. As language is basically a system of communication by means of sounds, *sound* aids are intrinsically more important than sight. If economy is a major consideration, as it is in many educational systems, then the only relatively cheap 'audio' device is the disc recording. As many language teachers know, this aid can be most effective. It is unfortunate that it is too often in contemporary technical literature rather passed over, as it was at the Ceylon seminar—though there the reason was lack of time.

As the seminar report shows, discussions at Ceylon centred principally on three topics: films, recorders, radio. The filmstrip was considered partly as a rudimentary form of language-teaching film and partly in its newer role when it is used in conjunction with the tape-recorder.

The collective experience of the participants at the seminar prevented any excessive display of enthusiasm for language-teaching films. This medium has, of course, great possibilities and these will surely be realized in the future, especially in conjunction with television. The fact remains that most existing language-teaching films are disappointing. It is perhaps natural that a gathering of language teachers should conclude that one of the principal causes of this relative failure lay in the fact that technical considerations were too often allowed to outweigh pedagogic ones. Whereas in the field of language teaching by radio a successful and harmonious working partnership seems to have been achieved in many countries between the radio technician and the language teacher, this state of affairs does not yet appear to prevail when it comes to making language films. The result is that many such films, though sometimes competent from a cinematographic point of view, are either linguistically or pedagogically unsound. Two classes of films escaped this general condemnation: the very short film that sets out to teach a given set of problems in phonetics or phonemics, and the straight documentary film designed merely to give background information on a foreign country.

The use of tape-recorders is constantly broadening and becoming more complex. Various machines of this type are now mechanically linked to filmstrip projectors, while successful experiments have been carried out, particularly in the Netherlands, to combine filmstrip projection with school radio broadcasts.

Of all the language-teaching devices, radio found the greatest favour with the participants at the Ceylon seminar. For this reason a separate chapter (Chapter VIII) has been devoted to this topic alone. The general subject of audio-visual aids also overflows into Chapter VII, which discusses textbooks. Because of this supplementary material only one document, in addition to the seminar report, has been included in the present chapter. This is a lively French survey of a number of aspects of the general problem. Readers will discover that its author does not always share the views expressed at Ceylon; he is dubious about the claims of radio and feels more sanguine about the language-teaching film. He is at one with the participants at Ceylon, however, in reiterating what they so often and so forcefully maintained: audio-visual aids are aids only; they can never replace the teacher.

THE SEMINAR REPORT

Films

Films which tell a story can profitably be utilized as a supplement to reading material, but are not likely to be of much use as a textbook. While a well-planned textbook can combine repetition with a sense of progress, once a film has been shown, a repetition of it and a detailed study of its several parts are likely to prove tedious and may fail to hold the pupils' interest.

Films can be an excellent vehicle for acquainting the pupils with the daily life of the people whose language is being studied. But it is important that the characters in the film should behave naturally and not be made to do things merely to bring home some linguistic lesson.

Films whose aim is to teach linguistic points can be of great value in showing the functioning of the organs of speech and in the teaching of pronunciation. Such films can also be utilized for the introduction of grammatical forms.

Any film is likely to have a powerful impact on the pupil, appealing as it does to the eye, the ear and the emotions. As a film will be regarded by the pupil as an authoritative document, it is essential that the utmost care be taken in the making of the film so that the result may be an artistic whole designed to achieve the desired educational end. Its themes and the characters it portrays should be such as to gain the sympathy of the pupils for whose use it is intended.

In the making of language-teaching films, whilst the advice of the film expert should obviously be carefully heeded, pedagogical considerations should be the determining factor in a case of conflict between the technical adviser and the language teacher.

It should be recognized that when a film is shown the class is frequently passive. Language-teaching films should therefore be short, and as a rule deal with only one linguistic point. If this latter is being introduced for the first time, it is essential that the class be brought rapidly into an active practice of the lesson that is being taught. If language-teaching films are used, they should be carefully integrated into the rest of the course.

Filmstrips

The filmstrip offers in a compact, economical and easily transportable form a large store of pictorial material which can be utilized for the teaching of almost any language structure. A strip showing a series of actions, for instance, can be used for the practice of all tenses and of both simple and complex sentences. The wise teacher will, however, take care not to forfeit the interest of his class by too frequently using the same strip for different purposes.

The pictorial material used as the basis of language teaching should be related to the country whose language is being learned and reflect the way of life of its people. Apart from their use in language teaching, filmstrips can and should be widely used to give background knowledge of civilization and institutions.

Filmstrips have the advantage of economy in production and flexibility in use. The teacher can arrest or accelerate the rate of showing whenever the situation requires it. The filmstrip projector is not only cheap but it can also be used in areas where electric supply is not available.

The Tape-recorder and Recordings Generally

The tape-recorder may be said to have two principal functions. First as an aid in linguistic analysis, it may be used to record the process of eliciting raw material, i.e. the sessions which the linguistic analyst spends with his informant. Such recordings may subsequently be used by the analyst as a check on doubtful points of his written record and coupled with the 'speech stretcher' (which is a device for reducing the speed of play back without distorting the frequency), as a record which may be slowed down to permit a closer examination. Secondly as a means of 'freezing' the utterances of a native speaker, it permits subsequent repeated play back of the same utterances, with the same rhythm, phrasing and intonation. As a model for imitation, such a recording may be used for additional drill outside the class.

A double-channel recorder may be used by the pupil for

recording his own repetitions of the model, and for subsequent comparison of original and repetition, by himself and by his teacher. The pupil may thus have his attention called to his errors and he may be led more quickly to correct them when he can be made to hear himself as others hear him.

The tape-recorder can also be used for the making of gramophone records to be used in schools. Portable tape-recorders can also be operated from batteries. The tape-recorder is, however, comparatively expensive, which may stand in the way of its being used very largely in educational institutions, especially in underdeveloped countries. Wire-recorders, gramophone records and other means of recording may be similarly used where such circumstances make them desirable.

Radio and Television

It was generally agreed that the radio was able to present a comprehensive course in language teaching. The flexibility and 'immediacy' of radio, it was felt, gave it certain advantages over other media, except, of course, television, which combines the immediacy of sight and sound.

It was stressed that there should be the closest possible co-operation between the educational and broadcasting authorities. Much of the success of language broadcasts depends on the close co-operation of teachers in the planning, use and assessment of broadcast services.

Language broadcasts should offer, among other things: satisfactory modes of speech, conversation and pronunciation; examples of imaginative presentation; supplementary and enriching activities; direct presentation of aspects of the culture of the people whose language is being taught.

The preparation of broadcasts calls for co-operation between linguists, teachers, script writers, producers and actors. In the final analysis, however, the responsibility for the educational effectiveness of language broadcasts must rest with the language-teaching specialist.

Educational broadcasting should be considered in relation to the broadcasting policies of national authorities. The opportunities for exploiting the medium depend in part on whether the system within a country is a nationalized one or is operated on a commercial basis.

Radio, it was stressed, was more than a means of communication. An art and a technique for presentation has been developed. Full use of all potentialities of the radio should be the aim of language broadcasts. Radio broadcasts could be recorded on gramophone records and thus fuller use of broadcast lessons could be made for classroom teaching.

Though sufficient evidence was not available on the use to which television could be put in language teaching, it was felt that television holds great potentialities for language teaching in the future.

General

It was emphasized that while teachers should exploit to the full the value of visual aids—whether in the form of films and filmstrips or in the older but no less valuable forms of well-illustrated textbooks, charts, felt-boards and sound blackboard work, and of audio aids in the form of radio broadcasts, gramophone recordings and tape-recordings—these were after all *aids* to the teacher and could not in any way replace him.

A REPORT ON AUDIO-VISUAL AIDS[1]

In general, people fail to understand one another for two very simple reasons, either because they do not listen to what the other party to the conversation is saying, or because they do not give the same meaning to the same words (this latter reason is yet another argument in favour of the study of languages).

Let us begin with a clear definition of the subject, 'audio-visual aids'. The meaning seems to me to be quite evident: the term includes all means, techniques, instruments—in short, everything which may help the teacher by catching the eyes and ears of his pupils. Let us at the very outset then cheerfully break down a door which should have been opened long ago. The teacher is always present—indeed, his presence is absolutely essential.

Why, then, do many teachers see red when there is any question of audio-visual aids? Because they have not been listening and because they fear that they will be ousted by these intruders.

Moreover, to call them intruders shows a lack of proper thought on the subject. When there is any talk of audio-visual aids, what is it that comes immediately to many people's minds? The cinema.

The limited view they take of the subject, combined with an obstinacy matched only by their lack of information, drives these teachers to pronounce finally against all those complicated pieces of machinery which lead to noisy disorder and waste of time.

---

1. This report, prepared by Mr. Paul Feraud, Inspector of Modern Language Teaching for the City of Paris, was presented to the Ceylon seminar in *L'enseignement des langues vivantes et la compréhension internationale* which was edited by the modern languages sub-committee of the French National Commission for Unesco.

But go to these teachers who are so bitterly opposed to the introduction of these 'revolutionary' techniques and ask them if they are willing to use the following aids, in the order given, in their teaching: specimen objects; small-scale models of objects; the blackboard; pictures; textbooks.

They will reply that the question is ridiculous and that there can be no question of the usefulness of those traditional aids. But do they realize that these things have really been used only for a comparatively short time and that each of them, in its time, was revolutionary because it was new?

This being so, why should we now decline to use aids simply because they are new and therefore not traditional? If our ancestors had been of that turn of mind, we should still be at the stage of purely oral instruction by the teacher. No one dreams of using that method any more, even in connexion with modern languages.

In point of fact, although there may have been opposition to their systematic introduction into teaching, audio-visual aids are indeed venerable. Writing itself is one. Hieroglyphs and idiograms are sufficient proof of the point, witness the Chinese saying that 'a picture is worth ten thousand words'. Audio-visual aids make explanations easier, clearer and quicker. All of them are therefore needed in some degree, but they are not all suitable for use in all circumstances. We have not yet found the universal audio-visual aid, the 'recipe' which would enable the inexperienced teacher to give faultless and efficient instruction from the very beginning. Perhaps it is just as well.

These aids are in fact merely tools, and we must know when to use them, just as a good workman changes his implements according to the raw material he has to work with. Their use is therefore a question of adaptation, i.e. ultimately, of intelligence. But we must begin by learning how to use them or we shall be unsuccessful.

Failure to appreciate this elementary truth has sometimes turned over-enthusiastic teachers into inveterate enemies. In the first place, they expected one particular audio-visual aid to do everything and, in the second, they did not know how to use it. Naturally, they could not see that they themselves were to blame, and they attributed their lack of success entirely to the method. I prefer the teacher who refuses to use these aids to the teacher who uses them badly; the latter is a much greater menace.

Does this apply only to new or technical aids? My answer to that, in the light of several years' experience of inspection, would be 'certainly not!'

I therefore consider it essential to revert, even if only briefly, to the traditional methods of the past, in order to see how they can be put to best use.

The textbook. This is probably the oldest of all and, while it is not, in itself, 'audio', it is most certainly 'visual'. For a very long time, it was the only aid the teacher had, representing the stored experience of the older members of the profession, the alpha and omega of the beginner, who followed it religiously step by step, taking lesson 10 today, after lesson 9 yesterday and before lesson 11 tomorrow. And that is the most serious mistake; it must be stated that even the best of textbooks is, in the main, no more than an experienced but unobtrusive guide, which we can trust but on which we ought not to rely all the time. It is designed for a certain ideal class and contains everything which may be useful to that class—which is a lot. The teacher must choose what is suited to his own class, adjusting the quantity and quality of what he teaches, just as a doctor prescribes different medicines for different patients. The teacher must therefore prepare his class; he must know roughly what he can teach in the year (with due regard to the Ministerial instructions), and exactly what he has to teach at each lesson, and how he has to teach it. He may perhaps be less ambitious than the textbook, but he will take better account of the actual material with which he has to deal—the 40 pupils in the classroom.

For this purpose he can call upon other aids.

Firstly, the *blackboard*. This is the symbol of the classroom, the point on which everything converges, and for which (except in the nursery school) the whole structure has been created. We can hardly imagine a classroom without one and in certain methods of teaching foreign languages used in other countries it provides the basis of instruction, the walls of the room being covered with blackboards on which the children come and write their lessons.

I have one preliminary complaint to make about it. It is *black* and therefore depressing. I would urge that, just as we have abolished the black pinafore, the traditional French schoolchild's dress, we should also abolish the colour (though not the board itself). In most nursery schools (coming back to them), where it is simply used as one aid among others, I have seen, for instance, light green boards, or panels of ground glass.

There are still teachers who do not know how to use this veteran aid, and who sometimes do not use it at all, even in modern language classes!

For what should it be used?

In the first place, for written explanations—words or phrases. Even for such a simple use—forgive me—there is a technique, which includes large, neat, legible writing, and the use of different coloured chalks to catch the pupil's eye (as in phonetic transcription).

In the second place, for explanatory sketches. Drawing seems difficult to some, but how many teachers have honestly tried to make clear, simple diagrammatic sketches of the plan of a house, for example, or match-stick figures?

There is, however, one point about which we must be careful. The board should always look neat and clear. It must not be a muddle in which hastily scribbled words run into the sketch or slope off into a space which happens to be unoccupied, and in which the children cannot see anything at all. What an example to set them!

The felt board (or flannelgraph). In passing, I should like to put in a word about a newcomer, first cousin to the blackboard, the felt board. This is a board covered with felt or billiard cloth, of any desired colour, on which the teacher can stick, by simple pressure, shapes cut out of thick material or paper backed with sandpaper. These can be fixed and removed in a moment, so that all sorts of combinations are possible—for vocabulary, for instance. The colours are cheerful, the teacher seems to be a conjurer illustrating the story he has to tell as he proceeds. There is only one disadvantage: considerable preparatory work is necessary. But, once it has been done, the equipment lasts a long time and can be interchanged.

The picture. All these aids finally bring us back to the picture—the picture which the teacher finds more and more often in textbooks and which he must not neglect, for, if well designed, it provides an illustration of the lesson, and therefore a subject for conversations and an opportunity for giving explanations or testing the pupil's knowledge. The only thing is that, even when well done, such pictures necessarily leave some gaps and cannot illustrate the whole subject. The teacher must bring other pictures to the classroom, and he has plenty of choice.

This is the age of the picture; we may regret it, but there is no denying the fact. We find pictures everywhere—photographs in an album, in the daily newspaper, in the pages of the weeklies, posters advertising holiday resorts or commercial products, illuminated signs. Pictures are forcing their way in and seeking indeed to take the place of written matter since, in addition to the 'comics', we find great masterpieces of literature condensed into pictures with a brief commentary on the back pages of our newspapers. There is too much of this, of course. But do not let us deprive ourselves of the enormous help this means of teaching can afford us. It is an inexhaustible mine and we can call upon our pupils to help us in exploiting it. They will bring us picture-postcards and cuttings from catalogues, and we shall sometimes be amazed at their ingenuity. All this will furnish the stock from which we shall draw the illustrations for our conversations about the foreign country we are studying, its general appearance, customs and inhabitants, all of which will be associated with centres of interest and much more lively than the ordinary discussion and appreciation of literary texts.

So much for the methods of the past, for I have said nothing about the use of specimen objects or models, which are obviously ideal for teaching purposes. After all, teachers of English cannot always lay hands on a plum-pudding or a kilt.

From the strictly 'visual' standpoint, therefore, the picture takes pride of place, and the new aids merely serve to ensure a wider use of pictures.

The epidiascope or opaque projector. There is a quite simple form of epidiascope for projecting, by reflection, enlarged images of brilliantly illuminated opaque illustrations on to a screen. This can be used in the same way as an ordinary picture but has the advantage of enabling the whole class to see the illustration. It is fairly expensive to buy. But it is above all the film, in its various forms, that enables us to make the maximum use of pictures.

The filmstrip. The advantages of the filmstrip are that it is extremely simple—and cheap. A 35 mm projector costs a few pounds, a filmstrip a few shillings, and both are easy to obtain. Moreover, a teacher interested in photography can very easily make his own filmstrips during his travels abroad. The strips are easy to project and can be shown even in a room which is only half blacked out. It is easy to give a commentary, since each picture can be kept on the screen for as long as is desired, and all the children can see it clearly.

As aids for the teaching of modern languages, we can at present make use of: films on geography and history; certain literary films, telling something about great writers; specialized films for use in commercial training (commercial methods, economic geography); films specially made for use in modern language teaching. There are very few of these last in France but some are beginning to come on the market in other countries (basic English, study of English by Americans, and films to accompany textbooks—a very interesting experiment).

There are certain dangers in the use of filmstrips: the danger of trying to show too many at one time, which hinders concentration and tires the children; the risk of being drawn into over-lengthy digressions on one picture; the danger that the pupils may remain merely passive.

The cinema. At last we come to the medium that has an impact on hundreds of millions of people throughout the world every day. Whether we like it or not, we cannot afford to neglect it or its enormous influence. It is the underlying factor in the transformation of which we spoke above, because of its power of suggestion and the spell it casts. Just think how much oratorical skill is required to conjure up certain ideas in people's minds. But the picture 'in the raw', with its light and movement, even when it is silent, makes its impact immediately without any other aid.

I shall not, however, dwell on the silent film, which is clearly inappropriate for modern language teaching, but shall pass on immediately to sound films, and, in the first place, to the 16 mm film, which is the only size suitable for classroom use.

This is the first time we have had occasion to speak of any sound other than that of the teacher's voice, and from the technical point of view, the sound in this case is very good. Projectors are simple; in many schools I have visited abroad, the pupils themselves work them. In any case, no teacher ought to be incapable of manipulating the apparatus after a few minutes attentive study.

This teaching aid therefore seems to combine the maximum possible advantages, but unfortunately it has at present one enormous drawback: it is expensive—a fact which will naturally affect the extent to which it can be used.

The number of 16 mm sound projectors is daily increasing, as is the number of films for certain subjects, such as geography, history and science. The number of films specially designed for modern language teaching is very small, since we generally find only about ten or so in catalogues as thick as an average length novel!

In these circumstances, what can the language teacher do? He has to fall back on what he can find, that is to say, on documentary films or those designed for the teaching of other subjects, and try to use them for his own purposes. There are many drawbacks. The sound film (and this is both an advantage and a disadvantage) carries a commentary which cannot be changed and which must be heard out to the bitter end.[1]

The films we have in mind have not been made for modern language teaching and are not adapted to the syllabus. Having been made for people who know the foreign language well, they are too difficult for the average class. All we need to do, then, you will say, is to make modern language films. Very true. But the problem is not so simple as that, for even a very short film is very expensive. Here we are in a vicious circle—no films because there is at present no market for them, no market because there

---

1. In most cases it is, of course, possible for the teacher to turn off the sound and make his own comments on the film. (Ed. note.)

are no films. I have no conclusion to suggest; the problem is principally one of finance.

The use of films in modern language teaching is therefore confined to specialized organizations with enormous resources at their disposal, but the results are extraordinarily successful. We ourselves are doing all we can. We use films whenever we can, wherever we can, and however we can, so that they are often not as successful as they might be. The film may come to be regarded as something external to teaching, as a relaxation and an entertainment for the pupils. They do not bring to it the attitude of mind essential for serious work, and remain slightly passive.

This passivity is not due, as has too often been suggested, to the film itself but to the way it is used. Experience proves, indeed, that a film, if well used, is a great means of encouraging activity, but, if it is to be so, several conditions must be fulfilled:

It must be related to the syllabus. It must be part of the class work and must be regarded as a normal means of teaching. It must be viewed in advance by the teacher, who should take notes. Preparatory work should be done in class, without 'spoiling' the film for the pupils, by setting exercises and putting questions to which the film will provide the answers. It should then be shown to the class once or more, after which an attempt should be made to answer the questions already posed and any others that the film may have raised. Finally the film may provide occasion for practical work in which the pupils are required to take as large a part as possible, such as conversations, class projects and assignments, etc.

What, therefore, are the features for which we should look in a modern language film? It should be short (with only one centre of interest). It should be very clear, even if the pace of the film suffers slightly as a result. After all, we are teachers first and foremost. The language should be very easy to understand, and suited to the standard reached by the class in question. It should be lively (be careful of films which are too academic). It should have an accompanying pamphlet.

Now it is up to the teachers. They must convince the technicians and help them to make these films which are so badly needed. A movement in this direction is beginning to take form abroad, and the atmosphere in France is favourable.

Negotiations are in progress for the exchange of films among various official organizations, while Unesco is active in connexion with the free circulation of non-commercial films. Such measures would give us quite a considerable choice of films, among which we should certainly find something to keep us satisfied for the time being.

Radio. Great hopes were once placed in the radio. It was to bring speech direct from the foreign country into our classrooms, and at the outset, many teachers were afraid of the competition of radio. Thirty years after the advent of radio, there are broadcast modern language courses, but I do not think that many of them are actually used in our classrooms.

The major drawback is that the medium is not sufficiently adaptable. The radio lesson, broadcast at a fixed time, does not fit in with the modern language classes, which are held at different times in each school. Nor—inevitably—are the subjects dealt with exactly suited to the school courses. And lastly there is something impersonal about the wireless which makes group listening difficult.

Except in certain special cases, as in Australia, where the wireless is systematically used, broadcast modern language courses are much more successful with such people as adults and invalids outside the school, where they provide additional information, and help in the revision and co-ordination of knowledge.

Television. This is the most recent arrival, the great unknown, in both senses of the term. What help can it give us? It is sure to be of some assistance, for so far no new aid has ousted any in use before but, on the contrary, has been employed in addition to the old.

Television suffers, to some extent, from the same disadvantages as the radio, in following a rigid timetable and having programmes designed for general purposes, but, in a measure, it also has all the advantages of the moving picture and therefore of the cinema.

Five or six years ago, fairly extensive experiments in educational TV were organized in France over a period of three years. I was in charge of the modern language programmes. The results of those experiments were extremely interesting. They were conducted with all sorts of audiences—beginner's classes, at the Sorbonne, and among the general public. In all cases, they were extremely well received and we were able to draw a few conclusions:

Television broadcasts can be effective only if they are arranged, in close co-operation, by the teacher and the technician. Suggestions made by a large number of teachers should be used in drawing up the programmes. They should aim at providing supplementary material, bringing the teacher what he cannot give his class himself (pronunciation, grammar or glimpses of the country's life and civilization, through the mouths of foreign assistants or prominent people). The class should be required to take an active part. The programmes should be known in advance (pamphlets).

The part such programmes can play is thus by no means

negligible. Unfortunately, all these experiments are more or less at a standstill, especially where modern languages are concerned. In the meantime, television which, in America for instance, is expanding considerably (millions of receiving sets, and seven broadcasting stations in New York alone), is making provision for a substantial proportion of educational programmes (one-tenth of the stations), in which modern languages are finding a place.

My list has been long and bare, but I wanted to show that, for teaching purposes, audio-visual aids are neither a panacea nor a poison. Like all man's works, they are both good and bad, and it is our responsibility to use them to achieve better results with less effort. In this they should be of assistance because they appeal both to the eye (visual memory) and to the ear (auditory memory).

We, the teachers, will then have to appeal to the other types of memory and the cycle will be complete.

Why, then should we refuse the aid they offer?

CHAPTER V
THE PSYCHOLOGICAL ASPECTS OF LANGUAGE TEACHING

The psychological problems inherent in language teaching and language learning occupy a field of human knowledge and endeavour which is at least as vast and as complex as that of the methodology of language teaching. Methods are conditioned by our changing, growing, knowledge of what takes place in the mind of a child or of an adult when that child or that adult is subjected to the process of learning a foreign language. But psychological research has failed to probe far enough, or has tended to shift uncertainly from one set of conclusions to another—witness the vexed question of the effect of bilingualism on the mental growth of children. Methods too have tended to fluctuate, and uncertainty has persisted regarding such questions as the optimum age for beginning second-language learning.

Indeed the language teacher who is not himself a professional psychologist sometimes grows sceptical and is tempted to wonder whether this is not a field which has so far yielded a larger crop of unsolved queries than of concrete results. Is there such a thing as linguistic aptitude? Can it be measured and diagnosed? What is the actual effect on a child of taking up the study of two new languages at once? At what age may a child be said to have acquired sufficient mastery of his mother tongue so that it is safe for him to start learning another language? Is language only a skill like learning to play the piano? This list of questions could be extended considerably; it comprises only a fraction of those problems whose solution could set language-teaching methods on a really firm foundation and permit their development along agreed scientific lines.

The seminar report on the discussions which took place on this general problem in Ceylon shows at least that they ranged widely. The rapporteur, Miss Panandikar of Bombay, was able to narrow the inevitable field of dissension and confusion considerably by a judicious use of categories. It is obviously a great convenience, for instance, to consider all aspects of the problem of language learning under three headings: as it affects pre-adolescents, as it affects adolescents, as it affects adults. It is also useful, following in the footsteps of Thorndike and McDougall, to divide the language-learning process into learning the elements of a new technique, using the intelligence to solve a number of new theoretical and practical problems, and making contact with a fresh set of ideas. Finally, the separate and ordered consideration of motivation, the process of acquiring linguistic knowledge (in its conscious and subconscious aspects), retention and recall, completes a mental tour of the main points at issue.

One reference in the seminar report may need elucidation: it is the allusion to the criteria of 'linguistic stabilization' and 'linguistic unstabilization'. What Mr. J. E. Weightman intended by the use of these terms was to establish a distinction between persons whose thought processes become fixed in their own language at an early stage and who, in consequence, prove refractory to the learning of another language and those, on the other hand, whose thinking is less distinctly verbal and who, consequently, experience less difficulty in 'thinking' in another language.

Two special aspects of the general subject were discussed with particular keenness. The first of these was the perennial question of the optimum age. Educational custom coupled with the laws of inertia have arbitrarily fixed this age in many countries at the first year of secondary school. There was at first a tendency to accept this practice as sound and not to question it, but a paper prepared and read by the director of the seminar, and which dealt with the experiments now being conducted in the United States with regard to language teaching for very young children, had a healthily unsettling effect. This paper, revised and brought up to date by its author, has been included as Chapter IX of the present volume.

The other discussion was on the subject of tests and measurements (including examinations in the traditional sense). Language teachers tend to regard many modern testing devices with considerable misgiving. They will admit that they do test 'something' but that this 'something' is often general intelligence or general knowledge and not the precise language factors that the teachers are really anxious to test. It is fitting, therefore, that the present chapter should end with a note specially prepared for this volume by an eminent educational psychologist. Dr. Wall's remarks on the general claims that testers now feel they can safely make will be read with interest, and particularly what he has to say on the validity of prognosis tests for language pupils.

Another section in this chapter deals with the interesting problem of regional or racial psychologies, in this instance the unsuitability of much of the language-teaching material prepared in the West when it is used for pupils in the East. This, according to

Dr. Jumsai, arises not only from the wider language gap but from a marked difference in maturity at given age levels.

Professor Closset in his note deals with the special learning problems of the language pupil at age 11–12, that is to say at the age when the average pupil begins his secondary studies. These factors are of special relevance to countries which, like Belgium, hold firmly to the view that the secondary rather than the primary school is the proper place to begin foreign language teaching.

Finally, Professor Gurrey makes some useful comments on the gaps in our present knowledge and gives information regarding recent research projects undertaken in widely scattered parts of the world.

THE SEMINAR REPORT

The seminar discussed as its fifth main topic the psychological aspects of modern language teaching. It was agreed that these psychological aspects formed the basis for the consideration of the objectives and methods of modern language teaching. The learner being at the centre of the teaching situation, neither the objectives nor the methods could be discussed without reference to him. Whether the learner would be attracted by any accepted objectives, whether he would be capable of realizing them, are fundamental questions which cannot be ignored in the discussion of aims and objectives on cultural or educational grounds. Similarly, questions of method must be decided with reference to the pupil who is to learn the language, and methods adopted must be in keeping with the pupil's capacity and with his mental make-up in general.

'What type of learning is language learning?' was the first question discussed at length. It was agreed that, in learning to speak and write a language, especially in its early stages, it was a skill as is also mastering the mechanics of reading the new language. It was also learning of the problem-solving type in its receptive aspects of understanding, speech or writing. In its cultural aspects it was learning in the sense of assimilation of ideas.

The psychological characteristics of learners at different stages were next discussed, and it was agreed that a child of 6–10 plus had certain distinct advantages favouring learning a new language over the adolescent or the adult: greater flexibility of his vocal organs, spontaneous oral imitation, sensitivity to the forms of speech heard and natural love of repetition. In the adolescent and the adult some of these would be weaker, but organized memorizing and greater capacity for effort would supplement them. On the emotional side, a small child would be less self-conscious and more of an extrovert, whereas an adolescent's growing self-consciousness was likely to stand in the way of learning a new language. An adult would, on the other hand, to a great extent have got over the self-consciousness of adolescence.

The four stages in learning, namely motivation, the learning process, retention and recall, were discussed in detail as applying to modern language learning. Whereas a child would learn a modern language just as a response to the situation and the demands made on him by the teacher and the school, an adolescent might tend to question its utility and might have a certain resistance towards learning the new language. However, in the modern world, with its various inventions bringing the distant parts of the world together through travel, the cinema and the radio, proper motivation of an adolescent would not be a difficult matter in terms of his characteristic attitudes and interests. An adult who usually learnt a modern language to meet some urgent practical or cultural needs was naturally better motivated.

In the process of learning a language the laws of use (exercise) and disuse would be evident in learning to speak it, and constant practice and repetition would be necessary to form the habits and reflexes necessary for speech. Such learning required the use of the intellect as in the process of spontaneous analysis and synthesis of the material presented that a pupil makes, and in the adjustment of speech to varying situations. A purely mechanical and automatic drill should have no place in human learning. In presenting material to pupils there must be grading in relation to the structure of the language, modified by psychological considerations such as interest, motivation and the relation between the mother tongue of the pupil and the language taught. In the case of reading and understanding, once the mechanics were mastered intellectual abilities and insight would be used to a greater extent. Hence a practical corollary for the teacher would be to emphasize practice, repetition and exercise in the matter of speech at the early stages, and to leave greater scope for the use of insight in the teaching of reading. Both exercise and insight, in varying proportions, would be necessary for learning the different aspects of language.

For retention and recall, it was seen that time and rest were required for proper consolidation in the mental structure and that judicious intervals of rest were as useful as periods of practice. A properly distributed learning would yield better results than concentrated learning, as proved in the case of some experiments with secondary school children.

In considering the qualities that make for success in language learning, the special question discussed was that of linguistic ability. From the results of a few experiments mentioned and a few case studies cited, it was seen that correlation between attainment in one's first language and in the languages learnt later was not high. An explanation, about which general agreement was not reached, considered that the distinction between 'linguistic stabilization' and 'linguistic unstabilization' as suggested by Weightman in his *On Language and Writing*,[1] or between conventionality and general inventiveness in terms of perseverance might also be useful. Generally, however, it could be said that children and adults of normal general intelligence were capable of learning a language if right methods were used and proper motivation secured.

The next question discussed was the place of various kinds of tests in the teaching of modern language. There was a considerable divergence of opinion. According to one view, new-type tests and standardized tests for purposes of prognosis, diagnosis and measuring a pupil's attainment in language were mechanical and could test only the mechanical aspects of language learning. These would be no measure of creative ability, or style, or thought. According to the other view, the tests, especially good standardized tests, would in the hands of a good teacher be a scientific and objective instrument and could be used with advantage, provided that they were used in combination with other devices of a broader and more personal type. The existing prognosis tests, it was felt, did not appear to have a high validity and could not be used by themselves. On this view, both objective tests and standardized tests would be of great use as a basis for research connected with the methods of teaching modern languages and research on all problems pertaining to modern language teaching. It was emphasized that research and classroom practice were intimately related, in so far as the needs in the classroom must be met by research and the fields of research must in turn be related to classroom needs.

The effect of modern language study on the pupil's general mental development was next discussed. It was seen that in view of the latest findings on the problem of mental discipline, a study of a modern language would go a long way towards disciplining and developing the mind, provided that in the teaching of the language an appeal was made to the interests of the learner and an opportunity given to him to use his insight and the ideals formed in his own mind. The study of a new language would enrich the mind not so much by adding to its content as by contributing to its maturation and development. A modern language taught in this manner, would, by securing the general mental development of

---

1. London, Sylvan Press, 1947.

the pupil, help to enable him to envisage the idea of a world community and be a worthy member of that community.

As regards the question of the optimum age for beginning the study of a new language, it was decided that in view of the experiments of introducing modern languages in elementary schools being carried out by various Member States, it would be wrong to discuss the question on *a priori* grounds but desirable to watch the results of the experiments. It was also agreed that, in view of the importance of this matter of the age at which a second language could be introduced, steps should be taken to keep all Member States informed on the success or otherwise of such schemes.

PSYCHOLOGICAL PITFALLS FOUND IN CLASSICAL WESTERN METHODS OF LANGUAGE TEACHING[1]

In many countries children learning English as a foreign language often use textbooks and readers written by those whose mother tongue is English. Although applying recognized methods of teaching a foreign language, these books are by no means satisfactory, since the writers take for granted as being understood so many of the small, trivial details that are confusing to a child brought up in surroundings entirely different from those of an English-speaking person. Such a child speaks a language the structure of which is very far removed from that of English. His environment is different, his living conditions are different, he has different social customs and religious beliefs, his historical background is different, and he thinks in a different way. Therefore he finds it very difficult to understand why such phrases must be spoken in such a way, why certain synonyms cannot be substituted for one another when they have the same meaning, why one word or phrase is used while another is not used, why a certain word must be spelt in this and not in that way.

It is my opinion that in order to understand the many local difficulties encountered both in teaching and learning English as a foreign language, one must be a native of the country, a person who knew no English for the first few years of his life and who, when he did start to learn it, had to struggle through the various difficulties of the language until he had mastered it. Only a person who has passed through this experience himself can comprehend the difficulties encountered by a child of his own nationality who is learning to speak a foreign language and grasp what the child is

---

1. This section is extracted from the working-paper prepared for the Ceylon seminar by Dr. Manich Jumsai who at that time was a member of the Secretariat of Unesco and who had previously been Head of the Curriculum Section of the Thailand Ministry of Education and Secretary of the Textbook Committee of the same Ministry.

thinking of when he interprets certain things in a certain way. Notwithstanding the theories put forward by various eminent specialists of modern languages, it is my firm opinion that the series of books on this subject will not be complete until consideration has been given to the complete cycle of effective development of the indigenous child's mind.

Let me speak as a Thai national, coming from a typical provincial town in Thailand, born in a village far from modern civilization, but eager to learn English, dreaming from childhood of strange lands where lived those funny white-faced people (of whom we sometimes heard) with blond hair, who spoke in a strange tongue and had strange customs.... I had never met any of these people. Why should I, when even my provincial teacher had never seen one of them, and our severe, grim-looking headmaster, most learned of the village people, did not know them? One day, my curiosity getting the better of me, I asked my master, and he in turn asked the headmaster, what was the name of the capital city of these strange white people who spoke the foreign language we now had to learn in all secondary schools, even in the remotest village, but neither of them could give me an answer. Such were the conditions in Thailand when I started to learn English 40 years ago. Of what use to us then were the direct method theories? My teacher did not speak English, he only read and translated words from the blackboard, together with their meanings, so that we could learn them by heart. At the next English lesson we had to tell him what were the meanings of the various words. As to writing, the teacher would avoid it very carefully so that, during my childhood, I did not have much chance of writing anything other than translations of sentences from English into Thai or Thai into English, usually from books. There was no question of free translations being made. Even when translating from books, an English-Thai dictionary had to be used. When we encountered a peculiar word or grammatical construction, we had to use it as instructed by our teacher. If we asked why it should be used in that way, we were told that that was the strange English way of saying it.

As for the meaning of words, there was no distinction in our minds between apples, pears, peaches, cherries, grapes, strawberries or raspberries, however large or small, whatever their colour, whether grown on vines or on trees. All we knew was that they were 'a kind of fruit'; the teacher said so. We had never seen them, and neither had the teacher. They were English fruits which could not be grown in a hot country like Thailand. They were strange fruits which puzzled our minds and our imaginations.

Similarly with trees, flowers, animals, insects, etc., while learning

English at school, I had stored away in my mind many strange names for each of them, but they were all the same to me—a kind of tree, a kind of flower, a kind of animal, etc., which the English people had but we did not have. At last I grew impatient, and one day I asked my teacher what were the English names for some of our local fruits, flowers, trees and foodstuffs. Of course, he could not tell me, and he looked somewhat surprised that I should ask such a silly question. Was I becoming insubordinate? Such things did not exist in English books, nor in English. Then I argued: 'Suppose one of these days I meet an Englishman. I will take him round to see things. I will show him the fruits we have (Noi-na, Lam-yai, Chompoo, Mafuang, etc.) and ask him to taste some of them. But what shall I call them?' 'Oh, curious child, what else would they be for these Europeans but a kind of fruit?'

I would therefore repudiate a list of basic words if it contained 'bread', 'apple', etc., instead of words appropriate to the food grown in the country where English was being taught. I consider that such a list should contain words which have a real meaning for the child because he sees and uses the articles described in his everyday life.

When it comes to English spelling and pronunciation, we people of Thailand find that the words are never pronounced the way they are spelt. It is of no use to learn any rules, but only exceptions. Then came a new invention: the international phonetic script. This is a device whereby we can see how the various peculiar English words are pronounced; but then we are introduced to new signs and symbols. This, again, is like learning a new language. Is not English difficult enough—must we now read a new language? Even this phonetic system is not a satisfactory solution to our problem. Whatever signs and symbols are invented for us, we do not pronounce them in that way since our own language is so different. We don't sound the endings of our words as do the English, we do not twist and roll our tongue to sound an *l*, or an *r*, we do not make sounds through our teeth like *th*, we do not have hissing sounds like *s* and *ss*. These are only English idiosyncracies to make things harder than they look. After a certain time, we go back to the ordinary English spelling, but what is the point when words are not all spelt in the same way? Our eyes see different words on paper, but our minds cannot identify them as being the same. We have to learn over again the quaint spelling and irregular pronunciation. Words are not written the way they are pronounced, as is done in the international phonetic script. But what is the use of struggling to learn all these quaint symbols if they are not going to be used? Also, there are exceptions and unusual things in the international phonetic script itself.

Then there are the various ways of expressing oneself. The Thai and English languages are fundamentally different, having absolutely nothing in common. Why should they? When all is said and done, the English and Thai peoples had never met until recently. They are not descended from a common stock with ancestors common to both races. While the original Thai people were still living in the valley of the Yellow River, in brick buildings, and with a fairly advanced civilization, the British were living in prehistoric times; Britons still wore leaves and animal skins and dwelt in the forests. The two peoples live in worlds far apart, each developing their own language to suit their different needs without ever having the opportunity to discuss what they should say for certain things, or how they should express certain feelings or ideas. Therefore, a Thai student starting to learn English would say: 'I speak English snake snake fish fish'. This does not mean anything to an Englishman, but it means everything to the Thai student. When a person knows only a few odd words of a language, such as snake or fish, and has to use the same words all the time because he knows no other, it is obvious to a Thai mind that he really knows very little of that language. On the other hand, when he knows so much of the language that the words flow from his mouth without hesitation, like water flowing from a spout, he will say: 'I speak English like water'. He understands this clearly, although it will not be understood by an Englishman.

Thai ways, sentiments, feelings and understanding are not the same as those of English people, and an Englishman must not be led astray by thinking that whatever he says is simple, straightforward and therefore easily understood by a Thai. For instance, look at these phrases which are perfectly obvious and clear to a Thai: 'I have ox two body'; 'he woman have son ox two body'.

Why should one say: 'I have two oxen'; 'she has two young oxen'; etc.? Why should the language be made more difficult by using 'has' on one occasion and 'have' on another? Why should the words be changed to plural when singular can mean the same object? Why should one use a new word 'she' when one can say 'a female he' or 'he woman'? Why should one say 'young oxen' when they are really 'sons or daughters of oxen', and so on?

There are instances when a Thai would say 'yes' and an Englishman 'no', and yet both expressions have the same meaning. A typical comparison is:

Englishman

   Q. Have you never been to England?
   A. No. (I have never been.)

Thai

   Q. Have you never been to England?

A. Yes. (The fact that I have never been there is 'yes' in this case.)

The English are great inventors; they make grammatical rules and then start to evade them by making exceptions and creating more and more language difficulties. The Thai language, on the other hand, has no tenses, no feminine nouns, no comparative and superlative adjectives and adverbs, no plurals, etc. It is quite straightforward. English grammar is perhaps one of the most difficult in the world to learn, owing to the number of tenses and irregular verbs. Compare these expressions:

English	*Thai*
He goes to school	He go school
He is going to school	He active go school
He went to school yesterday	He go to school yesterday
He has already been to school this morning	He go school already morning this
He went to school	He go school finished
He did not go to school	He no go school finished

As far as Thailand is concerned, I do not know of a single book which has been written by any of the eminent exponents of a number of accepted methods of teaching English which would be perfectly satisfactory and thoroughly understood by the pupils. English is made infinitely more difficult owing to the fact that the books are written about things which the indigenous child has never seen or heard of during the whole of his short life.

Attractive illustrations are not the special need of an English reader for a foreign country; the contents of the book are much more important. A Thai child starts to learn English at the age of 11 plus, by which time his mind is fully developed. He is a big boy or a small man—no longer a child. He has a thirst for true stories, for adventure, for culture, for his own social inheritance—something which is no longer childish, but which will fill his mind with ambitions, aspirations, adventures and heroism. He is not a fool who can be easily led to believe things which are untrue, such as fairy tales, spirits, goblins that inhabit the forests, and animals that talk. English primers written for children of a lower age level are therefore not suitable for him. The books are full of childish things, simple (not to say foolish or stupid) beliefs; they always contain the famous Grimm and Hans Andersen fairy tales, or stories taken from the Arabian Nights. What is more important, they contain strange words which are never used by adults and which cannot be found in ordinary dictionaries, thus making it more difficult for the average Thai teacher to understand and translate, his method being to translate everything. Instead of

'Bear', the books use 'Teddy Bear', 'Brer Rabbit' for 'rabbit', 'Jumbo' for 'elephant', 'Nanny' for 'goat', 'cot' for 'bed', 'pup' for 'dog'. Then there are all the terms of endearment which an English mother uses when speaking to her baby. Such things are outside the ordinary English vocabulary. Also, children in England start to learn by using words which are orthographically and phonetically simple and not too long. So, instead of the usual word 'sleep', they use 'nap', and in order to keep to simple monosyllabic words they use the most extraordinary words and stories. And a Thai boy of 11 plus has to learn this nonsense.

When writing primers for children of 11 plus, the mentality, curiosity, previous knowledge and experience, as well as the understanding of the child, should be taken into account. Special books should be written for children of this age in order to make them feel that English is not so difficult, confusing or nonsensical, books which will help them to master the simple normal language form.

Various primers have been written to cope with different factors, from the phonetic and from the orthographic angle, based on the monosyllabic word list, the nursery word list, the first basic word list, and so on, but none has dealt with the difficulties of grammar. English grammar and construction are extremely baffling for children whose mother tongue is Thai. So many differences and distinctions have to be accounted for. Grammar should be carefully analysed and graded, and explanations of the various points introduced step by step as those points occur in new phrases and sentences. If there is a list of basic words in English, there should be also a list of basic grammatical points.

Those who attempt to improve the teaching of English in Thailand should make a complete analysis of the Thai and English languages to see where lie the parities, similarities and discrepancies. When this has been done they will then be able to understand the mind of the child who is struggling to understand a foreign language like English. So far, no such analysis has been made.

ADOLESCENTS AND MODERN LANGUAGES[1]

How is it possible to arouse the interest of an adolescent of 12–13 years of age in the learning of a foreign language?

Adolescence is a period of anxiety and disharmony, an age of revolt and day-dreaming about adventures, travel and uncontrolled

---

1. This section is taken from the working-paper prepared for the Ceylon seminar by Professor Fr. Closset of the University of Liège.

freedom. Is it possible to confine this small turbulent universe within the narrow, and necessarily rudimentary framework of the study of a foreign language? How, if the principles of the direct method are to be observed, can the need for graduating the difficulties and for patiently applying the method of 'short steps' be reconciled with the impatience and curiosity which are so natural in an adolescent of 12 or 13?

In order to solve this problem, not the subject matter but the pupil himself has been taken as the starting point. The first question is not how much knowledge should be imparted to the pupil, but what his potentialities and capacities are. In short, choice of methods must be based on what psychological insight reveals.

If we compare the aptitudes of a pupil aged 10 with those of the same pupil when aged 12 or 13, we note that, at the latter age, there is a slight diminution in the flexibility of his auditory and vocal organs and that his mechanical, untrained processes of memorizing and his faculty of imitation, which are so useful in the study of foreign languages, have also weakened to a certain extent. On the other hand, these physiological shortcomings are offset by a development of other faculties—thought, organized memory the reasoned association of ideas, the capacity for synthesis, abstraction and voluntary attention, intellectual curiosity and a more conscious and disinterested sensibility.

The adolescent of 12 or 13 is still a child in many ways, but a child who now wishes to be taken seriously. His evolution is intermittent and spasmodic: sometimes we have to deal with a mere youngster who can be captivated by completely primitive methods, and sometimes with a young man or a young woman who demands that his or her personality be respected, revolts against all dogmatism and seeks the why and the wherefore of all things. The adolescent begins to be aware of himself and to observe the discipline of his own will. He no longer has complete confidence in others, any more than he has in himself. Only in action can he find self-assurance, as well as the answers to the innumerable questions that assail him. It is through direct action that he will discover his own capacities and the 'meaning' of things. At this age his conception of the world is a utilitarian one, dominated by the questions: 'What is the use of that? What will it lead to?'

The adolescent, therefore, who is obliged to stammer out the first words learnt in a foreign language experiences a natural feeling of embarrassment; he feels he is at a disadvantage and is even being made to look slightly ridiculous. He would inevitably fall a prey to discouragement and boredom if the teacher were not there to co-operate with his pupils in a spirit of understanding.

It is the teacher's task to take the mentality of his young charges into full account, and, from the outset, adapt himself to it.

In our opinion, certain rules must be observed by the teacher who is entrusted with the task of teaching adolescents a foreign language. He must: (a) use the pupils' need for individual and collective activity and encourage a spirit of co-operation by applying methods which, while ensuring that the teacher shall be a vigilant and active guide, reserve the most important and responsible role for the class; (b) create an atmosphere of friendly confidence and goodwill; (c) encourage initiative and inventiveness and all efforts to avoid the commonplace; (d) encourage the pupils to think for themselves and not simply to imitate; (e) choose subjects for his lessons which coincide with the interests of his pupils.

A pupil tends to remember only what he has actually experienced and what is in harmony with his personality. External phenomena alone cannot satisfy him, unless he is allowed to find out for himself their moral meaning and aesthetic value. Adolescents are highly sensitive to the manner in which things are presented to them; while they react violently against over-emphasized 'moralization', they are easily captivated by a beautifully worded text, a touching narrative, a human or social problem.

Although these rules obviously apply to all branches of teaching, we recall them here since in secondary schools, the beginning of language teaching coincides with that age which, at first glance, seems to increase teaching difficulties but which, on closer examination, is seen to be well suited to such study.

These rules conceive of the class as the scene of various activities, episodes, situations and pictures taken from life, and by the conception of the human body as a living, active organism. Objects are regarded simply as incidental to action. Descriptions and enumerations should serve merely to place scenes or anecdotes in their proper setting. The noun is necessarily accompanied by an action; it is emphasized by a gesture, an attitude; and the verb becomes the pivot of a sentence. This is the stage at which words are associated with gestures.

At a slightly more advanced stage, recourse is made to 'dramatization', based on the association of words, gestures and emotions. The essential thing is to 'humanize' the subject matter of the teaching, to centre the interest around what has been lived and experienced. Lessons will relate first to the adolescents themselves, or rather to the events of their daily lives; then to the lives of the foreigners whose language they are learning, these lives being studied within the framework of their environment, of their own 'atmosphere', as it were.

The question that comes to the lips of our pupils, 'What is the use of learning a foreign language?' thus receives an immediate answer: 'It enables you to get to know a vast new world, full of interest.'

Experience shows that we have not taken the wrong road: our first and second year pupils are passionately interested in the study of languages. Owing to their eagerness to learn they often increase the normal rhythm of their work, reading their textbooks in advance and asking for supplementary reading material. Every discovery in this new field, whether in the form of songs, poems, photographs, gramophone records or books, gives them genuine pleasure.

The adolescent not only likes discovering a new world, but wants to use the foreign language as soon as possible, so as to be able to speak about what interests and stirs him. Sports, technological progress, the cinema and theatre, animal life, travel, social problems and occasionally, in time of crisis, political questions, such are the subjects that absorb young people of 13–15 years of age and can stimulate useful exchanges of ideas in language classes. These subjects can form the basis of talks between the pupils and the teacher; they can be the material for 'commentaries' based upon personal observation or interviews on the spot (at the airport, the travel agency, a model farm, etc.), or for a 'newsreel' in which the pupils, individually or in groups, present their own accounts of recent events, illustrated by photographs taken from newspapers and reviews.

It is a golden rule to satisfy the curiosity of our pupils and to use it, at the same time, for the benefit of our teaching. But it is also necessary to meet the need for mental discipline which begins to reveal itself in adolescents of 13–14 years of age. Their desire to classify, associate, explain and understand the reasons for the various phenomena presented to them will be particularly useful in the study of languages and grammar. Our 13-year-old pupils do not shirk grammar, realizing that it enables them to discover the explanation of matters that are complex and obscure. The pupil is more interested in a problem if he is allowed to find the solution himself. Under the teacher's direction, he will train himself in observing, classifying and associating grammatical phenomena, and in deducing rules from particular cases. In other words, he will always employ the active method.

Those of us who have experimented with this method in teaching discovered from the outset that one of the most effective means of achieving our object is to 'dramatize', that is to put into dialogue form, the texts read by the pupils, which gives an impression of reality and life more readily than any other medium.

Such a method requires initiative, skill and tact on the teacher's part. Given this, however, it arouses the interest of the pupils, for a 'play' satisfies their instinctive desire for action. Instead of being obliged to remain passive listeners, they are invited to take an active part in the lesson, ask one another questions, offer criticism and make suggestions—all of which gives them great pleasure. They thus acquire, almost as it were by play process, new aptitudes and fresh knowledge, whose practical value immediately becomes clear to them.

TESTS AND EXAMINATIONS[1]

The rough testing which a teacher carries out for a number of lessons, or regularly at the end of a term, can go on at all times and perform a useful service. For instance the effectiveness of some procedure can be roughly estimated in terms of the pupils' responses and reactions to questions, e.g. did it promote active responses, were there many more mistakes than usual, were there plenty of words used by the pupils, was the standard in most of the answers high enough? So, too, there are many exercises to test achievement in all textbooks nowadays, though few indicate the percentage of correctness that should be accepted as a condition for allowing work to continue, or what percentage indicates that more revision is needed. Similarly, the use of 'composition scales' has not been widely recommended, though in the hands of a keen teacher a five-point or ten-point composition scale will be most helpful. It will estimate for him the general standard that that class should attain. It may also diagnose a prevalent weakness, and it will always single out the weakest pupils, one or two of whom may have escaped notice. It might be profitable for this subject of simple classroom testing to be discussed by experts with experience of teaching English abroad, and for particular techniques and procedures to be developed for general use in schools.

If the testing is to discover the better of two (or more) procedures, textbooks, plans in syllabus or organization, it will be reliable only if it is scientifically carried out. For this, valid tests with a known reliability will be needed, and the usual statistical analyses of educational research. This will require the full time of an investigator, or team of workers, and several years to secure results that are reliable enough for action to be taken on them. In order to discover, for instance, whether it is better (i.e. for

---

1. These notes are taken from the working-paper prepared by Professor Gurrey for the Ceylon seminar.

future success) to plan for pupils to begin English in their first year or their second, or whether it is better to have one, two or three years of oral work before any reading of English, or whether it is better to delay the use of English as the medium of instruction until the fifth, sixth or seventh or even eighth year of learning English, it is completely unsound, and a complete waste of time and money, to attempt to answer such questions by rough and ready methods, by observation, teachers' estimates, made once a week or once a term, or by school examination marks, even over a long period. A sound answer might be arrived at, but that would be almost accidental.

There has been little research on the learning of English. The only possibility for such work to be carried through is perhaps for specially appointed persons to undertake specific tasks, e.g. the construction of and standardizing of a battery of tests, or even of one test. So little has been done in this field that the preliminary stages take up much time and the preparing of tests is a protracted task. The second step in planning might be to discuss the project and the necessity of the research, and also its main focus, with those who have had practical experience of research in education. The recommendations of 'external' advisers would be valuable and would save much time. Their recommendations and advice would have to receive full consideration, for research can very easily go astray into theoretical channels or become entangled in relatively minor problems; or it can be wasteful by making use of unprofitable or unsuitable techniques. The third step in planning might well be to appoint a small committee of advisers for the researcher to consult and report to periodically. The members of this committee should be well informed, but not necessarily expert or experienced in educational research. The value of this suggestion is that it would save money and time if the research plan could be discussed thoroughly before it was begun.

Nothing is known about 'the learning burden' for pupils learning English, nor the comparative learning burden of pupils brought up in different cultures and civilizations—Arabic, Indian, Malayan, Fijian, etc. We also want to know the learning burden at the different stages, and its relation to the intellectual level of the pupils. No work has been done on the number of repetitions that are needed for the learning, say, of a hundred new words in a second language, or the ten commonest sentence patterns. It would be useful to know what is the number of new words that an average class can learn during a year, and what is the maximum number that can be learnt by a good class with normal teaching. Similarly some studies on the learning of grammar might throw light on the type of exercise that best promotes learning of inflexions; on how much grammar can be learnt in the first year of learning a new language.

There are a number of investigations, not requiring tests, that can usefully be undertaken to provide estimates and guides in the teaching of English. For instance, much can be done merely by counting. How much written work does this class or that actually complete during a year? What is the average amount of written work that can be completed at the different stages? How many new words learnt during the previous year appear in the pupils' free compositions? Then, an 'error frequency count' can be taken, though this needs expert guidance. But with care the most frequently occurring mistakes can be discovered, and if the count is spread over the written work of several schools, a check is provided and the total summed figures may be more reliable. Similarly, a count of tense usage can give us the kind of tenses that the pupils use at the different stages in written work. Informal counts can be made of the words outside the readers that the children use in speech and writing. Again, a concerted attack on such problems as these in a number of schools can produce reliable results. Information of the greatest value to textbook compilers could easily be collected by teachers, and even by pupils themselves, over a term of years.

The work that has been done in Fiji, the Gold Coast, South Africa and Madhya Pradesh (India) is outstanding. Investigation into teaching and teaching programmes is a permanent feature of educational administration in South Africa. This is, indeed, an example to all countries which points the way to improved teaching through more effective methods and better textbooks.

At the request of the Gold Coast Education Department in 1948, the new University College set up an English Research Department to carry out research into the teaching and learning of English throughout the country. The department consisted of two British and two African researchers: one professor, one senior English master of a secondary school, one middle school headmaster and one assistant education officer; it was helped for six months by an experienced educational researcher of professorial status from Canada. Research was carried out for four years, though with full staff for only two. The work consisted mainly of investigations into comprehension in silent reading, mental ability testing, a general survey of attainment in English over the whole country, including the Northern Territories, a study of written composition and the teaching of it, inquiries into the learning of grammar, with an extensive error frequency count of written work in every secondary school in the country and in a large number of middle schools, a study of children's out-of-school reading, the vocabulary and sentence patterns of children in their first three years of English (and first three or two years of school), and of the general standard of pronunciation in the colony, at all levels.

In all, close on 46,000 test-scripts and compositions were completed and analysed. Considerable statistical work brought to light much useful information. A test for comprehension in silent reading was constructed and worked over for reliability and validity; this brought to light the need for a thorough training in reading with precise attention to detail. A non-verbal mental ability test was the test finally chosen out of several others for experiment. It proved suitable for testing African schoolchildren with seven, eight and nine years of school. A composition scale for pupils with seven, eight or nine years of English was made and used in urban and rural areas. Grammar tests and the error frequency count established that the chief difficulty is tenses—not only in primary education but throughout the secondary stage as well.

In Madhya Pradesh tests of achievement in reading English and in middle school subjects have been constructed and standardized. A composition scale for written English has also been prepared: for senior high school level an eight-point scale, and for junior high and upper middle schools a nine-point scale, elementary schools a seven-point scale. The usefulness of these scales is explained for the teachers, the main points being: (a) they help in the judging of English expression apart from compositional ability, which is very complex; (b) they help to sharpen the judgment of teachers as to what is good work and what is not; (c) they help to standardize evaluation; (d) they help the individual teacher to evaluate more consistently; (e) they help teachers to differentiate between the standard to be expected in the different classes. Detailed instructions are also given for the use of these scales, and they are considerably improved in accuracy of application by the short list of 'characteristics' that is provided for each specimen composition.

In Natal, in 1949, an investigation into the work of secondary schools, including English as second language, was undertaken. It revealed that there has been a very substantial and encouraging improvement in the achievement of pupils in Natal Government secondary schools since before the war. Not all of this improvement, however, could be credited to teaching in the second language. Much of it was due to improvement in teaching techniques, and to the more understanding attitude of parents. It also became clear that the average Natal pupil was not yet bilingual enough to learn mathematics, history, etc., through the second language without some loss of time and comprehension of the matter studied.

Recommendations were made for a change which would make it possible to retain the advantage of teaching in the second language whilst avoiding the weakness which had been revealed.

As to Fiji, during the first year the work of the Educational Research Institute at Suva was largely concentrated on devising tests to provide a standard of attainment in all classes of the Fijian and Indian schools. These comprised tests in the basic subjects and a test of general ability. This was the first objective of the early studies, and a means of effective selection of pupils for secondary and further education. The preparation of attainment tests in English (which was at once recognized as a major factor in success in secondary and further education in the area) led to vocabulary studies which would assist in assessment of reading ability. The administration of the tests provided material for a survey of current standards of attainment in reading English. As a complement to this survey, a study was made of attainment in written English.

Assessment of the effectiveness of current practices in the teaching of English was hampered by lack of information concerning the retention of reading and writing skills in adult life. Therefore two pilot studies were prepared. The first was concerned with the reading habits and preferences of Fijian adults, and the second with their reading ability in English.

In the first study an investigation was made of the printed matter to be found in village homes in Fiji. The sample covered several villages and different levels of education and authority. It revealed that there were religious vernacular books (chiefly Bibles and hymnbooks) in all homes, English magazines or papers in 60 per cent of the homes, and English books in 40 per cent.

In the second study a small library was taken into a Fijian village by a member of the village community, and the choice of books and papers were noted. The most popular items were religious pamphlets in Fijian; but the absence of vernacular fiction made it difficult to determine whether this preference was due to language or content. A series of simplified English stories was read with interest, but full-length English novels were not popular. An interesting feature was the failure of comics to interest readers. A third part of the study examined the sales of books, papers and magazines: there was an obvious preference for vernacular newspapers, but a considerable percentage of literature sold was in English.

This study showed that Fijians who read were able to read both Fijian and English, but they preferred the latter, presumably because they found it easier. The interest in serious religious publications is a sign of the considerable impact of the missions.

There are indications in the study that serious literature—perhaps of the semi-technical kind—written in simple English would have a wide appeal. With modifications, this study seemed suitable for wider application in the Pacific.

The second of the pilot studies examined a sample group of Fijians who had left school more than three years ago but less than seven. These 'subjects' were tested in English reading with tests appropriate to the grade at which they left school. Although many of these 'subjects' did little English reading in their villages, their results in the tests were better than the average of the children still at school. It seems that greater maturity may have erased the effect of lack of practice.

This study appears to be of some importance in education not only in the Pacific, and preparations have been made for a widespread and thorough investigation of this problem. But the work of this research institute is concerned with all the problems of education in the Pacific area, and it is not possible to specialize in the teaching of English. We feel however that success in teaching English is an essential preliminary to the raising of standards of general education in all Pacific territories. For this reason, a large amount of our work has been, and will continue to be done, in this field.

There must be examinations of some kind as things are at present, and an examination will always influence teaching—let us face that fact. Protests against the domination of teaching by examinations are, however, usually justified; but they are protests really against the type and nature of the examination, rather than against having examinations. And often they are criticisms and protests directed to the teachers who succumb to the temptation of cramming their pupils for expected questions—and often for expected questions only. The remedy is not impossible: the examination should be framed on lines that cannot be crammed for. The teacher then does not gain anything for his pupils if he concentrates only on expected questions. Most of the recognized examining boards now announce the type of question that they will use for the various aspects of the paper, and there is no harm, and often much good, in doing intensive work on some types of question, for instance, comprehension questions. As the examination influences the teaching, we can improve the teaching by improving the examination—and that is what is badly needed, and is the obvious remedy. Work on the field of examining has been going on in the United States of America and in the United Kingdom for many years, and considerable knowledge has been accumulated; but administrators and other educationists in Africa and Asia who are responsible for examinations have not always availed themselves of the information that is readily provided by the bodies that have promoted this study. But as far as is known at present there is no adequate study of examining in English as a second language—a study would direct examiners to test the candidates' *command* of the language.

TESTS AND MEASUREMENTS IN FOREIGN LANGUAGE TEACHING[1]

All teachers at one time or another attempt to evaluate the results of their work with a class. In most cases they conduct internal examinations, annually or oftener; and, at the end of the course, most pupils are given some kind of external test or examination, the results of which are supposed to provide an index to the achievement of each candidate and a measure of the effectiveness of the education given.

The form and implications of such examinations, especially those set by official examining bodies like the Universities, came under very heavy criticism in the thirties[2] and the mental testing movement has brought about a considerable degree of re-thinking of the whole technique of measuring in education. There has been a marked change in methods and in concepts of what an examination or test might be expected to measure, and in particular a greater awareness of elements of unreliability in the instruments used and in the marker. So too we are now more aware of the possible effects of a syllabus-based examination and of the form of the examination itself upon the content and method of the course which prepares pupils for it.

It is important to realize that a so-called 'new style' or objective test of attainment is a form of examination that, though it may be very different in its method, attempts to serve the same kind of purpose as the traditional examination—that of assessing a level of ability or achievement. Many of the criticisms directed at this kind of test should more properly be directed against examinations in general, rather than at the new style test itself. The only essential difference—and it is a large one—between the traditional examination and the 'objective' test is that the latter consciously attempts to achieve a greater degree of accuracy both in the numerical assessment of the pupil's performance and in the comparisons drawn between one pupil and another.

It is important here to consider what we are attempting to do

---

1. This paper was specially prepared for the present volume by Dr. W. D. Wall, formerly Reader in Education at Birmingham University, England, and since 1951 a member of the Secretariat of Unesco.
2. See the publications of the International Examinations Enquiry initiated by the International Institute of Teachers' College, Columbia University, New York.

when we try to measure the results of language teaching. We may, and usually do, try to evaluate achievement, the results of a particular course of teaching; not infrequently however we are also trying to predict future success. We like to think that, for example, if a pupil gets a high mark for French or German in his matriculation or college entrance examination, he will also do well in a university or college course in the same language. We tend to assume too that the results of an examination in German composition or grammar, for example, mean that the ability shown in the examination room will also be shown if the pupil has to write a letter in German as part of his later employment.

The form and content of our examinations express another set of ideas. They embody what we think to be the objectives, knowledge or skills, which should be attained by our teaching. Much of the criticism levelled at tests and examinations of all kinds arises from the observation that they tend to stress unduly one particular objective—let us say a command of vocabulary, of accurate grammatical or syntactical usage—at the expense of others, for example knowledge and appreciation of the culture which the foreign language enshrines. Sometimes indeed the apparent ease with which certain aspects of language learning can be tested—such as vocabulary in the form of word recognition, or grammatical forms—gives these preference over more subtle elements such for example as oral expression or insight into the foreign culture.

This brief introduction may lead us to define some of the considerations upon which measurement in foreign language teaching might be based and some of the criteria to be used in devising tests and examinations. *Mutatis mutandis*, these considerations and criteria will apply to measurement and evaluation in the teaching of any foreign language, and indeed to most measurement in education.

The first important thing is to define the goals of the teaching given and, as far as possible, to resolve these into their simplest elements. Only when this has been done and the skills and attitudes involved defined in a reasonably concrete way can we begin to attempt to measure a given pupil's degree of mastery. If, for example, we take the ability to 'read' a foreign language as one goal, it will be seen that such an ability involves mechanical elements of word recognition, of vocabulary, and of fluency as well as the more purely intellectual ones of gathering the general meaning of a passage, understanding words in their grammatical, syntactical and meaningful contexts, and appreciation of style and of nuance. Most teachers would probably agree that there is a great deal of difference in the ability to 'read' a daily newspaper and that required to 'read' literary prose or poetry. Thus in considering any test of reading, or in constructing one, it is important to determine which aspect or aspects of the skill are to be measured, and, as far as possible to measure them separately. Not infrequently an examination in what purports to be reading is a crude test of intelligence, a vocabulary test, or something quite other than the examiner intended.

Most of the published objective tests of language proficiency concentrate upon one aspect of the complex skill at a time. They are frequently criticized because they do just this. Teachers are apt to complain that a test of word meanings or of grammatical rules is useless because it does not measure the ability to write the language or translate it. The answer is of course that such tests, if they are properly constructed, set out to measure only one aspect at a time; if other aspects are to be measured, other tests must be added to the battery. If however the maker of the test claims to measure all aspects of language learning by means of measuring one skill, then of course the criticism may well be justified.

This brings us to another elementary consideration in educational measurement. Language learning is a complex thing psychologically, the nature of which we know only imperfectly. We are certainly not yet in a position to say that by measuring any one isolable aspect of it, we are measuring all that may be implied. Even at a fairly advanced level, for example, success in written translation from and into the language may only correlate with success in oral work to the same extent as success in French correlates with success in English,[1] the correlation between the language and literature papers is much lower. It is thus clearly important to attempt to measure all the different aspects of language programmes rather than to think that any one will give an index to the whole. Among the elements which can be identified for this purpose and for which reasonably accurate measures have been, or could be devised are:

Vocabulary (recall and recognition), knowledge of idiom; grammar; syntactical usage; silent reading; comprehension of the printed language, comprehension of the spoken language; translation into the mother tongue; translation from the mother tongue; oral composition; oral reading; pronunciation; geographical, historical and cultural background.[2]

Most tests and examinations at present in use are too com-

---

[1]. See J. A. Petch, 'A Comparison of Orders of Merit of H.S.C. Candidates offering two Modern Languages', *Brit. Journ. Ed. Psych.*, vol. XV, pt. 3, 1945. The obtained correlations between the results of the language papers and the results of the oral tests ranged from +0.60 to +0.67 for French, Spanish and German. Language papers and literature papers correlate to the extent of +0.31 to +0.41.

[2]. For a fuller discussion of these and other points, the reader is referred to H. A. Greene, A. N. Jorgensen, and J. R. Gerberich, *Measurement and Evaluation in the Secondary School*, London, Longmans, Green and Co., 1943, 670 p.

prehensive; those devised by teachers and by official examining bodies are frequently so framed that they attempt to measure too many factors at the same time. For example a pupil's mark on a test of translation from a foreign language is a composite representing (imperfectly) his ability to recognize vocabulary, his use of the context to guess at meaning, his knowledge of syntax, his background of knowledge of the subject treated in the text, and his ability to express himself well in his own mother tongue.

Such a confusion, and the equally common one of ambiguity in the questions set, will affect both the reliability and the validity of the test used. If our estimates of progress and attainment are to be of use, the measuring instrument which we use must be *reliable*; that is to say, we must be reasonably sure that it will always give the same result under the same conditions. A test on which a pupil scored twenty today and forty tomorrow would be as useless as a thermometer which gave different readings when the temperature of the air was the same. Such fluctuations can be caused by a number of things—by ambiguous questions, by questions set in such a way as to favour lucky guesses or to allow the pupil to proceed to the correct result by a process of elimination; by questions which cover only a small sample of the skills or knowledge involved; or by questions which invite responses of different kinds and place too much stress upon the qualitative judgment of the examiner.[1] The last two are the commonest causes of unreliability in the examinations set by teachers. A test paper consisting of four or five questions which the pupil has to answer at length can easily fail to sample more than a small fraction of his knowledge. He may in fact have a competence in, say, three-quarters of the syllabus. If however two of the four questions cover the unknown quarter, he will get less than half marks. Conversely, if he is lucky, he may only get questions which he can answer and earn a credit beyond his deserts. So too a failure to understand one question out of four will lead to a loss of a quarter of the marks. If however the examination consists of a large number of smaller items—say a hundred questions—covering the whole of the syllabus equally, lucky shots are reduced in their effects and ambiguities in the framing of the questions are less important since we have taken a wider and therefore probably more representative sample of the pupils' knowledge or abilities. Such short

---

1. The theory and practice of the construction of reliable and valid tests can only be touched on here. The reader is referred to the pioneer work in the field, which still remains the best introduction: P. B. Ballard, *The New Examiner*, London, University of London Press, 1923. Also to E. F. Lindquist (ed.), *Educational Measurement*, Washington, D.C., American Council on Education, 1951; and (for those of a statistical turn of mind) to H. Gulliksen, *Theory of Mental Tests*, New York and London, John Wiley and Chapman and Hall, 1950. The work by Greene, Jorgensen and Gerberich previously cited should also be consulted.

questions, too, lend themselves to short answers and thus reduce the element of the subjective in the judgment of the marker. The long answer, usually in the form of some kind of essay, involves too many elements combined in too many different ways to permit easily an objective evaluation. Style, grammar, punctuation, spelling, handwriting may all be involved along with content, and influence the mark allotted.[1]

Unless a test is reliable in the sense described, it can hardly be valid; that is to say it can hardly be a true measure of what it sets out to measure. But validity is rather more than this. If a test is a valid measure then we should find, for example, that those who do best on, say, a test of oral French or Spanish, are also best when it comes to conducting a conversation with native speakers of the language. This may sound like a statement of the obvious; but we repeatedly find that examinations in school subjects correlate rather better with other examinations in the same subject than they do with the real use which can be made by the individual of the skills or knowledge involved. Validity in our measures will only be obtained when we state clearly the objectives of our teaching, analyse and define them in their separable elements, and measure each in situations which come as close as possible to the real circumstances in which they will be used. Thus, if spoken fluency in the language is an aim, then it must be tested in a variety of ways and with due attention to comprehension and expression to vocabulary recall and recognition, to pronunciation and to the finer discrimination of small differences in sound on which meaning may depend. Each of these and other factors should be tested separately, as well as being tested in a variety of situations in which they occur in combination. Each must be tested reliably in such a way as to eliminate so far as possible the effects of chance or embarrassment on the examinee and of subjective distortion of judgment on the part of the examiner.[2]

[*Editor's note:* An important advance in the testing of achievement in aural skill is the listening comprehension test, first developed by the Yale-Barnard Conference on the teaching of French and

---

1. This does not mean that responses of the essay type should never be used nor that they have no value. For the measurement of a pupil's capacity to sustain and express a train of thought, for example, or to marshal a complex body of fact, they are probably essential. They do however demand special precautions with which the naive examiner is often unacquainted; and even so it is frequently better to have the examinee write four or five shorter paragraphs rather than one long essay.
2. The testing of aural-oral attainment in foreign languages is the most difficult as it is one of the most important aspects of the topic. Most oral examinations are casual unstandardized situations which allow great play to the subjective judgment of the examiner and to the nervousness of the pupil. Some significant work has been done, by the use of uniform stimuli recorded on tape and on records, by Haley, Rogers and Clark, Seebert and Wood, Lundeberg and Tharp—for bibliography, see W. S. Munroe (ed.), *Encyclopaedia of Educational Research*, Macmillan Co., New York, 1950, rev. ed., p. 480 and p. 483.

now adopted by the College Entrance Examination Board. It is a fixed response test in which the candidate hears questions that come to him from a loudspeaker and chooses answers that appear on a printed page before him.][1]

With the aid of one or another of the simpler manuals mentioned earlier, the modern language teacher in the ordinary classroom can do much to improve his own testing and examining techniques so that he does come near to an objective and valid estimate of the progress of his pupils. There are however other purposes of measurement, for which from time to time he may have need of instruments specially prepared by experts. It is sometimes desirable to compare the attainments of the children we teach and the results of the methods we favour, with the attainments of children taught by other methods. It is here that the properly standardized and objective test is most useful.[2] Such instruments must of course conform to the criteria outlined above: they must be reliable and valid, and attempt to measure attainment in all the agreed areas of language skills and knowledge. In addition however they must be *normed*. A mark on a test or examination has no meaning in itself; a mark of 50 for example does not have the same kind of meaning as a length of six feet. A child's score on a test is meaningful only in comparison with the marks of other similar children on the same test. What is more, we do not know that the amount of difference in ability represented by two marks of 40 and 45 is the same as that between say 50 and 55. A properly standardized test is 'normed' by being administered to large groups of children of the kind and in the circumstances for which the test is intended. The crude scores obtained are then tabulated in such a way[3] that the performance of an individual child or of a class can be compared with that of children of the same age and circumstance.

This imposes certain limitations on the use of such tests. Not merely should the circumstances of testing be the same, and such things as the instructions and time limits be carefully adhered to, but it is also necessary to recognize that if the circumstances of the class to be tested differ markedly from those of the children on whose performance the norms were based, then the test may be invalid. Moreover every method of teaching has certain implications for the framing of questions, and the form of question may

---

1. cf. Henry S. Dyer, 'Testing by Ear', *College Board Review*, Yale University, May 1954, no. 23, p. 436-8.
2. For complete bibliographies and details of the available tests, see: O. K. Buros (ed.), *The Fourth Mental Measurements Yearbook*, New Brunswick, New Jersey, Gryphon Press, 1953 and the previous volumes by the same editor.
3. As *standard scores* (i.e. scores determined in relation to the mean score and dispersion of scores on the test concerned), *decile scores* (i.e. scores which indicate what percentage of children reach or exceed the same level), or as *age norms* (i.e. the mean score obtained by children of a given age).

raise difficulties of an extraneous kind for children working under different educational conditions from those of the standardization group. Hence, without special precautions in interpreting the scores and in some cases special adaptation, tests devised in one country cannot be usefully applied elsewhere.

Two other important uses of measurement may be mentioned in conclusion. To the ordinary teacher, the assessment of attainment is probably less important than the diagnosis of the weaknesses and difficulties of individual pupils. In the course of our teaching we want to know whether progress is inhibited by a faulty command of grammar, by poverty in vocabulary, by weakness in recall or by any other of the interrelated factors which may keep a child back. Much of this information is gathered by the good teacher in the course of marking class exercises; but we constantly find cases of children whose difficulties are overlooked for a long period until they become discouraged; or we may be faced with a new class whose status we do not know. Hence the battery of tests which systematically measures each aspect of attainment in isolation can be used to yield for each child a pattern of strengths and weaknesses on which remedial work can be securely built. If such a battery has been normed on large groups of children with separate and reliable scores for each sub-test, it is all the more valuable; but the teacher himself can devise useful diagnostic tests to cover all the main aspects of language learning and in the course of time build up rough norms that apply to the classes he teaches.

Prediction of ability to learn a foreign language is much more difficult, and little conclusive work has been done so far. In part this is because it is hard to find a criterion of success in a field so complex and where the aims and values aspired to by teachers have shown such marked variation over the past two or three decades. In part it is because the psychology of language learning has itself been very little explored. From general studies in the field of cognitive abilities we know that success in any school subject depends partly upon general all-round intellectual efficiency, or intelligence, partly upon one or more of what are called group abilities, and partly upon factors specific to the particular situation.[1] In those subjects which involve the use of words, it appears that, as well as general intelligence a group factor of verbal ability is involved. This group factor seems to consist of a number

---

[1]. Group abilities are so called since they appear to enter into some types of activity and not into others; 'practical ability' for example seems to determine success in such things as wood-work but not to enter into success in the mother tongue. Conversely *verbal ability* enters into success in language and literature, history and geography, etc. For an excellent short review of the extensive work in this field, see: C. Burt, 'The Structure of the Mind', *Brit. Journal Ed. Psych.*, vol. XIX, pt. 3, 1949.

of sub-abilities—for example a word factor involved in dealing with words in isolation and a language factor involved in dealing with words in context—and that these have executive and receptive aspects. So far as the writer knows, no really satisfactory prognostic test based upon the results of factor analysis has yet been devised.[1] It is indeed likely that the methods used in teaching the foreign language and the aims of the teaching itself would markedly affect the weight which should be ascribed to the various cognitive factors involved; and we do not yet know whether the acquisition of a foreign language at say the age of six or seven is the same thing, psychologically, as learning it at the age of twelve or later. As most modern language courses are at present framed, and assuming a start at around the age of eleven or twelve, it seems to be clear that the best predictive instruments are a test of verbal intelligence, a test of verbal fluency, and a measure of success in the native language. Certain special batteries have however been devised with some success. For example the *language aptitude test*[2] consists of 10 sub-tests of which four are artificial language tests, including the meaning of prepositions, memory for foreign language, use of prefixes and suffixes and use of language rules. Two other sub-tests constitute a measure of intelligence, two cover achievement in English grammar, and two others recognition of similarities in sound and knowledge of accent.[3]

The advocates of standardized or objective tests are frequently accused of wishing rather to weigh the baby than to feed it; and sometimes the jibe is not without substance. Testing and examining are a means to an end, an instrument of teaching like any other; and it has clearly defined uses in predication, evaluation and diagnosis. It also has an essential value in research, enabling us to determine how far we are achieving what we set out to do, the relative virtues of this or that method, and helping us to conduct the basic psychological research into language learning, a better understanding of which will improve our methods. Crude and unobjective measures are valueless; but, in collaboration with the expert in educational measurement, the modern language teacher can develop for himself serviceable testing instruments that will meet most of the legitimate criticisms and lead him towards a more thorough understanding of what he is doing and how far he is achieving his aims.

---

1. Three members of the Harvard Language Aptitude Project, J. B. Carroll, S. M. Sapon, J. E. Richards, are currently engaged in the construction and validation of a test battery for predicting success in spoken foreign language courses.
2. Centre for Psychological Services, George Washington University, U.S.A.
3. Other tests are listed in the *Mental Measurements Year Books* previously cited and in the annual *Reviews of Educational Research* published by the American Educational Research Association, Washington, D.C.

CHAPTER VI
THE TRAINING OF MODERN LANGUAGE TEACHERS

In the seminar report, which follows next in this chapter, considerable space is given to the ideal equipment and qualifications of the modern language teacher. Such perfection must necessarily remain the exception rather than the rule for a long time to come, particularly in those countries where the supply of suitable potential teachers is limited and proper training facilities more limited still.

Competent modern language teaching calls for exacting standards in teacher training—standards perhaps a trifle higher then those required of teachers in other disciplines. The language teacher must not only 'know' as much and cover as much ground in his special field as his colleagues do. He stands in greater need than they do of constant refreshment and revision of his knowledge. To teach a language and a civilization is to teach a growing, living subject, constantly shifting and changing, constantly threatening to leave far behind and hopelessly out of date people who thought they had once mastered it. Furthermore, the language teacher has to live in two or even more different linguistic worlds, his own and that of his pupils and the strange, exotic one from abroad that he strives to impart to them. He must, in a sense, live a life of carefully divided loyalties, being at one and the same time a normal, loyal citizen of his own country and, in the classroom, the unofficial ambassador of another.

Small wonder then that language teachers resent any tendency to deny them proper status and are particularly resentful of the fact that there are still some countries where language teachers receive *less* pay and consideration than their colleagues. This is a strange and intolerable survival of the age when school authorities thought any available unemployed foreigner could make a language teacher.

Insistence on proper status, and on the supervision of questions of status and of training standards through international agencies and through international language teachers' associations, was one of the interesting aspects of the discussions during the final week at the Ceylon seminar.

Interest also centred about types and patterns of teacher

training. These were classified by the rapporteur, Miss Panandikar, and were later listed in the seminar report. Such a list might be completed by some mention of those specialized institutions which have been set up fairly recently to train teachers of a given language or civilization who will do their teaching abroad. One thinks in this connexion of the special schools for the teaching of English as a foreign language which exist at London University or at the University of Michigan and which are intimately connected with the names of Pattison and Fries; also of the French École de Preparation et de Perfectionnement de Professeurs de Français à l'Etranger and of the help given to language teachers by organizations such as the Alliance Française or the Dante Alighieri Society.

The seminar report touches on all these questions of qualification, training and status as well as the all-important question of keeping in touch. It is followed by three seminar documents, two of which are practical illustrations of what is actually being done to train language teachers in two different countries. There should be no attempt to compare these two countries. In his brief note on the training of teachers of English and on the teaching of English in Turkey, Professor Gatenby deals with the teaching of a language which has only relatively recently been introduced on a wide scale; while Dr. Winkelmann, in discussing the contemporary training of language teachers in Western Germany, deals with a discipline which has formed a part of the educational fabric of the nation for nearly a century. She is also discussing a school system which must stand very near the top of the scale as regards the time and effort devoted to language teaching. Few countries can boast that their secondary school pupils devote seven years to the study of a first foreign language and often five years to the study of a second. Language teachers from many so-called advanced countries are likely to read Dr. Winkelmann's article with as much envy as enlightenment.

Like the German Federal Republic, Belgium is a country which takes modern language teaching very seriously. Professor Closset in his remarks on the training of language teachers has obviously had the problems of his own country in mind, but he has also transcended them to portray the optimum standards which those responsible for the training of language teachers in all countries should bear constantly in mind.

THE SEMINAR REPORT

In stressing the importance of the training of teachers of modern languages, the seminar was of the opinion that in addition to the training period proper, other factors, such as the home environment, the school, the university and life in general, played their part in the formative years of the future teacher.

Existing systems of training for secondary school language teachers seemed to fall into three main patterns:
1. Training spread over a four—or five—year university course and forming an integral part of such course.
2. Training conducted by a university or an educational authority subsequent to the normal academic course and sometimes separated from it by an interval of one or more years' teaching.
3. A university course of academic studies including an introduction to philosophy, as well as to the theory of education, followed by a training period of two years in training centres established by the educational authorities.

It was felt that the equipment of the future teacher in this field should include:
1. High standards of attainment in the language he proposes to teach: correct pronunciation, the ability to read aloud in a clear and expressive manner, fluent and correct speech, facility of expression in writing, and advanced reading ability.
2. Sound linguistic knowledge based on scientific study of the characteristic features of the language, past and present, such as system of sounds, inflexions, sentence patterns and word formation, and the ability to apply this knowledge in the classroom.
3. Extensive knowledge of the literature and civilization of the country under study.
4. An introduction to educational psychology and to the theoretical and practical problems of teaching, with special attention to the methods and techniques of teaching foreign languages and the use of audio-visual aids.

As the development of a balanced personality is of first importance for the teacher of modern languages, he will require for his task imagination, tenacity of purpose, and enthusiasm. The sustained study of the language and its literature, together with an ever-increasing knowledge of the way of life of the people whose language he is studying, will assist in broadening his culture and enhance his professional ability.

To enable modern language teachers to be properly equipped for their task and to help them to carry out their work under favourable conditions, the seminar was of the opinion that it was necessary for educational and state authorities to provide them with certain essential facilities.

The seminar would recommend that:
1. There should be provision for prospective teachers of modern

languages to spend some time, during their student days, in the country whose language they propose to teach.
2. Modern language teachers in service should be given opportunity to visit the foreign country periodically under Exchange of Persons Programmes, through the granting of leave, absence with pay, or under any other schemes.
3. There should be refresher courses for modern language teachers at regular intervals.
4. There should be a stronger bond between the universities and the training centres and also between universities and practising teachers, particularly in matters of educational research.
5. There should be easy access to books, journals and periodicals in the modern languages. In this connexion, well-conducted library projects would meet the needs not only of those working in cities but also of those in remote places.
6. Facilities for the supply and exchange of books, publications and teaching materials from one country to another should be provided, and all obstacles to the free circulation of such books and materials removed in conformity with the Free Flow Agreement sponsored by Unesco.
7. There should be opportunities for modern language teachers to hear native speakers when they happen to visit their country and to meet them socially.
8. Regular programmes in modern languages should be provided on the radio.

It would be incumbent on managements of schools to see that the modern language teacher was considered a specialist and given conditions under which he could teach the language effectively. He would need a modern language room, good audio-visual aids and a library well equipped with up-to-date books in modern languages.

It is important that at all stages of language learning the teacher should have the highest possible qualifications. In particular, it is vital that the teaching of beginners' classes should be of the highest quality. The seminar emphatically deprecates any system which puts junior classes in the hands of unqualified teachers.

The seminar also discussed the need for better organization of modern language teachers. It was agreed that, in principle, questions such as the improvement of the status and salaries of teachers, affecting the teaching fraternity as a whole, should be taken up by teachers' organizations of a general type, while the modern language teachers' organizations should concern themselves with improving the efficiency of modern language teaching and creating a sense of vocation with regard to their work among modern language teachers. It was stated that in some parts of the world teachers of modern languages are paid less than those of other subjects. Such injustices may very properly be the subject of action by modern language teachers' associations and the seminar strongly urges that these discrepancies be removed. It is also the opinion of the seminar that the status and salaries of the teaching profession as a whole frequently suffer in comparison with those of other professions requiring no greater academic qualifications or sense of vocation.

NOTES ON THE TRAINING OF LANGUAGE TEACHERS IN TURKEY[1]

The problem in Turkey, when work started at the Gazi Training College in 1944,[2] was to secure the most favourable environment both in the training college and the schools. Very little could be done directly to improve conditions in the schools, e.g. by reducing the size of classes or supplying equipment, and every effort was therefore made to train the teachers to a point where they would be able themselves to remove obstacles and secure better conditions. By familiarizing the teachers with the essentials of success it was hoped that the main difficulties might be overcome. In the result, this aim has been justified: our trained teachers have learnt how to deal effectively with a large class, how to get the best out of a textbook, how to make their classroom into a laboratory, and how to concentrate on speech first.

But every country, every area, has its own particular needs, and these have to be studied in order that teacher training may proceed along right lines. Effective classroom procedure differs greatly according to custom, background, mental attitude, etc., and a language has to be served to a class by a technique depending on national characteristics and habits. The particular technique best suited to the 12-18 age group in Turkey was studied at the Gazi Training College with the help of the students and in schools visited in various parts of the country, and it has been embodied in *A Direct Method English Course: Specially designed for Turkish Students*.[3] Nothing original is claimed, nothing that cannot be found elsewhere; the aim was to combine

---

1. This section was extracted from an essay originally prepared by E. V. Gatenby, M.A., Professor of English, Ankara University, as an appendix to Professor Gurrey's *Study on the Teaching of English as a Foreign Language in Countries in Asia, Africa and the Mediterranean*, which was commissioned by the Unesco Secretariat and used as a working-paper at the Ceylon seminar.
2. See 'Conditions for Success in Language Learning', by E. V. Gatenby in *English Language Teaching*, March and May 1950.
3. By E. V. Gatenby. London, Longmans, Green, 1952.

TRAINING OF TEACHERS

teaching elements in the right proportion and in the right order.

Among the points that may be emphasized are the following:

Although the *Interim Report on Vocabulary Selection* was the basis of the vocabulary of 2,000 root words to be used in the series of textbooks, we soon had supporting evidence of the assertion that word counts depend on locality, education, likes and dislikes, frequency of topic, etc., and that an 'average' collection of words such as that in the interim report may, in several of its items, be quite unconnected with the needs of a particular group of pupils. What seemed the necessary modifications were therefore made for Turkey, and common words of the Turkish environment were introduced.

Structure needs as much attention as vocabulary, and both must be taught together. The teacher who is not a native speaker of a language is notoriously weak on structure, and must be given special help with it in the teachers' handbook.

The non-native speaker also needs much more help with illustrative examples of the use of a word, definitions, questions and exercises than is given in most textbooks.

The point at which the purely oral approach used with beginners is no longer fully effective, but needs the support of eye and understanding, was discovered for classrooms in Turkey and found to come after approximately the first 300 words and their supporting structures.

The giving of meaning (by any method) was seen to be of secondary importance. It is the use and practice of words and structures that is the first essential.

Pupils benefit greatly by compiling their own dictionaries as they go along, showing meaning by drawings, illustrative sentences, opposites, synonyms, etc., without any use of the vernacular.

The untrained teacher with an excellent knowledge of English, but made over-confident by it and considering a teachers' handbook beneath his dignity, can do a great deal of harm.

Translation for comprehension, mentioned by so many textbooks as legitimate use of the vernacular, is a waste of time.

Dull children can best be taught not by translation, but by use and absorption of the language in association with interesting activities.

Limited objectives, e.g. a reading knowledge of the language, are a confession of failure on the part of teachers and officials.

The use of allegedly easy but synthetic English in the early stages is a waste of time, and delays advance.

An 'attached' school does not supply sufficient variety of practice and experience for intending teachers.

Pupils need to be shown how to learn just as teachers need to be shown how to teach.

Teachers and pupils need more opportunity for reading words and figures written by native speakers of English, and more attention should be given to correct the formation of letters. Much confusion exists at present.

For Turkey, the following sequence in a lesson—which may extend over a number of periods—gives the best result from the second year onwards:
1. The teacher reads aloud the main passage of the lesson.
2. The meaning of new words is given in a vocabulary known to the pupils. (The necessary material for this is given in the teachers' handbook.) The new words are written up on the board, with guides to meaning, and copied into vocabulary notebooks. Any new structure that needs explanation and illustration is dealt with.
3. The teacher asks miscellaneous questions on the text, with a view to ensuring complete comprehension.
4. The set questions in the book, which contain all the new root words and derivatives, are asked and answered by the pupils.
5. The textbook notes on grammar, etc., are read and studied.
6. The second reading passage, containing new words, is studied and discussed.
7. The structures, as listed in the handbook, are more closely studied and practised.
8. The dictation, drills, controlled composition, games, etc., follow as provided by the handbook.
9. The textbook exercises on the lesson are done, some of them as homework.

THE AIMS IN TEACHER TRAINING[1]

As can be seen from the information available on countries where the professional training of modern language teachers is well organized, we are, despite all appearances, still far short of the mark. Yet anyone who is really familiar with the problem knows that training for the teaching of modern languages is something that demands more than incidental attention.[2]

A man may be a university graduate, but he may not make a good teacher. He may have vast knowledge, outstanding culture and exceptional intellect, but that does not necessarily mean that he is able to stimulate pupils' interest, or transfer to them

---
1. This section is taken in slightly condensed form from the working-paper prepared for the Ceylon seminar by Professor Fr. Closset of the University of Liège.
2. For an authoritative view on the change to be made in the present position, see Fernand Mossé, 'Quelques considérations sur l'enseignement des langues vivantes en France', *Cahiers pédagogiques pour l'enseignement du second degré*, VIIe année, Lyon, Comité universitaire d'information pédagogique, octobre 1951, p. 7-8.

effectively the knowledge he has himself absorbed. Until he has come to realize and fulfil all the requirements of his task, and until he finds his right road, he should be able to rely on certain psychological and educational notions, on a clear-cut method, and on procedures that have been carefully tested. The important and urgent thing is to provide the future teacher with reliable procedures and a method that experience has shown to be sound. He should be trained how to make his university knowledge accessible to the pupils, while keeping their young brains alive and active, and whetting their desire for knowledge. The would-be teacher should be brought to cultivate a taste for pedagogical research as well as a desire for factual information. In order to save the pupils time and effort, as any teaching of modern languages should do, the prime requirement is not merely that the teacher should have complete mastery of his subject, but that he should be trained to use those techniques of modern language teaching that are based on the best and most up-to-date principles of psychology and pedagogy.

The teacher's training must be a twofold one, but these two parts of his training will be fully effective only if they are organically, not mechanically, linked together. It should be the purpose of this training to give the would-be teachers:

1. Such mastery of the foreign language as will enable them to use it for practical purposes, both orally and in writing.
2. Scientific notions concerning, firstly, the language as a 'human function' and, secondly, the place occupied in world culture by the foreign literature studied. Scientific (i.e. not dogmatic, but interpretative) study of a modern language must go hand in hand with practical study of that language, giving it greater depth. This type of training, because of the object it sets out to achieve, must be entrusted to instructors who are qualified from the standpoint of linguistics, literature, and the practice of teaching.

Accordingly, the work of training must not be undertaken solely by representatives of 'pure knowledge', whose daily labours do not at the same time bring them into contact with actual teaching practice. Nor, conversely, should it be entrusted solely to so-called 'practical' teachers, who are all too apt to discount pure knowledge or 'science'.

Few countries really appreciate the fact that if a teacher is to impart instruction about a civilization he must equip himself specifically for that task. Nor can it be said that, in most countries, university teaching has any very 'sociological' (*Gesellschaftskunde*) complexion. It is, however, possible to remedy this serious shortcoming, at least in countries where a *studium generale* is part of the curriculum. Here, once again, the principle of co-ordination must be observed. A course in the civilization of the country whose language is to be taught should everywhere, as in France, be one of the items of instruction leading up to the test to be undergone by the modern language teacher, since the latter must have a good knowledge of the foreign country and its language alike. The teacher will generally be influenced, throughout his whole career, by the habits of mind which his studies and his own reading have formed in him during his scientific and pedagogical training. Once they are embarked on their careers, few teachers have the time either to review their own notions or to readjust themselves and their knowledge with a view to teaching their subject from a new angle, although the country in question and (often) its language have evolved since the teachers previously studied them. This, of course, is wrong. To be satisfied with one's original knowledge is to confine oneself, throughout a career, to imparting instruction which is no longer adapted either to the needs of the pupils or to the realities of the situation.

Certain universities employ the services of foreign assistants from the countries whose languages they teach. These assistants supplement the instruction given in universities by teachers or professors who are, in most cases, nationals. The assistants' teaching, delivered in the language which is being taught, enables the students to acquaint themselves with the features both of the language and of its country of origin.

But it is a question whether (a) scientific and (b) pedagogical and didactic training should not be supplemented by practical linguistic training designed to produce teachers who are 'broken in' to the mechanics of the language they are to teach. Too many young teachers are, in this respect, regrettably weak. Their pronunciation is faulty, their conversational facility woefully slight, and their vocabulary too far removed from that in current use—and this in an age when the pupils have greater opportunities than the teacher himself of hearing the foreign language spoken and so, in consequence, of mastering its pronunciation during out-of-school activities (films, broadcasting, travel abroad, etc.).

Nowadays, few students—only those whose parents are comparatively well-to-do—have the means of spending their holidays abroad regularly. Association with foreigners and visits to clubs require too much time and are sometimes an expensive matter. In any case such activities are possible only for those who have the necessary opportunities. The State does not make the effort that would enable students to spend a whole academic year abroad. Seeing films or listening to the radio generally produces a purely passive reaction, whereas ability to speak a language comes through active effort in which at least two persons participate.

This being so, the State might consider solving these difficulties in a way that involves the minimum of expense for itself and the students alike: namely through the organization of essentially practical courses for students (practical exercises in pronunciation, conversations, readings, practice in idioms), each course being for a limited number of participants. Because of its practical nature, such a course should be given by a 'practitioner', a specialist acquainted with the students' scientific training and one who, since his departure from the university, has specialized primarily in the practical study of the language taught. The exercises would take place twice a week during the period of preparation for the licentiate's degree, in addition to the theoretical courses and in addition, also, to the study of the mechanism of the language which is carried out during the first two years at the university. After that the students would have been 'seeded' and there would therefore be fewer of them.

Modern language teachers should, ideally, also be required to make a more or less prolonged stay in the country whose language and civilization they are to teach. In some countries in fact this is obligatory. In most instances it should be unnecessary to compel modern language teachers to make a stay in the country of the language they wish to teach. Most teachers themselves feel a desire to acquire a better knowledge of the language and of the countries where the modern tongues they study are spoken.

The State could, in the case of students with slender resources, facilitate such stays. Fellowships are already provided by certain governments or education departments. Such fellowships are also provided for in bilateral cultural agreements between various nations. There are still, however, many countries where no such facilities exist. Why should young people not be granted loans on trust which would help them to make stays abroad? They have never refused to discharge a debt of honour, especially if time is given them to discharge it and they have the prospects of obtaining a university degree or some other qualifying certificate as a reward for their sacrifices.

The State, which is entitled to expect from its future leaders knowledge, skills and even sacrifices proportionate to their privileges, should make visits abroad a feature of the curriculum for most of the university examinations, or at least of the curriculum for the training courses for modern language teachers. Why should not the latter be compelled to spend at any rate one semester (term) in the country which can make the most effective contribution to their professional, scientific and humanistic training?

Teachers of modern languages are, of all teachers, those who most need to refurbish, continually, the knowledge they have acquired in the course of their studies. Their vocabulary contracts; they repeat the same expressions. As regards knowledge of the literature and study of the foreign civilization, errors of perspective are liable to arise if the teacher fails to remain in contact with the country about which he has to teach.

There is no end to the study of a foreign language and its methodology—any more than there is to the study of a science or an art. This is a fact that too many of us forget at the outset of our professional careers, with the result that we continue in the mistakes of our predecessors. Parents who entrust us with their children's education, and the pupils themselves, are entitled to expect a higher standard. The university provides no more than a foundation; it is up to each of us to consolidate that foundation, assemble materials, and build upon it.

Every teacher is entitled to be, and indeed must be, informed on the problems connected with his own particular branch of instruction. Do the central libraries of education departments provide documentation enabling established teachers to keep themselves up to date?—in many countries, most teachers complain that they have difficulty in obtaining the minimum of scientific and pedagogical information. Would it not be advisable for special experts, services or commissions to be attached to the larger libraries and to make the necessary purchases, and for a detailed list of those purchases to be sent to educational establishments, for consultation by teachers? Should not education departments, also, provide schools with a regular supply of specialized reviews and journals, see that the funds earmarked for this purpose are usefully spent, and ensure that teachers can find, in their libraries, full scientific and pedagogical documentation (books and handbooks of reference, recent publications, etc.)? Educational research centres, where they exist, should be easy of access to teachers who wish to consult new publications, information on teaching and methodology and articles on the teaching of modern languages and new departures in this field.

In some countries, the government and various associations organize 'refresher' holiday courses for the teachers, with the emphasis on methodology and teaching.[1] They invite foreign specialists to these courses, whose value is becoming increasingly apparent with every year that goes by, their influence on the improvement of the teaching being often decisive. At these gatherings 'quality' makes up for whatever may be lacking in 'quantity'.

Even for the purpose of teaching in secondary classes, it should

---

1. For a 'refresher programme' for established teachers, see Closset, *Didactique des langues vivantes*, p. 20–2, Brussels, M. Didier, 1950, 187 p.

always be the teacher's ideal, not merely to keep abreast of special techniques and to possess a substantial measure of general culture, but also to have an advanced knowledge of the language he is teaching to his pupils, of the literature whose vehicle that language is and of the civilization it reflects. He should make it a point of honour to have read, in that language's modern literature, as many works as any cultivated man of like age has read in the literature of his own country. He should have studied its great classical authors, as well as its history. He should have a thorough knowledge of the language's grammar, in its modern form. If in addition he has an elementary knowledge of historical grammar at his command so much the better. It will be of assistance to him in the preparation of his lessons. From the practical standpoint this ideal teacher should be able to pronounce the language perfectly, write a letter in it correctly and converse in it easily and freely. Finally, he should have made a prolonged stay in the country where the language is in daily use.

These, of course, are maximum standards, which are all too often unattained in practice. But, by dint of a constant effort at improvement, some teachers may reach them and many more approach them.

Success or failure in teaching depends on the thoroughness that the young teacher brings to his task. Pedagogically, and apart from the study of techniques, what matters is less the actual acquisition of knowledge than the work that has gone into acquiring it. A taste for methodical research, an observant mind, reliance on facts and experience rather than on formulae and appearances, a constant disposition to reason critically, and distrust of *a prioris*—such are the attitudes and habits of mind that will enable the teacher, where necessary, to remember what he has forgotten and, at the same time, to acquire fresh knowledge. In this whole process, active methods, which are so widely recommended today, are a great help.

All this, it should hardly be necessary to add, presupposes that education departments, either themselves or through professional organizations, will make available to young teachers the periodicals and books which at the outset of their careers they cannot, if only because of their family responsibilities, purchase out of their own modest salaries. Similarly, there should be fellowships to enable established teachers to spend some time abroad or attend the holiday courses organized in various countries.

Certain countries have summer or holiday courses that are held each year as refresher courses for modern language teachers coming from abroad. They are organized by universities, teachers' associations or other institutions. Summer courses also exist in various countries for the benefit of teachers who are nationals of the country concerned. Sometimes these are arranged by the cultural representatives of foreign countries. Occasionally governments help with the expenses. Finally, certain countries grant special leave to established modern language teachers for the purpose of stays abroad, and sometimes the teachers continue to receive their salaries during the period in question.

Financial aid of this kind seems to be granted more readily to established teachers than to students, at least in the majority of countries. Is this because the teachers have greater financial responsibilities, or possess smaller financial resources? While these suppositions may be well founded, it would not be right to convert the practice into a principle. Teachers in training do not come from well-to-do families and the cost of their studies prevents their parents from making additional sacrifices. In both cases, there would be an undesirable restriction on visits abroad if substantial and regular assistance were not forthcoming.

TRAINING MODERN LANGUAGE TEACHERS FOR SECONDARY SCHOOLS IN WESTERN GERMANY[1]

As in any other subject in the curriculum of our schools, the quality and the spirit of modern language teaching depends primarily upon the teacher, upon his personality and his views, upon the quality of his training. But before we approach this special topic of training, a few remarks on the type of school in which modern languages are chiefly taught and on the place of foreign languages in the curriculum of this school may be useful.

During the later nineteenth century, and largely as a result of the industrial age in Europe, the teaching of modern languages was introduced into the secondary school curriculum, and has rapidly increased since, in scope and importance, in Germany as in many other European countries. The more recent extension of foreign language instruction to the masses of children in elementary schools, mainly in some of the larger cities, has not yet shown fully satisfactory results, primarily owing to a widespread shortage of well-trained teachers. For this reason, and also because of the far greater amount of experience available, we shall confine our observations in the following study to the situation of language instruction in the secondary school. In type of pupil and in general curriculum our secondary school corresponds roughly to the

1. The author of this study, Dr. Elisabeth Winkelmann, a lecturer in the Teacher Training Institute at Hamburg, was the participant from the German Federal Republic at the Ceylon seminar. She wrote this paper at the request of the Secretariat of Unesco after the seminar was over and as an additional contribution to its proceedings.

English secondary grammar school or to the strictly academic stream of an American high school preparing pupils for college.

What languages are taught in these schools in Western Germany? With the exception of the classical type of secondary school (the *Gymnasium*, where Latin and Greek and one modern language are taught as compulsory languages, and the second modern language is taught for three years on a voluntary basis) the secondary school curriculum offers three languages, Latin and two modern foreign languages, all of which are required. In the majority of schools the two required modern languages are English and French, other European languages being offered as optional in various places. With regard to the order of languages studied during the nine years of a secondary school there is an almost unlimited freedom of choice, which has resulted in a variety of patterns, such as:

(a)	Latin	9	English	7	French	5 years
(b)	Latin	9	French	7	English	5 years
(c)	English	9	Latin	7	French	5 years
(d)	French	9	Latin	7	English	5 years
(e)	English	9	French	7	Latin	5 years
(f)	French	9	English	7	Latin	5 years

Of these six patterns of the order of languages taught, patterns (a) and (c) are probably the ones which have the widest distribution. Patterns (e) and (f) are found in the modern language *Gymnasium*, the emphasis being definitely on modern languages. Complaints from parents and from the public about too much variety, and about the difficulties caused by this excessive heterogeneity of programmes, suggest that there should be somewhat more uniformity with regard to the order of languages in our schools.

To sum up: the number of required modern languages in the secondary school is two. They are taught in 4–6 periods of 45 minutes each week, in language course varying in length from 5 to 7 to 9 years. It is obvious from these facts that a considerable amount of time is allotted in the secondary school curriculum for the study of languages and that the continuity of such studies is considered an essential factor in language learning. Modern languages have become a fully recognized, legitimate part of the curriculum and take a prominent place among secondary school subjects.

Whereas in the beginning, during the later nineteenth century, the new school subjects, natural sciences and modern languages, had to prove their educational value as compared to the traditional school subjects, above all as compared to the 'humanities', and in those days were mainly recommended for more or less practical, utilitarian reasons, modern languages are now being taught because of their educational and political value. The practical advantages of language learning have become so obvious in the course of time that they need not be mentioned any longer.

The impact of political developments in the last century, such as the 'shrinking' of our world, has been very effective in increasing and speeding up language study in many countries. Has this general development influenced language instruction in the German schools? While it has been deemed necessary by political leaders and educators in a number of countries to teach at least one foreign language to a much larger percentage of schoolchildren for a longer period of years, foreign language teachers in our country, though willing and eager to broaden the bases of language learning, have placed greater emphasis on the content and quality of language instruction, stressing the need for language study on a highly advanced level in order to enable pupils to approach the understanding of a foreign culture through the medium of its language. The traditional interest in a foreign language as a key to the reading of the foreign literature, chiefly for aesthetic reasons and for the study of literary history, was thus replaced by an entirely new approach. Emphasis on the spoken language, introduced earlier, and knowledge of cultural facts, *realia* that illustrated the culture of a specific country, were no longer sufficient. The promotion of cultural insight was considered a primary aim in the study of foreign languages. Thus, in defining the objectives of foreign language instruction, this aspect of international understanding was stressed above all and has given this school subject much greater significance and importance. It is the responsibility of the foreign language teacher that modern languages be taught with a view to promoting in the minds of his pupils a genuine interest in and readiness for international communication and co-operation.

A few other facts of a general nature should also be borne in mind concerning the teacher of foreign languages in our schools. Most language teachers in our public schools are not native speakers of the language they teach, but German nationals who had to study that language themselves. Only in a comparatively small number of schools do we have additional teachers of foreign nationality. These foreign assistants are mostly exchange teachers who stay in the country for a short period of one or two years. Secondly, the foreign language teacher is expected to be a highly qualified specialist, an expert in the subject he teaches. He has to teach at least two major subjects, both of which may be modern languages. He may, however, combine one foreign language with another secondary school subject, such as a classical language,

German, history, etc. The required standards as to proficiency in the language and as to the knowledge of the literature and culture of the country concerned are high.

Teachers of modern languages have become increasingly aware of their responsibility and of their decisive role in the basic political education of their pupils. They can only hope to approach these high educational objectives if intensive studies and training form the basis of their work.

In the pattern of pre-service training of secondary teachers we have to distinguish first between two completely different and separate phases: (a) four to five years of 'subject matter' studies at a university, and (b) two years of professional training in a training centre, organized by the respective school authorities. The German university student, it should be remembered, is expected to be a mature person, able and willing to plan his own studies, with the advice of his professors and instructors, chiefly on his own initiative; to engage in a high degree of specialization, and to perform individual research.

We come now to the specific training of the foreign language teacher, and to the five problems of his pre-service education. These are:

1. How can the required academic standards in the teaching subject be attained?
2. What proportion of academic studies and professional training —in terms of time devoted to each—is to be recommended?
3. Which is the most effective order of work in the preparation of a language teacher in so far as the sequence of 'subject matter' studies and professional training are concerned?
4. Is there any way of integrating professional training and academic studies during the university years?
5. What are the aims of professional training?

Academic subject studies in the university. It must be realized that the required academic 'subject matter' studies of a student of foreign languages consist of four distinctly different lines of work which are actually four aspects of his subject. The first two are the traditional subjects in the study of philology: (a) history and structure of the language; (b) literature, chiefly studied as the history of literature, but also with a view to principles and techniques of interpretation and the appreciation of literary works of art; (c) more recent developments have resulted in broadening language studies by placing new emphasis on cultural studies—to achieve an appreciation and understanding of a foreign culture the student has to add a considerable number of new areas of work to the traditional fields of study; (d) as a consequence of this new approach, language study as such became of vital importance. The aim of gaining insight into the culture of another people through the medium of language instruction made it imperative to study the language as a living and spoken language, as a skill and as a medium of communication. Practical language courses at the university of various kinds and purposes became of decisive importance.

The high degree of specialization and scholarship in the traditional areas of philology is still the same as it was during the first decades of this century, and requirements for the final examination demand a great amount of work in these fields. A slight decrease of interest in the purely historical aspect of the study of literature may however be observed, together with a shift of emphasis towards aesthetic interpretation and the study of aesthetic principles. However, just as before, the future language teacher has to be an expert in the field of philology and is expected to have accomplished a piece of research in a subject of his own choice. It is generally agreed that the level of knowledge of a secondary teacher should be considerably above what he will actually need in his classroom teaching. Only a wide and profound knowledge of the subject matter will guarantee the quality of instruction which is considered necessary in the German secondary school. On the basis of a general movement toward a modern 'humanism', the 'humanistic' approach in modern language teaching has brought about an extensive and thorough study of the 'classics' in foreign literature. To illustrate the manifestations of a given culture through the writings of great poets and writers, which are read in school partly in translations but as far as possible in the original language, was regarded by many educators as the core of the work of the modern language class. When these works of art began to form the central theme of modern language work in school, mainly because they were great and timeless, and were chosen on the grounds of their high educational and formative value, university students preparing for modern language teaching had to place special emphasis on such works of art in their studies as well.

The 'cultural approach' by which the transmission of cultural insights was made a fundamental aim of language instruction not only expanded and broadened the traditional studies of philology so as to include cultural facts and *realia* (*Sachkunde*), but involved an entirely new aspect of modern language instruction. It was hoped that by this new approach the study of foreign languages would contribute to the understanding of other cultures. This attempt at developing a comprehensive presentation of a whole culture received decisive support from such works as the book on

England by Wilhelm Dibelius. In his teaching as a professor of English in the university of Berlin, he showed his students the value and the difficulties of this broader aspect of foreign language studies, which added a whole range of subjects to be studied to the traditional lines of work—studies which even made a certain amount of interdisciplinary work necessary and would no longer permit the future language teacher to confine his work to the narrower field of philology. To understand the many facets and aspects of a foreign culture a great amount of work in history, sociology, geography, forms of government, education, art, religion, etc., had to be undertaken. Small wonder that this broader concept of the language teacher's work made its way rather slowly in the language departments of universities. For many students it seemed to ask for a superhuman effort, and a great many teachers were doubtful whether it could be done. In course of time, however, and in spite of all the additional work it involved, students began to take an enthusiastic interest in this type of work, largely because they began to understand the implications of this broader outlook for their future task of language teaching. They accepted the challenge, deeply convinced of the importance and dignity of their subject and of their own responsibility in the matter.

At the same time, an increase of interest in language as a spoken phenomenon added more practical work to the programme of the foreign language student. Students preparing to teach foreign languages had to attend courses in phonetics, pronunciation, intonation, grammar, style, and translation. Discussion groups with foreign-born lecturers and instructors, lectures held in the foreign language—all these things served the same purpose; to improve the student's proficiency in the foreign language.

Because of the many new requirements for the future language teacher a stay abroad was considered of even greater importance than before. Projects for student exchanges, for study at a foreign university, for scholarships and similar possibilities to help the foreign language student to live in the foreign country for a certain period of time were given full consideration. This experience became an integral part of the preparation of any foreign language teacher. How can the student learn to speak the foreign language well unless he has ample opportunity to use it, either in the various contacts offered in his own country or preferably in the country where the language is spoken? How can a teacher be expected to teach about the culture of another country without having studied it in the country itself? During periods of political tension and war, as in World Wars I and II, all these hopeful developments were, of course, interrupted, and thus for a great number of language teachers of the younger generation an important part in their pre-service training could not be carried through. At the present time, through refresher courses with foreigners in our own country, through courses for foreigners at universities abroad, and through an increasing number of exchange projects for students and teachers, a general improvement in this matter can fortunately be noted. To sum up: visits of future language teachers to the foreign country form an indispensable requirement in their preparation; in some places they have even been made compulsory. They serve the double purpose of improving the student's proficiency in the language and of facilitating the study of the culture in the foreign country in all its many aspects in order to promote understanding through sympathetic contacts.

Teachers who have once gone through such an experience will not easily fall a victim to stereotype views of another nation, which is one of the most dangerous barriers to international understanding. If the foreign language teacher is to be held responsible for the attitudes caused by his teaching about another country, it is his own first-hand knowledge of the country and its culture, his intellectual integrity, modesty and sympathetic understanding that will exert a sound influence on his students' minds. As we must admit that the systematic analysis of a culture lies within the province of the social sciences, the foreign language teacher must know his own limitations in teaching about a foreign culture. Teachers often try to do too much in too short a period of time, and with too few facts available. Pupils and students are only too apt to generalize and to venture hasty solutions for very complex questions. The foreign language teacher, however, must not allow his students to perpetuate those superficial and popular misconceptions of nationality that exist everywhere in the world. Otherwise they might continue using such nationality stereotypes without even realizing the danger involved. Should we not, instead of stressing differences more than similarities in our teaching, instead of using generalizing statements about the French, the English, the Russians etc.—should we not rather warn our pupils against such dangerous temptations and help them to work toward genuine and sincere understanding of another people on the basis of first-hand knowledge about a foreign country and its culture?

The work of the foreign language teacher must rest on solid ground. He must be prepared for his task by a tremendous amount of academic work and by as many real contacts with the foreign country as possible. That such studies will never be completed goes without saying. Language learning is a never-ending process and the teacher must always strive to extend and deepen his knowledge and understanding of the foreign culture. The education of a language teacher cannot end with the completion of his pre-service training programme; there will always have to be some kind of in-service education, for the language teacher as for any other teacher.

Proportion of academic 'subject matter' studies and professional training, in terms of time devoted to each. In the nineteenth century and even earlier, it was generally assumed that the scholar, i.e., the teacher who really knew his subject well, would automatically be the best teacher in the secondary school. There is just enough truth in this assumption to influence a number of teachers and students even today, who remain doubtful whether professional training is of much importance for the teacher. It may be questioned, they argue, whether there is any real need for it at all. Of course, a high academic standard of knowledge is a *conditio sine qua non* for teaching in a secondary school. But experience has shown that a good scholar is by no means always a good teacher, and certainly not necessarily a good trainer of teachers. If we apply this to the preparation of the foreign language teacher, we must ask, what amount of professional training, if any, should be added to the 'subject matter' studies described above? What could be regarded as an ideal proportion of time spent for each? This being one of the current problems of teacher training in general, it is not easy to find a quick and satisfactory solution. Numerous educational conferences have dealt with the problems involved. For some time in this century, along with the growth of educational theory into a fully recognized academic subject, the pendulum seemed to swing to the other extreme. More and more work in professional education was required in addition to the traditional 'subject matter' courses in the university. This tended to endanger standards in the subject matter field. If, for example, a high degree of language proficiency, and extensive and thorough knowledge about the foreign culture, are to be attained by the student, he will certainly need all the time available in his university years to meet these requirements. The situation is aggravated by the fact that he must study two majors (as compared to one in the case of his French opposite number). It should also be mentioned that—no matter what his teaching subject may be—a general background of work in philosophy forms an essential part of his required academic work. How much time then will he be able to spend during his university period of training on any type of professional work, either theoretical or practical? 'Very little, if any' will be the answer given by the majority of students and their professors.

This leads to a discussion of the appropriate order of 'subject matter' studies and professional work. When should professional education begin? It has been recommended from time to time that even for the secondary school teacher a certain amount of practical work should be required at rather an early stage of preparation. Though this might seem to be very helpful in testing the student's teaching ability and talent and in introducing him into his future duties, it would, in most cases, mean asking too much of the young student. Teaching in a secondary school requires advanced work of a comparatively high level. The student cannot and should not be asked to teach a foreign language unless he has achieved a fairly high degree of proficiency in it. His cultural teaching will necessarily remain ineffectual until he has completed a considerable amount of university work in his teaching subject. It is for such reasons that in the preparation of secondary teachers the professional training period of two years was made to follow the long period of academic studies. But is it a really satisfactory solution of the problem to have two separate training periods—one strictly academic, and the other professional? Should there not rather be some form of gradual transition, introducing the student from the one to the other? This problem of transition without a break has become urgent, for students who were good in their subject matter areas have run into difficulties or even failed in the professional work in school.

Is there a way of integrating professional training and academic studies? This complex question should not be discussed without referring to recent experiments carried through in a number of universities in order to study the results, on the part of the student, of adding a professional aspect to his university studies. Of course, the lines along which this was attempted had to vary from place to place, according to conditions in the universities concerned. The general problem of teacher training—of how to introduce educational work into the phase of 'subject matter' studies, without endangering the quality of this work—has been widely discussed in German universities. The question arose whether the theoretical study of education and psychology, which had been offered for many years in several universities, would be made more meaningful for the student by giving him opportunities for observation and experience in the schools. In this respect, an experiment which has been conducted during the past five years by the Pedagogical Institute at the University of Hamburg may be of interest.

While he was doing the academic work required in his teaching field and, at the same time, completing his general education through studies in philosophy and educational theory, what were the activities (besides the theoretical lectures) which might help to introduce the future foreign language teacher to his specific task? It has been noticed that in the long period of pre-service education of secondary teachers, a period of six or seven years, there was a gradual shift of emphasis from pure subject matter interest toward interest in educational problems. On the assumption that this shift was desirable for the majority of students preparing to teach, an attempt was made at Hamburg to offer, in the later phases of university work, certain practical educational opportunities which were to be evaluated in the light of theoretical educational work. These opportunities, it was hoped, would have a good effect on the personal development of the future teacher and on his academic studies as well. In close connexion with practical teaching opportunities in schools, with opportunities for observation and participation in language instruction in secondary schools (which, however, does not pretend to be 'training' of any kind), courses are also held from time to time about such questions as the aims and objectives of language teaching and about the values and principles of language learning. In discussing such basic problems, which are of direct concern to their future work, students may begin to see their responsibility in this task, and they will also make progress in their understanding of various new aspects of their academic 'subject matter' work.

The first results of this experiment seem to suggest that this may be a valuable way of integrating academic and professional work. Always providing that the amount of professional work is kept within the necessary limits, such opportunities seem to be appreciated by the students who are preparing to teach languages. In conclusion it should be repeated, however, that the period of real professional training follows graduation. All attempts, in an earlier phase, towards professionalizing academic studies are bound to prove a failure if they should tend to interfere with academic standards.

The period of professional training. As pointed out earlier, there are two full years devoted to professional training in the pre-service education of secondary teachers. The Training Centre, (which may have different names and slight differences in its organizational pattern in the different parts of Germany) is called a *Studienseminar* in Hamburg. It is organized by the state (or city) school authorities, and its members, the *Referendare*, are thus no longer university students. They receive maintenance grants from the city during the two years of training and are not expected to have any teaching duties, except the ones which are part of their training.

The seminar is organized in the following way:

A fairly large group of *Referendare*, about twenty to thirty in number and specializing in all the different teaching subjects, are grouped together in one *Studienseminar*, which is directed by an experienced educator appointed by the school authorities. He is responsible for the professional education of the whole group. The weekly general meetings of the *Studienseminar* as well as the supervision of the practical teaching programme which is carried on in many schools of the city, are some of the primary duties of his work.

The *Referendare* are also grouped by teaching subjects, and each group of a certain teaching subject receives theoretical and practical advice from an experienced subject counsellor or *Fachleiter*.

They do their practical work during the two years of their training in at least two different schools. This school practice consists of a comprehensive programme integrating observation, practice teaching and evaluation. All practice teaching is done in the presence of a subject teacher of the school who acts as an adviser. The emphasis in this phase of the training is definitively on the practical, professional, side. However, to promote a sound interrelationship between educational theory and practice is one of the major objectives.

In the general meetings of the seminar group educational concepts and ideas, acquired as part of the educational studies at the university, have to be clarified, extended and deepened on the basis of these first teaching experiences. While academic study of the history of education, educational psychology and systematic problems of education and learning are considered part of the student's university work, all of these matters are taken up again in the seminar, where they are discussed with constant reference to the practical work in the school. The ultimate aim of this work, throughout the training period, is for the *Referendar* to acquire a professional attitude which is based on his academic studies as well as on his educational ideas matured through educational experience.

In the group meetings of the 'subject matter' group, the topics of discussion are primarily problems of methodology. For the foreign language teacher there are such questions as the psychology of language learning, language ability, teaching language as a skill, the basic skills in learning a foreign language, aural-oral methods of teaching, the teaching of pronunciation, vocabulary selection, grammar reading approach, use of textbooks and readers, selection of reading materials, translation, written work, the use of modern teaching aids, the teaching of current events, introduction into the foreign culture, etc. Of course, in addition to questions of teaching methods, such basic questions as the aims and principles of language instruction, the interrelationship of modern languages and other school subjects and facilities for further study and in-service training for the language teacher also have to be dealt with. The core of the work, however, is the actual teaching done by the *Referendare* and the critical evaluation of it by the group and by the subject adviser. Most discussions start from real teaching experiences and the problems arising in the practical work.

School practice in a number of secondary schools, teaching in many different classes, on all levels, work with several subject teachers, ample opportunity for observation in different language classes, all of this, practised throughout the two years, serves to give the *Referendar* enough teaching experience in his subject field to make him understand the problems and difficulties of foreign language teaching and, at the same time, to encourage him to work independently and on his own responsibility.

If the young teacher is expected to apply modern aural-oral methods in his language teaching, and to extend his instruction so as to provide cultural insight in his foreign language classes, he should also be able during this period of his training to increase his proficiency in the language he teaches and to learn about the culture of the foreign country. Projects for the exchange of young teachers in training are therefore of primary importance. It may be debated, however, whether it is advisable to interrupt the training period for several months. There is no doubt whatsoever about the value of such a period of teaching abroad, but the practical question, at what point such a stay in the foreign country can best be included, remains to be solved. No fully satisfactory answer has yet been found. Suffice it to say here that, irrespective of an ideal solution of this problem, it would mean a great improvement in the training of foreign language teachers for a visit to the foreign country to be considered an indispensable part of the training.

We must not forget either that, at least in the larger cities, lectures given by foreign scholars and experts as well as other contacts with people from another country are no longer a rare exception and that, in addition to radio broadcasts, there are many facilities available, in the libraries and in the exhibits of such institutions as *Die Brücke, Amerika-Haus*, the *Institut français* and others, to study current cultural developments in foreign countries. International meetings of teachers and exchange visits of groups of teachers and pupils create contacts with people from abroad which may promote understanding and good-will among nations. All these contacts are valuable factors which add to the education of a foreign language teacher. In conclusion it might be mentioned that the development of modern methods of language teaching in other countries, particularly in Europe, is another of the many subjects of study in the seminar. The knowledge of such new developments enables the young teacher to join in discussions on language instruction with international groups of language teachers and to read foreign modern language journals with interest and understanding.

To sum up regarding current trends in the training of teachers of modern languages. Among significant trends, as we see them, the following should be stressed:

The emphasis on study of a living, spoken language has made language teachers think of language learning primarily in terms of acquiring a skill. The four basic skills of studying a foreign language—hearing, speaking, reading, and writing—are to be introduced in the order given. Teachers must be trained in using aural-oral teaching techniques.

The study of *realia*, i.e. more or less unrelated cultural objects (*Sachkunde*), in vogue mainly at the end of the nineteenth century, was dropped to a great extent and now as a rule forms an adjunct to instruction only in the earlier phases of language study. Readers used in the lower language classes contain materials of this kind.

Through the 'cultural approach' to language teaching which replaced the traditional study of literature the basic concept and methods of language instruction were changed completely. New ways of teaching had to be devised, for the study of a foreign culture in language classes and the training had to be broadened accordingly. This is probably where the greatest difficulties lie for the beginning teacher.

Only recently another shift of emphasis took place. The predominant interest in contemporary literature, in newspaper articles, and current reading materials of various kinds and value—which had been so prevalent in the last few decades, due to a misconception of the term 'cultural' as applied to language study—began to decrease somewhat under the impact of the 'humanistic' movement in foreign language instruction. Teachers were reminded of their primary duty to introduce pupils to the understanding and appreciation of the great works of literature. The 'classics' are now again being studied because of their timeless, eternal values.

Finally, in the course of time, and mainly in the last decade, education for international understanding has become one of the most important objectives of foreign language teaching. How language learning can be made a tool for communication among nations and how efficiently this can be done is the great task for the immediate future.

Teachers of modern languages have begun to appreciate their 'mission', which is to help to overcome the misunderstandings and tensions that exist between nations. This work for international understanding and co-operation through language instruction is what the younger generation of language teachers should learn to understand above all else in their period of pre-service education. Only then will they be able to share in the great task in which language teachers of all countries should feel united: the task of making the teaching of modern languages contribute towards education for living in a world community.

CHAPTER VII

TEXTBOOKS

One of the successful features of the Ceylon seminar was an exhibition room, where over one thousand modern language textbooks sent in by 23 different countries were on display. These books were almost without exception samples of the best that highly specialized publishers in this field have produced in the last few years. It was clear to anyone who browsed through this collection that techniques of language textbook production have improved immensely since the last war. Typography, page presentation and illustrative material are, in a majority of countries, all much more attractive than they were. Most textbooks designed for the teaching of a foreign language in its early stages now pay a commendable regard to vocabulary selection, even if structural grading is still too advanced and abstruse a proposition for many textbook publishers. It is still possible, however, to criticize the political and cultural bias of a good many language textbooks; some are not without a patronizing chauvinism, conscious or unconscious. In this respect, it may be worth mentioning that one national delegation requested the seminar authorities to withdraw a textbook published in their own country as it was realized that it might well give offence to participants from certain other countries.

The seminar report makes it clear that it is the duty of modern language teachers everywhere to exercise constant vigilance on this point. Steady progress has been made since the last war, along lines laid down by bilateral agreements, in the revision of history and geography textbooks. There are however still modern language textbooks in current use that contain material that is just as offensive and just as much an obstacle to the cause of true international understanding. This is particularly true of certain books that include superficial cultural surveys of a foreign country. Inaccuracies, out-of-date information and undesirable stereotypes abound in some of these texts. It is therefore particularly gratifying to record that, as a direct result of the Ceylon seminar, the first series of bilateral consultations on the revision of modern language textbooks—in this instance between France and the German Federal Republic—has already been started.

Originally, owing to lack of time, it was not intended to hold special discussions at Ceylon on the subject of textbooks and the question was not included among the six main general topics. However, in this case the participants showed more wisdom than the organizers and insisted during the discussions on audio-visual aids that the subject of textbooks should receive adequate treatment. There were panel discussions in consequence and a special committee was appointed to draft the report that appears below.

This seminar report, which, it is suggested, both publishers and educational authorities could study with advantage, is followed by a brief extract from Professor Gurrey's working-paper dealing with an important aspect of the subject of vocabulary control and by a similar extract on the same theme taken from Dr. Jumsai's paper.

THE SEMINAR REPORT

Procedure for the Selection of Textbooks

Wherever possible, the maximum freedom should be left to teachers in the choice of textbooks.

Teachers teaching the same language in the same institution should agree on the same series of textbooks to be used for a definite period in that institution, in order to avoid disconcerting changes of textbook when a pupil moves from one class to another.

Though it is recognized that in some countries it is considered necessary for the Ministry of Education to prescribe or recommend textbooks, teachers should be consulted before such prescription or recommendation comes into effect. In this connexion, the setting up of language teachers' associations, where they do not already exist, is recommended.

It is recommended that similar machinery should exist for conveying teachers' criticisms of textbooks actually in use, and suggestions for their revision or replacement, to the prescribing or recommending authority.

The list of prescribed or recommended textbooks should be subject to review at reasonable intervals. At these reviews, the comments and suggestions received from teachers using the textbook should be taken into consideration.

Suggestions to Authors

The author of a textbook is obviously expected to be well acquainted with the language and the country with which he is dealing in his book. For modern languages, an inadequate knowledge will be found to be less tolerable than in most other fields.

The author should have had adequate experience in language teaching and should be familiar with the results of the latest relevant research in the fields of language teaching and general linguistics.

In preparing either a series of books or a single book, the author should never lose sight of the requirements of a course of study covering a given number of years.

The author should be familiar with the pupils' mother tongue, with their general background and their attainments in other subjects according to their mental age, or he should collaborate with someone who is familiar with these matters. He should show aesthetic and literary taste.

Suggestions for the Selection and Preparation of Textbooks

Attention should be paid to clarity and attractiveness of presentation on the page, bearing in mind that all material placed in the hands of the young should contribute to the training of their aesthetic sense.

Textbooks at any level should be appropriately illustrated. Pictures should be clear, relevant and accurate in detail. Though there is a tendency in some countries to use photographs extensively, drawings should still have their place.

A textbook should contain a clear and detailed statement of its aims, the principles and methods followed in it, and its scope.

Textbooks for the earlier stages (that is the stages during which the main features of the language are being taught step by step). New learning items should be presented one at a time and each completely mastered before another is attempted.

New learning items, whether sounds, intonation patterns, words (or new meanings of words already known), inflexions or sentence patterns ('structures'), should be introduced in an order graded according to difficulty, although no attempt should be made to concentrate on one type of item at a time: i.e. the first lesson may include phonological, lexical and syntactical items, provided the principle of presenting one individual item at a time is followed.

Great care should be taken to keep within the limits of vocabulary, sentence patterns, etc., covered at each stage.

It should be remembered that each new meaning of a word may have to be treated as a fresh learning item.

Guide-books for teachers, giving detailed advice on how to

present and review each item in a methodical, interesting and attractive way would be welcome.

An index of vocabulary and sentence patterns used should be provided, either in the textbook or in the teacher's book. In the case of vocabulary, an indication of the meanings in which words have been introduced should be included.

So that pupils will not forget what has been learnt in the first stages, provision should be made for revision of earlier items by their reintroduction at later stages where they fit in with new items.

Only normal language in current use should be employed.

While the simplification of original texts by the replacement of words deemed too difficult is condemned as a perversion of the original, the practice of rewriting such works within predetermined limits of vocabulary and sentence patterns is considered necessary in the early stages, provided the suggestions given in earlier paragraphs of this report are observed.

In selecting works to be abridged or issued in adapted form for the use of young children, care should be taken to see that they represent the best in the literature of the country in whose language they are written, due regard being paid to their moral and cultural content.

It is desirable that a wide range of such readers be made available, suited to different age levels.

Later stages. As soon as possible, pupils should be introduced to extracts from the works of creative writers in their original form.

At these later stages, both literary study and more advanced language training should be pursued. The language training could well be based on the study of passages by creative writers.

Suggestions to Publishers

An appeal is made to publishers all over the world to grant special facilities to authors of textbooks who wish to include selected passages from copyright material.

In order to help both Ministries of Education and teachers in the selection of textbooks, an appeal is made to authors and to publishing houses to send specimen copies of textbooks to Ministries of Education, teachers' training institutions and teachers' associations.

The price of textbooks should be kept as low as possible. The various means of achieving this end should be explored in close co-operation with Ministries, teachers' associations and publishing houses or publishers' associations.

The Textbook and International Understanding

The author of any textbook intended for language teaching should make sure that his work offers a fair and accurate picture of the country concerned.

If a writer deals with a language and a country other than his own, he should submit his textbook in advance for advice to one or more competent persons belonging to the country or countries whose language and civilization are presented in the book.

If the textbook is intended for use in a country other than that of the textbook writer, care should be taken that it avoids any prejudice against the country where it is to be used.

Language teachers' associations should be aware of their responsibility for publicly pointing out linguistic and cultural inaccuracies concerning their own country in textbooks produced in or brought into their own country.

LOCAL FACTORS IN VOCABULARY SELECTION[1]

Many countries or territories in Asia and Africa now have textbooks for the learning of English that have been written within the scope of the 2,000 word-list of *The Interim Report on Vocabulary Selection*.[2] Educationists have been aware for some time that this interim report could not be the final authority, and that it needed revision. There is still some ill-informed textbook writing; nevertheless, the work that has been done on vocabulary selection by Thorndike, Horn, Palmer, West, Maki and Faucett has had an extremely beneficial effect. The principle of vocabulary selection has been accepted by all—as it must be accepted—for every teacher of young children makes a vocabulary selection, even though he may not realize it. But there has been no agreement on the criteria for selecting words.[3]

In Malta, the Sudan, the Gold Coast and other countries, additional lists of words to be taught in the lower classes of primary and middle schools are being drawn up, and would form a sound nucleus for a revision of the interim report if they could be collected and collated by a representative committee. These words are ones usually current in the daily life of the towns, and ones of common occurrence in the country concerned, and perhaps not in wide

---

1. This section is extracted from the working paper prepared for the Ceylon seminar by Professor P. Gurrey.
2. P. S. King & Son, Ltd., London, 1936, 506 p.
3. For a thorough treatment of this subject, we must refer readers to the valuable study made by Dr. H. Bongers entitled: *The History and Principles of Vocabulary Control*. Published in 1947 by 'Wocopi', Woerden (Netherlands); in three parts.

use elsewhere, but they are words which have been found by experience and careful and critical observation to be needed in the work of the higher classes of a middle or secondary school, or during the first years in one of these schools. These words can easily be incorporated into special lessons, or introduced gradually, according to a simply worked out plan, into existing texts and lessons. This can be a very useful step in the long process of determining the vocabulary to be acquired by the children at each stage of their education. The work can be carried on incidentally to teaching and inspecting for many years, and each word can be tested over a long period for its usefulness and ease of teaching and learning, and gradually an authoritative word-list can be drawn up by each country according to its needs, though it would have to be revised as new ideas or things arrive in the country (e.g. 'jet aircraft landing'). It is likely that every country or homogeneous area should have its own 'additional word-list' to supplement the interim list.

Care of course must be given to the selection of technical words, for some of these are more easily, or more effectively, taught when the need for them arises; for instance, the terms of the physical sciences are very often best taught when the apparatus or picture in the textbook presents a clear reference and concrete meaning. Words such as these should not be included in an additional list. Similarly, words with 'local meanings' that are not commonly used in English need to be included only after weighing up their usefulness; for instance, in West Africa, 'I will meet you at the junction', means 'at the *road* junction', for the scarcity of railway lines and side roads outside the large towns makes a road junction a distinctive feature. This work of collecting words for additional lists and for revision of the accepted list should be begun now, as it is too late to begin when a revision is called for; and the collecting can be done without much trouble. Secondary school teachers of the lowest classes need only jot down words of common occurrence that they find are not known, or that are not easily learnt, and a useful working list then can be compiled by collecting these teachers' lists from each school in the country.

It has been found by those who have seriously studied the problem of the textbook as the best 'aid' in teaching English, that the only acceptable solution for providing suitable textbooks is for each country or region to have its own specially adapted ones. The adaptations of the original Oxford English course to suit Mauritius, Malaya, Papua, and New Guinea, Africa, and the special course for Malta, show that this policy is sound, acceptable and possible. Malaya has an almost complete series of readers, composition, grammar and speech books, as well as supplementary readers, all specially designed for Malayan pupils. These have been a great help for general education in Malaya as well as for raising the standard of English there. So too it is evident that the course by Gatenby for Turkish students is more suited for the linguistically able Turkish pupil than any other. That compiled by D. C. Miller and Selim Hakim in Baghdad is especially suited to pupils in Iraq, and those written by L. W. Leavitt and by I. Morris are more suited to the comparatively well-read student in Lebanon and in Israel than for the African junior school pupil. These writers have done important work for the countries they have worked in or are still working in, particularly Mr. H. R. Cheeseman, C.M.G., sometime Director of Education, Malaya, Professor E. V. Gatenby in Turkey, Professor L. W. Leavitt in Lebanon, Mr. I. Morris and Mr. J. S. Bentwich in Israel.

It is not necessary to retell the story of the use of limited vocabularies for the writing and compiling of readers, courses and other textbooks for the teaching of English, but the plea for the inclusion of 'local' words into these books is a recent and fairly widespread factor for writers to consider. This, however, was always the intention of the compilers of such word lists as *The First Two Thousand Most Frequently Used Words*. Those with wide experience of teaching in Africa, Asia and elsewhere have noted that there are a number of words, outside the interim vocabulary word list, that children in towns know or see daily in public notices, advertisements, announcements outside shops, schools, offices, etc., or that they hear spoken in shops, post offices, inquiry bureaux and in the streets, public vehicles, garages, workshops, markets and of course in cinemas. Obviously a limited number of these, selected from the most useful and the commonest, could be used in compiling English textbooks. No general list could be entirely satisfactory. It would be best, therefore, for each country or region to draw up its own list, though some words might eventually be found to be common to all, or to a large majority of the lists.

Like vocabulary selection before word-counts were carried out, the selection of the information or thought-content of the sentences presented to young pupils to enable them to learn the language has been left to common sense and teaching intuition, and this has often worked well enough. But research has shown that many of the sentences included in well-known courses for the learning of English give no real understanding of the things referred to in them. In the Gold Coast, for instance, it has been found that the ideas of the schoolchildren of things that they had never seen, but had only learnt about in their reading with the help of perhaps one picture, were utterly vague. For instance, middle school pupils' ideas of a camel were so imprecise that they could have had no clear visual image of the animal—right or wrong; similarly, girls at the top of a town middle school had not a single idea among them of how a gun was fired or how one worked. How could they know? Yet they were reading about such things. Similarly, it was found that pupils who had read about life and work in other countries in their English readers had the queerest ideas of what things are like, for instance, the conception of a river flowing in a channel higher than the fields along its course was ludicrous to them; the rivers they knew all had steep banks below the level of the land; and even what a field is like puzzles many pupils, though of course they are not aware of the vagueness or inaccuracy of their ideas. It is evident that, at first, the ideas and content of the sentences and passages that are being used for language learning should be those which are familiar to the pupils. But for how long an English course should keep to familiar ideas, topics and 'subjects', it is impossible to say at present. This again is a matter for research. But we can dogmatize here in saying that if topics and 'subjects' outside the pupils' experience are introduced into language learning lessons, then these topics must be dealt with thoroughly; otherwise, the language remains largely on a verbal level without relevance to reality.

ENGLISH TEXTBOOKS AND TEACHERS' MANUALS FOR THAILAND[1]

Thailand has been a good and faithful testing ground for all kinds of foreign readers. It is my opinion that a whole series of readers ought to be written especially for Thai children, as existing readers are incomplete and unsatisfactory in their selection of words and ideas. Apart from the readers, students must use some form of grammar-book.

I am convinced that, however good foreign textbooks may be, they must be replaced by books written in Thai which teachers and students alike can understand. Grammar is a subject sufficiently difficult without having the additional hindrance of English explanations. There are many grammar books in Thai which have been written during the past ten years, but many of them are open to criticism. English is a difficult language for one who has not studied it in an English-speaking country. There are certain things which are grammatically correct but which one would not dream of using in ordinary speech. It would be a difficult matter to write a good series of books on grammar and practical exercises

---

1. This section is extracted from the working-paper prepared for the Ceylon seminar by Dr. Manich Jumsai who at that time was a member of the Secretariat of Unesco.

for use in schools when the type of reader most suitable for teaching Thai students to speak English is not yet fixed, nor the curriculum definite, because such books should not be written as separate entities, but should borrow ideas, words, phrases and incorporate sentences taken from the readers in use in the schools.

The present readers should be modified, the students taught to use them and to observe various points, and they should be encouraged to explore variations of the texts so that they will learn to express their thoughts and ideas independently by sentences other than those used in the readers. Before producing readers and other English books to go with the readers, we should first of all make up our minds definitely what our aim in producing such books is. Do we intend them to be read for pleasure, or as a source of facts or knowledge? Do we want just one series or several series for the country as a whole, setting out different ideas to suit various local surroundings? Then again, one person wants the books to be written with an English background, while another prefers a Thai background with names, objects and stories all derived from Thailand. I think that it would be best to write the first book or two using the boy's own environment as a background, and discussing the things he knows and understands. Then as his vocabulary increases, English subjects could be introduced— English boys and girls, their homes and customs, and the things the student would see and do if he were to visit England. A Thai is proud of his own social heritage, and if he reads and hears about the doings of brave men of England, great institutions and so on, he wants to express his personal pride in Thailand and in his own countrymen. Thailand also has traditions, a proud history, men and women whom he can look up to, and a culture and a religion no less important than those in Great Britain or the United States. However, while on this voyage of discovery, gathering information and observing things, he becomes interested and enraptured. He understands the people on the isolated island of his dream, and appreciates their way of thinking.

In order to gain a complete understanding of English people, their customs and the things they do and are capable of doing, the textbooks must give comparisons between the things that happen in Great Britain and Thailand. This is the only way in which a student can be made to realize and appreciate the facts. With each new textbook the way should be open to him to learn more and more facts, not only new ones but interesting facts that he feels are true. This leads me to the conclusion that the student should be given true stories to read, rather than the usual fiction which tells of an imaginary family making an imaginary voyage to England, meeting with fictitious incidents and seeing supposedly true objects and things. There is also another very important point to be considered, and that is that children are not always interested in the things that appear interesting to adults. One should consider this point carefully and find out what things interest the average student, what he observes and what vocabulary he picks up.

Class readers are by no means complete in themselves. The habit of reading should be inculcated so that once the student has mastered a certain vocabulary he should be encouraged to read by himself and on his own initiative. A number of supplementary readers should be supplied for the use of the students—short stories of varied interest, a small collection that each student would be proud to possess.

At the same time, we must not forget the teachers who, even with the best textbooks available, cannot teach English if they do not know the language sufficiently well themselves. In order to help these teachers, a series of books should be compiled for the purpose of educating the teachers; also handbooks giving instructions on the method of teaching English. There are a few books for adults on the market, but they have no set aims and describe things which would not interest the teachers nor aid them in any way in their teaching.

I am convinced that, at the present stage, if teachers are to teach English at all, a series of handbooks must be written for them, giving sample lessons which they can study before going into a class. The sample lessons could be accompanied by explanations to help them and, if necessary, by records so that they could learn the correct pronunciation from English people by just putting on the records and following the lessons prepared for them. Although not the ideal way, this method would be a means of helping some 6,000 teachers of English in the country who, at the present time, are teaching inadequate English to about 200,000 students now in secondary schools.

If we expect the teachers to speak English to their students, we must prepare sample graded dialogues for them. If they are to teach the writing of essays, then essays on all possible topics should be prepared for the teachers, so that they have a wide selection of subjects to choose from and will be able to make a sensible choice of subjects. Students learn better by imitating the teachers than by writing original essays when their knowledge of English is not good enough. Apart from the sample grammar exercises for the various classes, sample letters could also be written for use by the teachers.

CHAPTER VIII
THE TEACHING OF MODERN LANGUAGES BY RADIO AND TELEVISION

The main advantages and disadvantages of radio as an aid in the teaching of modern languages were summed up in succinct fashion in the introduction to a paper presented to the Ceylon seminar by the English-by-Radio Department of the British Broadcasting Corporation. The four chief advantages are:
1. The radio presents the true spoken language, on which modern opinion agrees that all good language teaching must be based.
2. In doing this the radio can bring to all the services of the best native speakers of the language, combined with those of the most expert teachers.
3. The radio can reach all kinds of listeners in all kinds of places. It is unhampered by problems of accessibility or of the availability of teachers and classrooms.
4. Given the existence of a broadcasting network and of a sufficient number of receiving-sets among the audience, it is remarkably cheap—cheaper in relation to the number of learners served than any other mass teaching medium.

Over against these the paper very fairly listed three disadvantages:
1. The outstanding one is the learner's 'blindness', his lack of visual aid.
2. The second main disadvantage is one which is by no means confined to sound radio but is shared by other mass media, including books, gramophone records, films and even television. It is that it is a one-way street. The traffic is all from the teacher to the learner, and there is no opportunity, as in the classroom, for the teaching to be modified according to the needs of the individual pupil or the circumstances of the moment. And bound up with this is the danger that the radio lesson may induce too passive an attitude in the pupil, that because the teacher is not there to observe his reactions and test his understanding the learner may remain too easily content to listen but not to speak, to absorb half-comprehended information without attempting to clarify it in his own mind and re-express it in his own way.
3. Finally, it must be admitted that over long distances radio

still remains dependent on the vagaries of reception conditions and that in a broadcast where it is important for the learner to hear every sound as clearly as possible this can sometimes be a handicap.

The Ceylon seminar was able to learn more about the purely classroom aspect of language teaching from a survey prepared beforehand by the Secretariat of Unesco and which was based on recordings and information received from radio networks in Austria, Canada, Denmark, Japan, Netherlands, Northern Rhodesia, Norway, Sweden, Switzerland and the United Kingdom. In most of these countries radio has proved a useful adjunct to the classroom teacher and besides helping in ordinary language instruction has, to use the words of the Swedish report, increased pupils' knowledge of foreign countries by 'giving the listeners a feeling of being physically present in the country whose language is being spoken.'

It is clear that radio as a language teaching medium is still expanding rapidly and is discovering new tasks or new aspects of the main task to perform. In India it is proving a valuable tool for the mass teaching of Hindi, the new national language. In Japan it is used in schools, in elementary and intermediate classes, not only for teaching the traditional western modern languages, English, French and German, but for Chinese as well. Some national radio systems, such as that of the United Kingdom, have plans far advanced for the use of radio language lessons as a medium for combatting illiteracy.

Two documents on the successful exploitation of radio as a language-teaching aid are included in the present chapter: one chronicles the steps taken to facilitate the exportation of a language and deals largely with the techniques required to reach an adult audience; the other outlines the measures taken in a special set of circumstances to import a language on a widespread scale and may be said to be more directly connected with the problem of school broadcasting.

Language teaching by radio has been a reality for over a quarter of a century (regular programmes were broadcast for schools in Germany as early as 1928), but television as a language teaching medium is still in its infancy. It is true that closed-circuit experimental telecasts were conducted at Creighton University, Omaha, Nebraska, U.S.A. as early as 1946–47, but it was not until about three years ago that any appreciable number of commercial and educational television stations in the United States began to televise regular programmes, or that television was used to supplement foreign language teaching in the schools.

It would seem that so far nearly all the pioneering has been done in the United States. This fact emerged fairly clearly during the Unesco-sponsored study course for producers and directors of educational and cultural television programmes which was held in London in July 1954. It is equally clear, however, that other countries are on the verge of availing themselves of this medium to further language teaching both in the schools and to adult audiences outside them. The early achievements in the United States are now being chronicled, and teachers in other countries who are interested in the possibilities of television would do well to consult the existing literature.[1]

Meeting in the summer of 1953, the participants at the Ceylon seminar hardly had enough factual information to carry on a fruitful discussion of television as a language teaching aid. They were, however, keenly aware of its possibilities and urged the widest international exchange of information on this subject.

EXPORTING A LANGUAGE: THE UNITED KINGDOM[2]

What are the requirements of a radio language course? How best can we exploit the advantages of the medium and how best overcome its disadvantages? Before examining some of the problems of the individual radio lesson we must first consider a question which will to a large extent determine how we tackle those problems. It is the nature of the audience for the course. Until we know this we cannot begin to define the methods to be employed.

Though some other types of audience are possible, we find in practice that the majority of radio language courses are addressed either to children in schools or to the adult general public. There could hardly be a greater difference of circumstances. The function of broadcasts to schools is very largely auxiliary. The children are being taught already by their own teacher, and the responsibility of the broadcaster to convey essential information is correspondingly smaller. It follows that in a broadcast to schools there is no need to force the medium in any way. There is no need to put into elaborate spoken descriptions what would be clearer from an actual demonstration in the classroom; or to lose time in dictating words and examples which could much more quickly

---

1. See particularly *The Teaching of Foreign Languages by Television* (*Foreign Languages Bulletin* no. 25), June 1954, published by the Modern Language Association of America, 6 Washington Square North, New York, 3, N.Y., U.S.A.
2. This paper is condensed from 'The Teaching of English as a Foreign Language by Radio', a working-paper prepared for the Ceylon seminar by the English-by-Radio Department of the British Broadcasting Corporation. It first examines the kind of problems that have to be faced in attempting to teach a foreign language through the medium of radio and then gives an account of how these problems have been met in one particular instance.

be written up on the blackboard beforehand. Any teaching functions not suited to the medium can be left to the classroom teacher, and the radio period used above all as a means of bringing the language to life, of letting the children hear it spoken by native speakers in natural, realistic situations. There are other important advantages enjoyed by the organizer of a broadcast course to schools. He knows that his audience will be reasonably homogeneous, all about the same age, with roughly the same kind of interests, and learning under similar conditions. Moreover, through his co-operation with the teacher on the spot he can be given a reliable indication of how much the pupils know before they start the course and trustworthy reports of their progress while it lasts. He does not have to work in the dark.

With the course for the general public it is clearly quite otherwise. The age-range may be anything from 18 to 80, the degree of previous education an unknown quantity, and the occupations and backgrounds of the learners as far apart as those of businessman and bus-driver, labourer and lawyer. The only safe assumption to make is that the listener knows nothing except what the broadcast course tells him; and having made this assumption we realize that we can no longer simplify the task by leaving part of the teaching to be done by others. Whatever the handicaps they must be tackled somehow.

Another important difference is that the lessons have to be addressed to the individual listener in his own home: they cannot count on the stimulus which comes from study along with others in an organized group. As against the school broadcasting situation there is perhaps the advantage that listening is in no way compulsory. Most listeners will be studying of their own free will and so be spurred on by a genuine urge to learn. On the other hand, it must be remembered that many of them will have lost the habit of planned and regular study. They will have lost too the child's easy adaptability and un-selfconsciousness when asked to make strange sounds or imagine itself in strange surroundings. Without personal contact with the teacher, confusion can more easily arise and discouragement more easily set in. The radio course for the individual adult must therefore make special efforts to win the learner's confidence and to persuade him that he can succeed. Even the best teaching material will fail if it is not presented so as to give this feeling. It is so easy to switch off.

A factor of almost equal importance with the nature of the audience itself is the provision of texts to accompany the radio lessons. Obviously, if we can provide a leaflet or a book for the learner there is again no need to force the medium, no occasion to attempt to teach through the ear what would be better done through the eye. Pictures are possible, which will make up for the radio's blindness, and tables, vocabularies and exercises can be included, which will help the learner to consolidate his knowledge. A text can also create an immediate association between the spoken and the written word and make it unnecessary to spend time on spelling or dictation. For these reasons a text is specially desirable in a course for beginners. Otherwise the teaching has to go infinitely more slowly and, apart from any notes he may succeed in taking, the student has no permanent record of the lessons from which he can refresh his knowledge later on. Even in a more advanced course, where reference back is perhaps less necessary, the existence of a text can still greatly affect the pace at which it is possible to proceed.

In general then a text is always helpful, and every listener should have one. But it is easier to recommend this than to realize it in practice. The cost of production is often an obstacle, and even when the text is produced it still has to be distributed. Again the situation is easier in a course for schools, for here one can usually count on the co-operation of the educational authorities in ensuring that it is provided. In courses for the general public the broadcasting organization itself must make this provision, and in some areas the possibilities of distributing and selling books are very small. A cheap and much-favoured solution is to publish the texts of the lessons serially in a radio-programme journal. But whatever solution is adopted there usually remains a fair proportion of listeners who for one reason or another do not get a text. What is to be done for such listeners: are they to be ignored or should we, for their sake, still try to make the broadcast lessons reasonably complete in themselves? Clearly the answer may affect the whole planning of a course.

Yet another important general consideration is the level of the course. Are the audience beginners, intermediate or advanced students? The degree of help needed in the form of texts or spoken explanations will vary from one level to another and widely differing techniques may be required. A striking example is the problem of the use of the learner's own language over the air. Teachers accustomed to employ direct method techniques for the whole of their classroom work would no doubt question using the vernacular at all, even for beginners. But a moment's reflection reminds us that in the early stages these techniques depend entirely for their success on the ability of the pupil to see what is being referred to. Meaning is conveyed by visual demonstration, by the teacher pointing to objects or himself performing, or getting others to perform, the actions he describes. Deprived of this demonstration, the pupil must be helped in some other way to visualize the situation behind the words. We have already noted that this can partly be done by the provision of texts with illustrations, but only partly. The teacher in the classroom also achieves his result by establishing good relations with his pupils, by the timely use of the encouraging gesture, the friendly smile, the occasional joke. On the radio such encouragement can be conveyed only through the voice; and one cannot be encouraging or crack a very effective joke in a limited vocabulary of a few dozen words! Nor can one stretch the meaning of those words by the use of subtle intonations which would be quite lost upon the elementary learner. Not to recognize this is to run the risk of defeating the whole purpose of a radio series by losing the audience at the outset.

The vernacular then is essential in the early stages, though it may be progressively discarded for more advanced students. It should also be clear that as the knowledge of the language widens the actual forms of lessons may vary. Continuous talks, dialogues and discussions in the foreign language will become possible; and from the mere giving of information about the language itself we may pass gradually to its indispensable corollary—the portrayal of the life and manners of the people who speak it. Along with grammar and advice on pronunciation there will be simple descriptions of national institutions and customs. Contemporary events can be referred to, or the lesson can introduce glimpses of the country's history or specimens of the literature which the language has produced; until at last the broadcast may no longer appear a 'language lesson' in the ordinary sense, and the learner will have reached the point where he no longer needs any help or where he can be left to find his own material for further study in ordinary radio programmes in the language.

Let us now consider some of the requirements for the individual radio lesson. The word 'lesson' is used here in the sense of a single teaching broadcast, just as in the classroom it is used in the sense of a single teaching period. And herein lies a great difference; the classroom language teacher is accustomed to think of lessons in terms of 45 minutes or an hour, but experience has shown that without the support of the eyes effective concentration cannot be maintained for as long as this. In a recent experiment on the comprehension of broadcast talks it was found that after about 15 minutes the amount retained by the average listener not only does not increase any more, but actually begins to decrease. A broadcast talk is thus not quite the same thing as a language lesson, though the parallel is sufficiently close. Probably the maximum desirable limit is about 20 minutes, and the minimum 10. Anything less will hardly be worth while.

Hand in hand with the question of length goes the question of the amount of teaching to be attempted in the time allowed. A few points clearly stated, often repeated, and summarized at the end are the golden rule. The teacher at the microphone must constantly remind himself that his unseen class have no opportunity to ask him questions and that they cannot as in a book turn back to re-read something they have not fully understood. He must seek to be as clear as possible from the beginning.

Repetition is necessary in all teaching. It serves both to ensure understanding and to drive home what is learnt. It is even more necessary in broadcast instruction, where the learner has not the help of his eyes. Possible difficulties of reception are a further strong argument. A point made only once may be lost in the trough of a fade or in a burst of atmospherics. But with average listening conditions a point well reiterated will still get through. There must therefore be the maximum degree of repetition within each broadcast, whether obvious or concealed. And though the aim must certainly be to make each broadcast stand by itself there will always be value in repeating it as a whole at a different time, in order to provide the chance of a second hearing.

Liberal repetition will also help to solve another problem of the radio language teacher: the rate of speaking in the foreign language. In the elementary stages this must obviously be slow. The learner's stock of words and phrases is very limited and his command of them not very secure. He must be given time to recognize and absorb each item before being asked to take in the next. But too much slowing-up is dangerous and leads to speech-distortion: exaggerated stresses, unnaturally lengthened vowels and the separation of sense-groups. To avoid this the learner must be introduced as quickly as possible to the normal sentence-rhythms of the language and become accustomed to them by hearing them over and over again.

Even though the lesson is kept to the right length, with a proper measure of repetition and limitation of matter there is still the danger that the listener's attention may wander or flag. There are obvious ways of countering this danger, but the cardinal requirement is good speakers. It is not enough simply to bring a well-known language teacher to the microphone and let him follow his own devices. His success in the classroom will have been achieved through many other personal qualities besides that of his voice, perhaps even in spite of it. Divested of these qualities he may make far less appeal, and may lack the skill of the professional broadcaster to put over meaning and feeling by voice alone. Either he must gain command of the medium himself or he must be replaced by a more practised speaker. In any case a single speaker is insufficient for a good language-teaching broadcast. However good his voice may be, it may still prove monotonous in the end, and to hold the listener's attention to the full a change of voice will often be required. A change of voice in broadcasting may be compared to a change of type in the printed word. It can recapture our waning interest or underline an important new point. To do so successfully, good contrast between the voices is needed, and none can be more effective than the natural contrast of man and woman speaker.

Also useful as means of recapturing the listener's attention from time to time are the recognized radio devices of a change of pattern in the material or of tempo in the production (provided this does not interfere with understanding). Learners who have been inactively listening for most of the broadcast will benefit if they are suddenly called on to answer a question or to repeat a phrase or a sentence themselves. A passage of solid, factual information is best followed by something lighter and easier in vein, giving time to digest what has gone before. And of course suitable incidental music may be employed, whether to create a mood, effect a transition, or 'curtain off' one part of the broadcast from another.

It is clear that one of the greatest services the radio course can perform is to place expert teaching within the reach of every listener, wherever he may be and whatever his financial resources. For an audience which may be numbered in tens of thousands only the best teaching material will do, and a course which does not provide this is failing in its purpose: every effort should be made to ensure that the broadcast lessons are based on sound pedagogical experience and linguistic research.

It must be equally apparent that one of radio's foremost attractions in this field is the chance it offers to hear good native speakers of the language, and a course which does not do this will again be failing in its best purpose. There is indeed a case, as we have already seen, for the early stages to be presented in the vernacular by someone who can identify himself with and win the sympathy of the audience. But as an incentive and experience for the learner nothing can exceed the value of listening to the native speaker, or rather speakers. For here we come back to the need for more than one voice. It is a weakness of much classroom language teaching that it must always be given by one and the same person, and that the learner becomes accustomed to the language in only one shape and dimension. Even if the class teacher has no actual defects in his pronunciation which could be passed on to his pupils (he may after all be a native speaker himself), he still cannot offer them experience of all those slight variations of pitch, tone, and accent which make up the fullness of a language and help us to distinguish one speaker from another.

Moreover, language is not a string of words or unconnected sentences which can be learned by rote at the teacher's behest. It resides in situations, in situations among people, in the daily encounters of life among those who use it. Only after experiencing these situations a sufficient number of times can we automatically produce the language which applies to them. But the teacher, unaided, cannot readily create such complete situations in the classrooms. However well he may teach, however good is the textbook he uses, he is still only one person able to speak the language standing in front of many who cannot. True conversation is impossible and the sense of reality lacking. But modern radio can provide these things. With its highly-developed production technique, its battery of sound effects and its sensitive microphones it can conjure up for us in the space of a few seconds almost any scene, any situation we choose. Not to take advantage of this by introducing a variety of speakers into the broadcast lessons would be a mistake.

From all that has been said it will now be plain that the successful radio language course is something which calls for a high degree of co-operation between teacher and broadcaster. Whether the teacher who prepares the course takes an actual part in it himself or not, he will still need the services of an understanding radio producer, able to translate his material into forms and terms truly suited to the medium. And the producer in turn will need the help of trained speakers, able to interpret his directions in a manner which does not sacrifice interest for clarity or clarity for effect. It is indeed a task demanding much team work and a wide basis of experience. A great deal of such team work and experience can now be said to lie behind the name of 'English by Radio'.

The BBC's English-by-Radio Department is now entering on its eleventh year of regular broadcasting to oversea students of English, and during the past decade has seen a steady expansion of its activities from a mere five-minute 'refresher' programme for listeners in wartime Europe to a comprehensive service of lessons directed to all parts of the world. Over 100 of these lessons weekly are given direct from London in the BBC's own external services and twice as many more are radiated from stations oversea with the help of scripts and recordings ('transcriptions') supplied by the corporation. In keeping with the general character of BBC programmes to other countries the lessons are aimed primarily at the adult listener abroad, though the claims of younger learners in the family circle have also been borne in mind.

What is the nature of these lessons and how are they produced?

Clearly, with such an immense and varied audience no one type of course would be sufficient and in effect there is a whole range of lessons for listeners at different stages of progress. They may be divided into two main categories. First, for beginners and elementary students, there are courses with explanations in the listener's own language. Then, for those who already have some foundation on which to build, there are lessons given entirely in English, so graded and arranged that they will take the learner to the point where he can comfortably follow an ordinary broadcast in English. The lessons entirely in English have the practical advantage that they can be directed to more than one country at the same time, thus making it possible to cover a wider area and provide a more frequent service of English teaching programmes in the time available.

The courses with foreign language explanations are generally progressive in kind and designed to run for about two years, after which the learner can transfer to the all-English lessons, and a new course for a fresh set of beginners can be begun. The task of organizing and co-ordinating all these various courses is carried out by a special department, working in conjunction with the BBC's foreign language and transcription services on the one hand and the authors of the lessons on the other. Some of the lessons are actually written by members of the staff with language-teaching experience. But in the main the policy followed has been to call on the assistance of recognized outside experts and to join with them in producing suitable courses to go over the air. Thus most of the names famous in the field of teaching English as a foreign language have contributed at one time or another to the programmes, and a few years ago a permanent source of guidance was provided by the setting up at the London University Institute of Education of a special chair and department for research in this field. The holder of the chair, Professor Bruce Pattison, has served as the department's educational adviser, and three members of his staff have been responsible for writing the principal English-by-Radio course for beginners, 'Listen and Speak'.

It will be of interest to take a closer look at this course as a specimen of a combined teaching effort taking full account of the peculiarities of the medium. It was decided at the outset that it should be suitable for people with no previous experience of learning a foreign language and that it should be adaptable for audiences of many different nationalities. There was considerable experiment before it was begun and the three authors, Mr. A. V. P. Elliott, Mr. W. F. Mackey and Dr. J. A. Noonan, submitted each script for studio testing and discussion before it was finally recorded.

Their teaching material is based on the most recent linguistic research and in particular on an extensive study of the essential sentence patterns of English. Believing that the real problem for the student is the learning not of individual words but of the structures or patterns in which they operate they have graded the structures of English according to their usefulness, frequency and difficulty; and each lesson introduces a limited number of new structures in a carefully controlled order. The basic course comprises 150 15-minute lessons (supplemented by a varying number of special pronunciation lessons for each particular audience, usually about fifteen), and is normally given at the rate of two lessons a week.

Although, for the reasons already given, 'Listen and Speak', as a beginners' course, has to be presented in the vernacular, it is still in one sense a direct method course. It is direct in the sense that it seeks to show the meaning of the words taught by presenting them in complete sentences and associating those sentences immediately with the sort of situations in which they are used. Each lesson consists of three parts. First the radio teacher describes in the learner's own language what is happening in the studio, so that a mental picture is built up with which the English sentences that follow can be linked. Sometimes an individual word or phrase has to be translated in order to provide the necessary starting-point, but routine translation is rigorously avoided and the listener is always encouraged to make a direct link in his mind between some simple, typical situation and the sentences he is asked to learn. Whenever a new structure is introduced it is explained in this way by reference to a simple situation and in terms of structures already taught. The learner then has the opportunity of hearing examples of the new structure in a piece of continuous English dialogue. A story about an English family, the Grey family, runs through the course, and the dialogues present episodes from the life of this family. As he gets to know the personages and their characteristics—the father's impatience, the son's untidiness and the mother's love of order—the listener can more readily imagine the situations in which he hears them talking.

At the end of each lesson, after the dialogue, there is an oral exercise in which the learner is called on to speak under the direction of the radio teacher (hence the title: 'Listen and Speak'). Care is thus taken both that the listener's interest is maintained and that he makes some active use of what he learns. Obviously his response to the exercises cannot be heard in the studio, but they are so framed that he cannot go far wrong and can test his degree of success for himself. Apart from the Grey family dialogues, the lessons are always given by two speakers, the radio teacher, who is assumed to be bilingual, and an English-speaking colleague. In each of the exercises the second speaker acts as the pupil; and after a pause during which the listener makes his own reply, gives the correct answer, so that the listener can judge how far he was right. As the course proceeds, more and more use is made of English as the means of actually conducting the lessons until at the close a number of them are given entirely in English. Because of this, and because of the very small extent to which it relies on actual translation to convey meaning, the course has indeed proved readily adaptable to widely different language audiences, from Europe to the Far East.

Again, for the kind of reasons given earlier in this paper, 'Listen and Speak', as a beginners' course, is intended to be used in conjunction with a printed text, and corresponding books or serially-published editions have been issued. These texts have been designed to supplement the broadcast teaching as much as possible and contain much more than a mere abstract of the spoken lessons. There are illustrations to teach the structures through the eye, there are substitution tables to help him build parallel examples for himself, written exercises to drive the points home and grammatical summaries and vocabularies to enable him to look up quickly anything he has forgotten from an earlier lesson.

In passing on to the subject of the lessons entirely in English, it is no longer possible to take any one course as being fully typical of the work which is done. There is in fact a 15-minute lesson of this kind every day of the week throughout the year. Each lesson is given a number of times (at present seven) during the course of the day in order to serve different areas in turn. This arrangement has the advantage that it also provides a choice of listening-times and allows many listeners to hear the lesson more than once.

The audience for these lessons consists not only of those who have followed one of the beginners' courses, but also includes large numbers of people who have already had a good deal of teaching at school or elsewhere and whose main need is to become more familiar with the spoken language. Since these listeners would not be so interested in a complete and strictly progressive course there is only one series, called 'Listening and Speaking', which forms a direct continuation of 'Listen and Speak'. The remainder of the lessons are more loosely organized, to allow some freedom of choice according to individual requirements. There are however two broad levels of difficulty, differentiated by the range of vocabulary, subject matter and the average rate of speech employed. These elementary and advanced lessons are given on alternate days, and it is left to the individual listener to make the change from one series to the other, as soon as he feels ready for it. Many indeed listen to both. Moreover, each lesson is made as far as possible complete in itself so that learners may join or come back to the series at any time.

Typical themes for the elementary series (apart from the 'Listening and Speaking' course) are pronunciation, stress and intonation, and the vocabulary of everyday conversation. One series, called 'What to Say', is based on the sort of situations in which a student of English might find himself on a visit to Great Britain: asking the way, getting into a train or a bus, going into a shop or restaurant, and so on. The listener first hears a short and rather slowly-spoken conversation in one of these situations; any difficult points in it are explained and the conversation is repeated at a faster speed. Then he is given practice in speaking useful sentences from it himself, and finally the conversation is repeated once more at a completely normal speed. Another favourite conversational series is called 'Ann and her Grandfather'. Here too the basis is a short conversation which is repeated with comments and explanations in between, but the particular attention is the character of 'Grandfather' and the humour of the situations. Most people find that they can remember new words and phrases more easily when they are associated with an amusing incident or a sympathetic personality, and as we saw earlier familiarity with a character and the way in which that character is likely to act can be a help to understanding.

At the advanced level there is a still wider range of types of lesson: perhaps 'programme' would be a better word. There are dialogues on English idioms; there are dramatized serial stories and readings from English literature, with an explanatory commentary; there are programmes illustrating commercial English and other specialized terminology; there are answers to listeners' questions on points of English usage and talks giving general advice on the study of the language. These are the weekday programmes. The Sunday programmes have even less the character of formal language lessons and include programmes on British history and institutions, traditional songs, accounts of popular customs, and competitions.

With such a variety of subject matter for the programmes, variety of form and presentation are highly important. Apart from actual talks all the programmes introduce a number of voices. There exists a panel of speakers of both sexes specially chosen for their clarity of diction. They are none the less sufficiently varied among themselves to give the student a thorough training in understanding the spoken language. The department also has its own specialist script-writers and producers whose experience and training have taught them how best to employ their team of speakers for particular language teaching purposes.

To meet the demand from other radio organizations for help in broadcasting English language courses, a considerable service of transcription has been built up. These 'transcriptions' are programmes supplied in script or recorded form to other radio stations for local re-broadcasting. They have the particular advantage, from the language teaching point of view, that since they can be put out locally they can be heard under the best possible reception conditions.

A selection of some of the most generally useful series has been made, including items suitable for students at various levels. At the more elementary levels this again raises a problem over the use of the vernacular. Complete recordings of 'Listen and Speak' have been made in such major languages as French, Spanish and Arabic. But elsewhere a compromise had to be found, a compromise which in the event has proved to have its own advantages. It is to provide recordings of those parts of the lessons which are entirely in English, together with basic scripts from which the vernacular explanations can be translated and produced locally. This makes the minimum demand on the local station's production resources (a translator and one or two voices at most are required), and has the attraction that the vernacular portion can be presented in exact accordance with local linguistic taste.

The issue of records for use on gramophones might not at first appear a normal activity for a department concerned with teaching English by radio. But many educational authorities have wanted to have the broadcast lessons in recorded form for their own teaching use. Despite the high cost of making permanent records, combined with limitations of copyright an important selection of courses, corresponding broadly to those also issued as transcriptions has now been made available, and the records are being widely used in schools, universities and teacher-training colleges. Other types of users are adult educational organizations and trade unions. The records are not on sale to members of the general public.

Texts of the courses are provided with the records and, as with the transcription courses, help can often be given over issuing special local editions where occasion demands. With the 'Listen and Speak' course another form of assistance is given. As this is a beginners' course it is patently necessary for the classroom teaching to be carefully controlled and co-ordinated with the recorded material from the beginning. For this reason a special teacher's handbook has been prepared showing how the course as a whole can best be adapted for classroom use.

IMPORTING A LANGUAGE: SWEDEN[1]

In Sweden the co-operation of the broadcasting system with public education began early in the 1930's. It is now managed by a special section in the semi-public broadcasting corporation, Radiotjänst. Broadcasting for schools is carried out under the supervision of the central government department for the educational system, the Royal Board of Education. Between the latter and Radiotjänst there is an officially sanctioned agreement, which lays down the responsibilities and rights of the two sides. The programmes, which are drawn up half-yearly, are scrutinized by the board, which also has a voice in the appointment of the officials who run school broadcasts. Otherwise the activity is administered by Radiotjänst, which is thus responsible for programme production and—in collaboration with the central department for the relevant technical questions and with the Telegraph Board—for transmissions. As with the whole organization of Radiotjänst, financing takes place by means of the income from radio licences.

In general, broadcasts for schools have only had the purpose of supplementing the teaching of the schools on suitable points, not of guiding it continuously. However, one particular branch of the work, the so-called combined correspondence and broadcast teaching, has formed an exception in this respect. Circumstances have led to its development as a distinctive innovation in Swedish school broadcasting, and it is perhaps also worthy of international attention.

During recent decades, the teaching of a modern language (English) has gradually been introduced into the syllabus of the compulsory school in Sweden, but it has been necessary to obtain special permission for this in the case of each individual school. However, the training of elementary school teachers has not included qualification for this English teaching; language teaching at the training colleges has only had a general educational function. Certain qualifications have been laid down for language teaching in the elementary school, which have to be acquired by the teacher by private study. The number of teachers with these qualifications has increased year by year but is still far from adequate. In particular, it has always been difficult to obtain English teachers for the purely rural districts. It was primarily this shortage of modern language teachers that led to the feeling that it might be advantageous to make use of radio.

The question was taken up by an expert commission, the 1940

---

1. This section is a slightly condensed version of the working-paper prepared for the Ceylon seminar by the Swedish National Commission for Unesco and entitled 'The Teaching of English in Sweden by a Method Combining Correspondence Courses and Radio Broadcasting'.

School Committee, which considered that there ought to be a more general introduction of English teaching in the elementary school, from at least the sixth class (the last year but one of compulsory education). At that time the Swedish educational system was still organized in such a way that pupils from the elementary school who wished to transfer to a secondary school could do so either after the fourth class or after the sixth. In the former case the pupil had a further five years (i.e. a total of nine years) before taking the *realexamen* (school certificate examination), and in the latter case a further four years (i.e. a total of ten years). The immediate task was to discover whether, even in schools lacking a teacher with the prescribed qualifications in English, a detailed broadcast course in English for the sixth class, combined with written guidance, could achieve with the more gifted pupils results roughly corresponding to those obtained in the first year of the four-year *realskola* (middle school). School broadcasting was begun as an experiment, under the supervision of the Royal Board of Education, in the autumn of 1945 after special material had been made available. At first the experiment included only the districts around Stockholm and used only one broadcasting station. In the academic year 1946–47, a continuation course was organized for the seventh class.

A new body, the 1946 School Commission, favoured a more rapid development and the introduction of English teaching from the fifth class of the elementary school. At the same time, the goals of language teaching were to be made more practical. With this objective in view, in the year 1947–48, the combined teaching went on with a certain selection of pupils in the fifth class of specially chosen schools. The following year the sixth class was also included. At that time there were involved some 1,500 pupils in about 170 schools in 15 different inspectorates, and seven stations were used; the field had thus been widened considerably. It was now desirable, without aiming at comparisons with the results of the 'middle school', to see how far it was possible to go with pupils who had to some degree been selected.

Since 1949–50, there has been more general participation in the teaching: only obviously unsuitable pupils may be excluded. Teaching has also been extended to cover the seventh class and the broadcasts are directed to groups scattered over the whole country. Use is made of all of Radiotjänst's transmitter stations. At present (1953) the number of pupils taking part in the combined correspondence and broadcast teaching of English is about 8,500, and the number of groups taking part about 875. This teaching by a combination method (which is still regarded as experimental) is planned year by year.

Schools that are unable to obtain an English teacher with the stipulated qualifications, but that wish to take part, are instructed to send in an application with the necessary information to the relevant elementary school inspector. The inspector assesses the suitability of the teacher for acting as supervisor in the subject and gives his opinion on the need for the teaching. The applications are then sent through the Royal Board of Education to the School Broadcasting Service, which selects the schools.

The number of schools taking part has been, and to some extent still is, held down to a rough maximum figure, as it has been necessary to keep within the financial limits permitted by Parliament. The expenses involved consist, first, of the direct costs of transmission, which fall on the Telegraph Service. Since all transmitting stations are now used, these expenses are not affected by the number of schools participating in each area. Other overhead expenses are the production costs of the school broadcasting department, e.g. for radio teachers and for administration. On the other hand there are expenses that vary directly with the number participating, i.e. the cost of the correspondence course, of the written tests, of the correction of the pupils' work, and of the supervisors out in the schools. At an earlier stage the costs of the material sent out to the individual pupils and the costs of correction were met, like the other items just mentioned, out of the specially assigned grant. These costs rose, at their peak, to about 800,000 kronor a year ($154,800). Later, they were transferred to the local education authorities. The correction of the written tests is now carried out by the supervisors in accordance with instructions obtained from the school broadcasting service. The cost of the supervisors, which is the most expensive item, has been transferred from the special grant for combined correspondence and broadcast teaching to the large grant for elementary school teachers' salaries. In this way the special public outlay for the work has been reduced, and for the financial year 1953–54 is estimated at 400,000 kronor ($77,400). The supervisors receive a fee for each hour of supervision outside their statutory weekly hours of work. The fee is the same as that for other extra teaching in elementary schools, and may not exceed three hours a week for each class. There must, however, be at least three pupils in each class at the beginning of the academic year.

As a result of the transfer to the local authorities of all expenses that vary with the number of pupils, it is to be expected that it will gradually become possible to achieve the aim of introducing this form of teaching pretty generally into schools where English teaching cannot be organized in the normal way.

Administratively, it is the school broadcasting service that directs the work, but always under the supervision of the Royal Board of Education. The shaping of the courses and transmissions is thus the responsibility of the broadcasting service, but in other respects the work forms a part of the regular education system. The supervision of the work enters into the duties of the elementary school inspectors, and inspection of the functioning and results of this form of teaching is undertaken by the board. Requests for the State grant are made in the board's general budget proposals.

As already stated, combined correspondence and broadcast courses in English are now given for the fifth, sixth and seventh classes of the elementary school. The timetables and syllabuses for the ordinary English teaching in these classes are also intended for the combined teaching. The timetables allot five lessons a week to the subject in the fifth and sixth classes, and four lessons in the seventh. The total number of lessons a week in these classes is 32, excluding handicrafts (two to four lessons a week).

Two of the weekly English lessons are broadcast lessons. These, however, are somewhat shorter than ordinary lessons (30 minutes as against 45). The intention is that the supervisor out in the school shall immediately use a quarter of an hour for further emphasizing what has just been taught and for arranging homework. The supervisor himself is responsible for the remaining lessons in the subject; in these, the content of the broadcast lesson is gone through and written work is done. Timetables are drawn up by the teachers concerned and scrutinized by the headmaster. It is difficult to produce suitable plans of this kind for classes consisting of more than one age-group, but, practicable solutions have been found, even in cases where the supervisor has been drawn from a class other than the one where English is being studied.

The teachers responsible for the broadcasts ('radio teachers'), who must obviously have high qualifications in several respects, are selected after special test lessons. These are judged by a committee appointed by Radiotjänst. Special weight is attached to the 'radiogenic' quality of their pronunciation and intonation, and their ability to hold the attention of the invisible audience.

A broadcast lesson usually begins with a catchy tune to attract attention. Music is also employed in other ways. There is a short break for music about half way through the lessons, and at this point pupils have the opportunity of making the acquaintance of characteristic English songs and melodies. The lesson itself begins with conversation exercises about everyday things and then goes on to the study of a passage in the correspondence course which has been worked out for the various age-groups. The pupils are gathered near the loudspeaker under the eye of the supervisor.

They answer in chorus the questions of the radio teacher, underline important passages in the correspondence course and take notes. The supervisor is there to give a hand if necessary, writes on the blackboard as instructed by the radio teacher, and sees that all the pupils take an active part in the lesson. Sometimes the radio teacher addresses himself direct to the supervisor and explains how the work that follows is to be handled. It is necessary to insert suitable pauses for the pupils' replies or repetitions and to strike the right tempo and tone. The lessons are highly concentrated, and place great demands on the radio teacher, the supervisor and the pupils.

The class teacher is certainly not left out of the picture; when the broadcast lesson is ended his work begins. All the new knowledge that has streamed out of the loudspeaker in a fleeting half-hour has to be explained, practised and assimilated.

Special gramophone records have been recorded to supplement the teaching and a special songbook compiled. The correspondence lessons are in general written by the radio teachers. In addition to texts they contain a large number of suggestions for conversation practice and for written exercises. All explanations, naturally, have to be both clear and detailed. Illustrations and anecdotes are added to avoid stodginess. As supplementary material there are occasional tests that are worked out by the school broadcasting service and marked by the supervisors in accordance with instructions given them. Information about the results is sent in to the broadcasting service. Previously, tests were given more frequently and were also examined at a special centre by a group of university students, but the organization has now been simplified.

The quality of the teaching depends in the first place on the radio teachers, and here it has been possible to fulfil extremely exacting requirements. The supervisors, whose qualifications are assessed by the elementary school inspectors, usually have a knowledge of English corresponding to that required for the *student-examen* (roughly equivalent to the old Higher School Certificate in England), or have at any rate reached the standard required in the normal training for the class teacher in an elementary school. However, certain minimum qualifications are insisted on. In order to improve the supervisors' qualifications, grants have been obtained for courses of instruction. These are usually held in the summer under the auspices of the school broadcasting service. It has been established by experiment that the results of the combined broadcast and correspondence courses do not always stand in direct proportion to the qualifications of the supervisor.

In addition to the supervision exercised directly by the board and by the school broadcasting service, it has been possible during recent years, thanks to special grants, to appoint regional advisers. Each regional adviser, who is normally a language teacher at a secondary school, usually has allotted to him either one or two of the country's 51 inspectorates' districts. He visits each group at some time during the year, gives advice and instructions and reports on his experiences to the school broadcasting service.

In view of the conditions (groups that are still largely not homogeneous, the lack of qualifications on the part of the supervisors, and the real teacher's purely oral-aural contact with the pupils) it must be expected that the results will be uneven. According to the computations which have been made on various occasions, it can be considered that between a quarter and a third of the groups have got very little profit out of the teaching. About the same number of groups have been found to make good use, often outstandingly good use, of the course, while the remainder have been about average. In practically all groups there have been individual pupils who have shown very good results.

In this kind of teaching pronunciation practice offers special problems. The direct broadcast gives a model to be imitated. Whether the object is attained depends very largely on the extent to which the individual supervisor can assimilate the instructions and diagnose and correct his pupils' faults with their aid. Success is dependent to a particularly high degree on the supervisor's interest, language sense and energy.

In general it has been found that, in this form of teaching, justice is done to conversation practice. By the technique of the broadcast lesson, by choral reading, dialogues, various kinds of dramatization and assiduous practice, the pupils have often made great strides in the will and the power to use English in simple everyday contexts. The ability to understand the spoken language is obviously encouraged by this kind of teaching. Above all it has been possible to show that in general the factual content of passages has been grasped, both in listening and in translation work even if exactness of detail has not been adequate.

The grammatical course has had to be relatively limited. Great importance has been attached to its being treated in its natural linguistic context. The written exercises done for the supervisor and the test papers provide a necessary complement to the oral side of the teaching. Here the results are particularly uneven, but the great majority of the pupils have nevertheless been able to give satisfactory evidence of their knowledge of, for example, tenses, the use of the progressive form of the verb and the periphrastic use of *do*.

To sum up: it has been shown that, for the majority of pupils, combined correspondence and broadcast teaching can furnish an effective general course in English. The question of the future organization and use of the combined correspondence and broadcast teaching of English in Sweden has not yet been decided; however, in the curricula of the experimental schools, which are the testing ground for the future educational system of the country, this method of teaching is included as an alternative. It is clear that if English is to be introduced more generally into the elementary schools there is great need for the combined method. It will therefore probably be used for a long time to come in schools which lack an English teacher but in which a suitable supervisor can be found. The experience so far obtained indicates that in this way it will be possible to be of special assistance to isolated rural schools where classes are made up of more than one age-group and where it is always most difficult to obtain fully qualified teachers. When at some future date the need for competent teachers has been met, the school broadcasting service will have as its natural function in the sphere of English teaching that of supporting by more isolated broadcasts the direct instruction in the schools—as it now does with other school subjects.

CHAPTER IX
MODERN LANGUAGE TEACHING IN PRIMARY SCHOOLS

In the final paragraph of the seminar report published in Chapter V the following sentence occurs: 'As regards the question of the optimum age for beginning the study of a new language, it was decided that in view of the experiments of introducing modern languages in elementary schools being carried out by various Member States, it would be wrong to discuss the question on *a priori* grounds but desirable to watch the results of the experiments.' The decision to include this statement in the report arose out of the lively discussion which followed the reading of a paper by Professor Theodore Andersson on 'The Teaching of Foreign Languages in the Elementary Schools in the United States of America'. It was realized that the subject was a controversial one and likely to remain so for some time, but it was also felt that in at least one country the question was being studied pragmatically and that the progress of this experiment was well worth watching.

In the year that has elapsed since the Ceylon seminar, the practice of introducing language teaching at the elementary stage has continued to make progress in the United States and to arouse increasing interest among educators in that country. The paper that follows chronicles the genesis and development of this experiment.

It is realized, of course, that the practice itself is not new. Although many countries adhere strictly to the custom of introducing language teaching only in the first year of the secondary school, others have found it advisable to begin at an earlier age. In the City of Hamburg, for instance, there is an unbroken tradition of foreign language teaching in the elementary schools that goes back for over three quarters of a century. Readers who are interested in discovering what the prevailing practice is may, besides consulting the source suggested by Professor Andersson, find further information in a study on modern languages in the schools which is planned to appear in 1955 as a companion volume to this study.

TEACHING MODERN LANGUAGES TO YOUNG CHILDREN IN THE UNITED STATES

In his stimulating book on *The National Interest and Foreign Languages*[1] William R. Parker includes a table showing graphically the offerings in modern foreign language study in the public schools of 35 countries. The table shows that a second language is offered for a period of from three to ten years in this group of countries, and indicates the starting age, which varies from 7 in Austria to 14 in the United States. It will be seen that in most countries a second language is begun at the age of 11 or 12, an age which generally coincides with the beginning of the secondary school. The introduction of a second language at the elementary school level is as yet quite exceptional, and therefore the rather extensive experimentation going on in this field in the United States will perhaps be of interest.

A survey of the status of second language teaching in the elementary schools of the United States as of the autumn of 1953[2] reveals that French, German, Italian or Spanish were being taught in at least 145 communities in 33 states and the District of Columbia. Children varying in age from 5 to 12 were learning Spanish in at least 409 schools in 27 states; French in 251 schools in 20 states; German in 30 schools in 6 states; and Italian in one elementary school in Atlantic City, New Jersey. French, German and Spanish were being taught in the public schools of Washington, D.C. Until Professor Mildenberger has brought his study up to the autumn of 1954, no one can know exactly how rapidly the movement is now growing, but that it is growing rapidly—'snowballing' is the term commonly applied—is certain.

A backward look will show that the trend towards introducing second language study in the American elementary schools has already reached the beginning of its third stage. During the first stage, almost exactly fifty years in length and dating from around 1870 to the end of the first world war, German was taught in many public elementary schools in centres of heavy German population, particularly in the Mid-West.[3] This was part of an Americanization programme made necessary by the fact that many immigrants founded German schools to instruct their

---
1. William R. Parker, *The National Interest and Foreign Languages, A discussion guide and work paper for citizen consultations*, initiated by the U.S. National Commission for Unesco, Washington, D.C., U.S. Government Printing Office, April 1954, 148 p.
2. Kenneth Mildenberger, *Status of Foreign Language Study in American Elementary Schools, Fall Term, 1953*. Washington, D.C., U.S. Department of Health, Education and Welfare, Office of Education Committee on Foreign Language Teaching, 1954, 28 p.
3. 'Historical Account of German Instruction in the Public Schools of Indianapolis', an unpublished study by Frances H. Ellis of Indiana University.

children in German. This first period was brought to an undignified halt by the political events of 1917-18.

The second period began almost immediately (1921) in Cleveland, where French was offered to selected children as a part of an enrichment programme from Grade I through Grade VI, that is, throughout the elementary school.[1] French and occasionally Spanish are now offered in from 15 to 20 of the Cleveland schools. It is estimated that some 25,000 Cleveland children have profited from this unusual opportunity. Two other programmes which have continued up to the present began in the 1920's, one in French and one in Spanish; 6 began in the 1930's, 5 in French and one in Spanish; 29 in the 1940's, most of them this time in Spanish because of the Good Neighbour Policy advocated by President Franklin Delano Roosevelt. The largest programme, that of Los Angeles, had in 1953 an enrolment of about 75,000 pupils and, since the programme began in 1943, has had a total estimated enrolment of 300,000. Ten new programmes began in 1950, 9 in 1951, 32 in 1952 and at least 66 in 1953.

While there was a marked acceleration in the number of programmes begun during the forties, it seems natural to date the beginning of the third stage from 3 May 1952. It was on that date that Dr. Earl J. McGrath, then U.S. Commissioner of Education, addressed a large meeting of modern language teachers in St. Louis and advocated the general introduction of modern foreign languages into the elementary school programme. The effect of this pronouncement by an educator who was not a teacher of languages was electrifying, and the fact that the number of programmes begun in 1953 almost equalled the number of durable programmes begun since 1921 is, I think, to be attributed to the action taken by the Commissioner.[2] As Professor Parker remarks in his account of the elementary school language movement in *The National Interest and Foreign Languages*,[3] 'The development of this education "trend" during the past few years has outraced statistical analysis. At least fifty-four new programmes started in the fall of 1953, and

---

1. See Emile B. de Sauzé, 'How the Administrative Problems Connected with Modern Language Instruction in Elementary Schools were Solved in Cleveland', A Report to the National Conference on the Role of Foreign Languages in American Schools, January 1953. Washington, D.C., U.S. Office of Education; 'Teaching French in the Elementary Schools of Cleveland', *The French Review*, vol. XXVI, no. 5 (April 1953), p. 371-6; William McClain, 'Twenty-five Years of the Cleveland Plan', *Education*, vol. 65, Boston, Mass. (May 1945), p. 541-7, also in *The French Review*, vol. 18 (February 1945), p. 197-201.
2. See his three addresses: *Foreign Language Instruction in American Schools*, printed and distributed free of charge by D. C. Heath and Company, Boston, Mass; *Language Study and World Affairs*, the address delivered at the meeting of the Central States Modern Language Association, St. Louis, Mo., 3 May 1952, which may be obtained from the U.S. Office of Education, Department of Health, Education and Welfare, Wash. 25, D.C.; and 'Broadening the Base of Language Study in America', *PMLA* (Publications of the Modern Language Association of America), vol. 68, no. 1, New York (March 1953), p. 25-9.
3. p. 91-2.

many were scheduled to start in the early months of 1954. "Workshops" to prepare teachers to meet the unprecedented challenge are being planned by at least twenty-five institutions for the summer of 1954'.

Such is the factual background against which we may examine some of the theoretical and technical problems involved. The first question which presents itself is this: Why should this movement command such interest in the United States of America, where the study of foreign languages has been notoriously unsatisfactory and where the linguistic needs of World War II caught the nation completely unprepared? The question itself suggests some of the answers. The very fact that the nation was so completely unready made it necessary to take stringent measures to make up for lost time. The intensive method elaborated by certain linguistic scientists for use in the armed services demonstrated to the public in a dramatic way that even Americans could learn to speak other languages quickly and well. The research and the practical work done by these same linguistic scientists and by some language teachers brought about a better understanding of the nature of language and of the process of language learning.

The fact that the United States ranked so low in the matter of language instruction set the stage ideally for a thorough reform. Among the 35 countries listed in Professor Parker's table, the United States ranks next to the bottom and, in some ways, at the very bottom of the list. Thus, the customary beginning age for the study of foreign language in the United States is 14, the latest of any of the 35 countries listed. Although a four-year sequence is theoretically available for language study in the United States, as compared with three in Argentina—which is in thirty-fifth place—language study is obligatory in Argentina and only elective in the United States. It is well known, moreover, that although a four-year sequence is available for language study, a two-year sequence is much commoner and represents the average length of time spent in language study by those who take language at all. This situation is so much at odds with the present-day needs of one of the leaders among the nations that jostle one another uneasily on a shrinking planet that American educators have the best kind of incentive for improving the quality and the status of language instruction.

A second explanation may be cited to account for the present interest in our country in elementary school language instruction. Unlike most other countries, we have a decentralized system of education, in which the individual States are responsible for public education, and we are therefore well situated to conduct local experiments or pilot programmes without getting permission from a central authority. This situation makes it necessary also for each community to be aware of what is going on in other communities. Thus, if a successful experiment is reported, it is likely to be repeated in a variety of patterns in different parts of the country. This is exactly what is happening. If, as Professor Parker remarks,[1] the movement 'has as yet no centre, no directives, no guiding philosophy', this is not necessarily an unhealthy situation. In fact, it is normal that there should be a fairly extended period of trial and error, after which a guiding philosophy may be expected to develop. As for a 'centre', it may be the Modern Language Association itself which will turn out to be that.

In fact, the Modern Language Association *is* the centre of the movement—the hope that the U.S. Office of Education might assume the leadership was disappointed when Commissioner McGrath resigned in 1953—and has undertaken several enterprises in support of the movement. It sponsored a conference of outstanding authorities among language teachers in December 1953, and as a consequence of this meeting published a valuable report.[2] A second conference, held in June 1954, brought together elementary school authorities and language teachers for a joint study of some of the problems involved. In June 1954, also, there was held, again under the sponsorship of the Modern Language Association, a conference on the teaching of foreign languages in the elementary schools.[3] On this subject Professor Parker, again in his book on *The National Interest and Foreign Languages*,[4] has this to say: 'An additional touch of "modernity" has been given the new movement by considerable use of radio and television to supplement the language skills of elementary school teachers and to arouse and maintain the children's interest. After an experimental year of Spanish lessons over station WTHS–FM, Miami educators hopefully planned to involve 20 schools (Grades III–VI) during 1953–54 and met with requests for participation from 82 elementary schools. Over WRGB–TV, Schenectady, third through sixth-grade youngsters have "fun with French" on Monday mornings (and adults learn Spanish on Thursday mornings). In Buffalo, after-school classes receive TV Spanish lessons and in Washington, D.C., elementary school foreign language classes receive weekly 15-minute TV lessons in French or Spanish. During 1953, Iowa grade-school youngsters learned German from TV broadcasts. In El Paso, a Spanish programme is broadcast three times a week

---
1. Op. cit., p. 93.
2. *Foreign Languages in Elementary Schools: Some Questions and Answers*, Modern Language Association, 6 Washington Square North, New York 3, N.Y. 15 cents.
3. See Report: *The Teaching of Foreign Languages by Television*, Modern Language Association, 6 Washington Square North, New York 3, N.Y. 15 cents.
4. p. 94–5.

to the fourth to eight-grade classes of 17 schools. In Cleveland, weekly 20-minute lessons in French and Spanish are broadcast to classes under the guidance of voluntary teachers. Radio station KSLH in St. Louis recently received a grant to produce a series of 13-15-minute kinescopes for the teaching of French over TV, and this series will soon be distributed to the TV member stations of the National Association of Educational Broadcasters.' And, finally, the Modern Language Association publishes about once a month its *FL Newsletter* containing current information on foreign languages in the elementary schools. This newsletter goes to all known elementary school language teachers, already some 1,300 in number.

What is the theoretical basis for a belief that a second language may be profitably introduced into the curriculum of the elementary school? In the first place, it rests on simple observation of the fact that young children placed in a foreign environment and exposed to one or more foreign languages learn to understand and speak them with such ease as to induce feelings of envy in the adolescent or adult who contemplates his struggles with a second language. It is unnecessary to cite cases of this wonderful language-learning ability in children; everyone has seen or heard of examples.[1]

Not only has observation finally led language teachers to explore the possibility of making use of what may turn out to be the best learning age, but a good deal of research has already been done in the field of teaching languages to children. The most complete and up-to-date account of such research is contained in a report by the Central Advisory Council for Education (Wales) of the British Ministry of Education on *The Place of Welsh and English in the Schools of Wales*.[2] The members of this council, who have made what is perhaps the most thorough study of the vexed question of bilingualism and who have had at their disposal all available works[3] on the subject, come to the following cautious conclusion: 'It appears wisest at the present juncture to accept that body of opinion that maintains that bilingualism in itself is neither an advantage nor a disadvantage to the mental develop-

---

1. One of the most interesting cases, involving British children in India, is told by J. W. Tomb in his article entitled 'On the Intuitive Capacity of Children to Understand Spoken Language', *British Journal of Psychology*, vol. 16, part. 1, July 1925, London.
2. Published by Her Majesty's Stationery Office in London, 1953.
3. To be recommended in particular are the following titles: Seth Arsenian, 'Bilingualism and Mental Development', Teachers College, Columbia University, N.Y., *Contributions to Education*, no. 712, 1937; and 'Bilingualism in the Post-war World', *Psychological Bulletin*, vol. 42, Washington, D.C. American Psychological Association, 1945; W. S. Leopold, *Speech Development of a Bilingual Child*, vols. 1-4, Northwestern University Press, Evanston, Ill.; and Jules Ronjat, *Le développement du langage observé chez un enfant bilingue*, Paris, Champion, 1913.
4. p. 47, paragraph 218.

ment of a normal child'.[4] According to this view, the enthusiastic opinions of those who believe that knowledge of a second language contributes to the mental capacity of the individual and the view of the sceptics who suspect, on the contrary, that the learning of a second language threatens to disturb the use of the first, and even to cause such mental disorders as stuttering, tend to cancel out. We are forced to conclude that more research needs to be done before we can reach a definite conclusion.

The experience so far acquired in connexion with the study of a second language in the American elementary schools tends to bear out the conclusion of Arsenian that 'bilingualism, that is, simultaneous learning of two languages from infancy, has no detrimental effect on the child's mental development provided: (a) that at the earliest stages of the child's language development a consistent method of source and presentation of the two languages is observed, i.e., *une personne, une langue*; (b) that psychological barriers or negative affective conditions such as inferiority or superiority of the languages involved, or national or religious animosities are absent; and (c) that the languages are learned by spontaneous informal or play methods, and not by formal and task methods'.[1]

In an interesting chapter on language,[2] Susanne K. Langer, writing on the phenomenon of language learning in the child, suggests that in the babbling stage the child not only begins to imitate the sounds heard around him but also experiments with all kinds of sounds, by no means confined to the language of his environment. There is no reason to believe that a child cannot learn to reproduce with accuracy any sound contained in any one of the three thousand or so languages spoken on our planet. The further suggestion is that the reason he does not learn all these sounds, or at least retain those with which he experiments, is that the process of conditioning sets in. He gets from the grown-ups surrounding him a response only to the sounds existing in their own language or languages. So the child, conditioned by his social environment, is confined to the narrow dikes of his own language.

Both observation and research done suggest the importance of imitative learning in the acquisition of linguistic skills. In the young child imitative learning predominates over analytical learning. But this capacity for imitative learning declines steadily, while the child's analytical or conceptual learning capacity increases. It is in this early period that the child appears to learn a second language particularly well and easily. Here is the way that

---
1. Op. cit., p. 47, paragraph 219.
2. *Philosophy in a New Key*, Cambridge, Mass., Harvard University Press, 1942; New York, Mentor Books, 1953.

Professor Emile B. de Sauzé, for 30 years director of foreign languages in the Cleveland public schools, compares the learning of the child with that of the adolescent: 'All children who know their own mother tongue can of course learn another language during the years which in methodology are called the bilingual period. Nature has endowed a child up to 11 or 12 years of age with the precious gift of learning a language empirically, by imitation, by absorption, without ever being conscious of analogy with or differences from his mother tongue. At the mental age of 11 or 12, nature progressively withdraws that gift. The student then begins to compare the new language with his own; he notices similarities and especially differences; he analyzes linguistic elements; he seeks to generalize and is impatiently critical of purely empirical teaching.'[1]

Further light on this central problem of the psychology of language learning is shed by the research done on the human brain by the well-known neurological surgeon, Dr. Wilder Penfield, Director of the Montreal Neurological Institute. His extensive work in this field has led him to the strong conviction that young children are, for purely physiological reasons, more adept than adolescents or adults in learning the language skills: 'Speaking, and the understanding of speech, also reading and writing depend on the employment of certain specialized areas of the cerebrum. There is an optimum age when these special areas are plastic and receptive, and my purpose in this rambling, pseudo-scientific discussion is merely to remind educators of this fact.'[2] He sums up his argument by saying, 'To everything there is a season and a time to every purpose under heaven. Educators, before all others, must realize that this is particularly true of the "organ of the mind". Physiological evolution causes it to specialize in the learning of language before the ages of 10 to 14. After that gradually, inevitably, it seems to become rigid, slow, less receptive. In regard to this function, it is soon senescent. But it is ready for life's fulfilment in other directions, ready for reasoning, self-discipline, understanding, even wisdom.'[3]

Another authority who contributes to a better understanding of the process of learning a language is François Gouin, whose book, *The Art of Teaching and Studying Languages*, created such a stir at the end of last century. Much of his writing is dramatic and does not always inspire confidence, and much of it is completely

---

1. 'Teaching French in the Elementary Schools of Cleveland', *The French Review*, vol. 26, no. 5, American Association of Teachers of French. April 1953, p. 373.
2. 'A Consideration of the Neurophysiological Mechanisms of Speech and Some Educational Consequences', *Proceedings of the American Academy of Arts and Sciences*, vol. 82, no. 5, p. 202. Also in *Bulletin of the American Academy of Arts and Sciences*, vol. 6, no. 51. Feb. 1953, Boston, Mass.
3. Op. cit., p. 213.

out of date; but one part is still enlightening for the present generation of language teachers. This is the description of the author's three-year-old nephew as he is taken by his mother to the mill for the first time. It will be remembered how amusingly Gouin describes his many efforts to learn the German language, first by one method, then by another, always without success, first in Hamburg and then in Berlin. Finally, full of discouragement, he returned home and found to his delight that his nephew, whom he had left a year earlier in the awkward middle stage of learning to speak, had in the meantime learned to speak French perfectly, within the limits of his own experience. This miracle intrigued him, especially in view of his own futile linguistic efforts, and he speculated as follows: 'To surprise nature's secret I must watch this child.... The child has not yet seen everything, has not yet perceived everything. I should like to surprise him in the presence of some phenomenon entirely fresh to him, and see what he would do—on the one hand to express this phenomenon to himself in the aggregate and in all its details, and then to assimilate the expressions gathered, attempted, or invented by him on the occasion of this phenomenon.' A visit to a mill afforded this opportunity, and Gouin describes vividly the child's reaction to everything that he saw. Then he continues, 'He came away deafened, stunned, astounded, and went back home absorbed in thought. He pondered continually over what he had seen, striving to digest this vast and prolonged perception. I kept my eyes upon him, wondering what could be passing within him, what use he was going to make of this newly acquired knowledge, and, above all, how he was going to express it.

'At the end of an hour he had shaken off his burden. Speech returned.... So he told his story, and told it again and again ten times over, always with variants, forgetting some of the details, returning on his track to repair his forgetfulness, and passing from fact to fact, from phrase to phrase, by the same familiar transition, "and then ... and then ..." He was still digesting, but now it was on his own account; I mean, he did not stay to think any further over his perception; he was conceiving it, putting it in order, moulding it into a conception of his own.

'After the discourse came the action; after Saying came Doing. He tormented his mother till she had made him half a dozen little sacks; he tormented his uncle till he had built him a mill. He led the way to a tiny streamlet of water near by; and here, whether I would or no, I had to dig a mill-race, make a waterfall... manufacture a simulacrum of a large wheel, and lastly... arrange it so that it would turn and the mill would work....

'When the mill was ... set agoing, the little miller filled his sacks with sand, loaded them on his shoulder... then, bent and grunting beneath the weight, carried his grain to the mill, shot it out and ground it, so reproducing the scene of the real mill—not as he had seen it, but as he had afterwards "conceived" it to himself, as he had "generalized" it.

'Whilst doing all this, he expressed all his acts aloud, dwelling most particularly upon one word—and this word was the "verb", always the verb. The other terms came and tumbled about as they might. Ten times the same sack was emptied, refilled, carried to the mill, and its contents ground in imagination.'[1]

This spectacle of a three-year-old child first perceiving something new, then digesting it and translating perception into conception, and then translating into speech, and finally into action accompanied by speech, all of this constituted for Gouin a veritable revelation, the force of which has not diminished with the passing of time. This point of view is no different from that of the linguist-anthropologist who in the year 1954 defined language in these terms: 'Language, most broadly conceived, may be said to include all the ways of behaving which serve to communicate with other persons and to reaffirm an individual's own integrity. Among these ways of behaving are stance, bodily movement, facial expression, oral movement, and speech.'[2] Experience, behaviour, the prime role exercised by the ear, patterns of sound followed by patterns of meaning, the intertwining of speech and action, these are the elements on which are built today, as they were in Gouin's day, the best language-teaching techniques.

It is these considerations having to do with the language learning process that have led me to express the belief that a second language should be introduced ideally in the early grades, and that every year lost in a later start represents the loss of the most precious language-learning time.[3] A good deal of observation and experimentation is still required before we can be certain that this theory is well founded. There is the danger that the misinterpretation of the results observed will also hinder us from reaching a sure answer. Thus, for example, observers of language classes in the early primary grades are tempted to compare them sometimes unfavourably with classes observed in what we call the middle grades, four, five, and six, because they observe that the latter children learn patterns more quickly and cover more ground. One

---

1. François Gouin, *The Art of Teaching and Studying Languages*, Second edition, London, George Philip and Son; New York, Charles Scribner's Sons, 1892, p. 35-8.
2. Norman McQuown, 'Language-learning from an Anthropological Point of View', *Elementary School Journal*, vol. 54, March 1954, p. 402. Chicago, Ill., Chicago University.
3. Th. Andersson, *The Teaching of Foreign Languages in the Elementary School*, Boston, Mass., D. C. Heath and Company, 1953. An expanded and definitive edition of this book is planned for September 1956.

should, however, remember that the younger children take in rather than put forth and that it is this absorbing process at which they are particularly good.

A teacher who has contributed an interesting point of view is the Dane, Aage Salling, who, applying to the learning of a second language the basic principles at work as one learns one's own language, elaborates the concept of 'the little language'.[1] Basing himself on the direct observation of children, Salling points out that, though in the early stages a child's vocabulary may consist of only twenty words, these twenty words are adequate for his needs in the given situation. They constitute a full functional vocabulary permitting him the behaviour he craves. When he develops the need for greater behavioural elbow-room, he will learn the words and patterns necessary in the new situation. Vocabulary, therefore, grows out of a situation.

This suggests that a language teacher should start from a situation and not from language patterns, and most assuredly not from a list of words arbitrarily presented to a student because they happen to occur in a particular text which has been selected by the teacher. It will be remembered that this form of teaching, called situational teaching, is already in use in many parts of the world, perhaps most notably in the teaching of migrants in Australia.[2]

By a happy coincidence these principles, which undergird the best language teaching in the elementary schools in various parts of the United States, coincide strikingly with the principal element of elementary school theory in general. In the three-cornered relationship which exists between the teacher and the pupil or student and the subject, it is a commonplace in our country to say that teaching in the elementary school tends to be child-centred whereas teaching in the high school tends to be subject-matter-centred. The good elementary school teacher believes in general that little real teaching is done unless the child is ready and motivated and unless the teaching is given in a way that interests him. It is therefore common practice to build on the child's immediate environment and experiences. But the child's world of reality is bipartite and, after a period of neglect, teachers have come to understand that the child's imagination is capable of creating a world of fantasy which is quite as real as the prosaic world which surrounds him. Due regard must therefore be given to the child's real nature and, more particularly, to the characteristics of his age-level. By tailoring the school-room situations

---

1. *Det Lille Sprog: En Sprogundervisningens Teori*, København, Grafisk Forlag, 1952. This book contains a summary in English, 'The Principle of Simplification', p. 129–39.
2. *English, a New Language. A bulletin for teachers*, Sydney, vol. 4, no. 1, September 1953. Commonwealth Office of Education.

—and indeed seeking or creating learning situations outside the classroom—to the natural learning process and interests of the child, the sensitive and progressive elementary school teacher feels that he is challenging the child's capacity to the full.

A quite different point: if the teaching of a second language has met with so much favour in many parts of the country, it is often because it has been closely correlated with the teaching of social studies in the elementary school. Thus, for example, in San Diego the presence in the curriculum of a unit on Mexico makes it natural to introduce Spanish at the fourth-grade level. One of the really heartening results of many of these programmes has been the lessening of tensions between linguistic and cultural groups and the improvement in the social status of foreign-language-speaking children and their families. It was with this aim in view that the Superintendent of Schools in Los Angeles introduced the teaching of Spanish in 1943, and his hopes have been justified by the results.

In Louisiana, where there are 400,000 speakers of French, the situation in many communities has been greatly improved almost overnight. A few years ago children of French-speaking parents were not allowed to speak French in the schools or school-yards (playgrounds). Now, after the introduction of French in the grades in many communities, these same children are looked up to and admired because they know the language which the others are eager to learn.

The Modern Language Association is planning a conference on foreign languages and inter-cultural understanding, the purpose of which is to explore further ways in which foreign languages can, in this country, where over 20 million inhabitants have a mother tongue other than English, be used to improve the relations between ethnic and linguistic groups.

The higher language teachers, who follow precisely the same line of thought as the regular teacher, are beginning to construct materials which reflect this point of view. Thus, for example, El Paso, Texas, has embarked on a 12-year Spanish programme beginning in the first grade of the elementary school and continuing all the way to the twelfth grade in high school. Carlos Rivera, the supervisor of Spanish in the elementary schools of El Paso, has already prepared and published for his teachers—the pupils receive no books in the primary grades—material[1] of this kind covering the first and second years of instruction, and a volume containing the materials of the third grade will appear shortly. In addition,

---

1. *A Manual of Materials, Aids, and Techniques for the Teaching of Spanish to English-speaking Children, Grades I and II*, published by the School Board of the El Paso Public Schools, El Paso, Texas, 1952, 1953, 2 vols.

PRIMARY SCHOOLS

the audio-visual staff of the El Paso public schools has prepared an 18-minute coloured film with sound illustrating a sequence of language classes in the first, second and third grades. In September 1954 the programme moves into the fourth grade.

One of the best Spanish programmes in the middle grades, begun in 1944, is to be found in the San Diego, California, public schools, Here, Mrs. Margaret MacRae, assistant supervisor of Spanish in the elementary schools, has, together with a team of competent collaborators, prepared a handbook[1] for teachers and a guide to resource materials. This programme, built on situations of real interest to children and involving the active use of the spoken language, emphasizes, in addition, the use of stories of the kind that children aged 9 to 12 enjoy.

The Los Angeles programme is also built around a carefully planned syllabus.[2] Far less rich in its materials than those of El Paso or San Diego, it leaves a great deal of scope to the ingenuity of the individual classroom teacher. The Los Angeles public school system has also produced a coloured sound film which gives an excellent idea of the elementary school techniques used.

In the French field, the outstanding syllabus is entitled 'Juvenile French', prepared by the Cleveland public schools and containing a wealth of materials in the form of language patterns, poems, songs, games, and dramatic pieces.

One of the issues most discussed is whether a second language in the elementary school should be taught by the regular classroom teacher, in order to integrate it thoroughly with the rest of the programme, or whether it should be taught by a language specialist coming into a classroom each day for a period of 15 or 20 minutes. The Los Angeles and San Diego systems stress the use of the regular classroom teachers, although the supervisors do all they can to assist and some use is made of travelling teachers. The El Paso system is built around the use of specialists, who, however, endeavour to adapt their teaching to the rest of the curriculum. The Cleveland plan makes use only of specialists. Some programmes—Fairfield, Connecticut, is an example—use several different patterns. Thus, for example, a regular classroom teacher will teach French or Spanish to her own class and exchange a lesson with a neighbouring teacher in order to teach the second language to another class. A second pattern consists in allowing the high school foreign language teacher to teach one or more classes in the elementary school. A third pattern provides for the

---
1. *Handbook for the Teaching of Spanish in Elementary Grades*, published by the San Diego City Schools, San Diego, California, 1952; *Guide to Resource Materials for the First Year of Spanish in the Elementary Grades*, San Diego City Schools, 1953.
2. *Instructional Guide for Teaching Spanish in the Elementary Schools*, Los Angeles City Schools, Los Angeles, California, 1946.

use of a travelling specialist. Perhaps the most reasonable conclusion to be drawn from these diverse practices is that a second language can be taught satisfactorily either by a specialist or by the regular classroom teacher, provided both are aware of the needs, interests and capacities of children and have a fluent knowledge of the spoken language.

So great is the shortage of teachers that the following makeshift arrangement is used in some places. Many teachers, though very much interested in introducing a second language into their classrooms, feel that they are not fully qualified to serve as a dependable model for the speaking of this language. Such teachers sometimes make use of tape recordings prepared by native speakers of the language. In this case, the teacher acts more as a master of ceremonies guiding and sharing in the learning experience of the children. Other ways in which individual qualified teachers may reach a larger pupil audience is by the use of radio or television.

Another issue which often causes lively discussion is whether a second language should be offered to all children or only to selected pupils. Some programmes operate on the selective basis, such as Cleveland, St. Louis, and Springfield, Massachusetts, but many more follow a more democratic plan and allow all children in a grade the opportunity of a second-language experience. Nowhere is a second language required in elementary school, but it is found in practice that, if it is offered on an optional basis, practically all children wish to be given the opportunity to study it. Most educators believe that there is no really satisfactory basis for selection, that there is no dependable correlation between language aptitude and an intelligence quotient or reading ability in the first language. In fact, a number of remarkable cases have been reported of slow children who have done so well in the second language that soon their confidence and later their achievement in the rest of their work has improved. Those who defend the principle of selectivity contend very properly that there are not enough teachers to go around and that therefore it is better to select those students who are likely to make most rapid progress. It is also easier to administer a small programme than a large one.

The really stubborn problem to be solved is that of preparing qualified teachers in sufficient numbers to meet the anticipated demand. Here the universities and teachers' colleges have not been fully alert to their responsibilities. Only a few have made special provision for the training of elementary school language teachers. A hopeful sign was the announcement by some twenty-five universities of workshops offering special courses in this field in the summer of 1954. Among many others, the University of

Wisconsin and Middlebury College held three-week workshops involving courses on the teaching of foreign languages in the elementary schools and particularly demonstration classes with children. The shortage of really qualified teachers is clear, but some contend that as soon as the educational authorities and the citizens—who in the last analysis determine educational policy—realize the urgent need of modern languages as a matter of national interest, many qualified teachers not now teaching can be found and many others can either be trained quickly or be invited to come to this country on educational exchanges.

Only the future can tell whether this trend can live up to the promise which it seems to hold. If full advantage is taken of the powers of very young children to learn the basic linguistic skills, and if teachers of a sufficiently high calibre can be prepared quickly enough, it should soon be possible, at least in the more favoured communities, to teach children to understand and to speak a foreign language within reasonable limits in the primary grades. It should be possible to teach the elements of reading and writing, starting with the notion of eye support for ear learning, in the middle grades. By the time the student reaches the junior high school, his analytical sense should permit the study of the more formal aspects of the language, or grammar, as well as progress in understanding, speaking, reading, and writing. This, in turn, would allow greater concentration at the senior high school level on systematic consideration of the civilization of the country whose language is being learned. Literary and civilizational elements should of course be introduced from the very beginning but can be systematized at this point. Such a programme in the schools would permit in the college and universities teaching of a really advanced nature, appropriate to the university.

It is small wonder that language teachers and other educators look upon this new trend with considerable hope, as well as some fears. If it succeeds, it can in time renew completely the methods used in high school and even on the college level. Besides providing a larger number of citizens with knowledge of a language advanced enough to convey a deep sense of achievement and satisfaction, it should serve to make the average American citizen much more international-minded and much more sympathetic towards his neighbours who speak other languages, whether they live within the national boundaries or without, and it should lay a sound base for the preparation of the many specialists who will be needed if the United States is to deal on an equal footing with other nations. In fact, the concept 'foreign language' might in time yield to the more appealing concept of 'second' or 'third' or 'fourth language'.

CHAPTER X

SPECIAL AIDS TO INTERNATIONAL UNDERSTANDING

For seven years Unesco's Exchange of Persons Programme has concentrated much of its attention upon the factors which contribute to the effective planning and administration of international exchanges for educational purposes. The aim in so doing is based not only upon a desire to promote more numerous international exchanges and co-operation among nations in such activities, but also to ensure that the exchanges that are made will contribute both to increased international understanding and to a transfer of knowledge and skills among the different countries of the world.

Anyone with experience of such problems will readily appreciate that educational exchanges do not necessarily contribute to international understanding unless certain basic prerequisities have been ensured. These prerequisites include careful preparation on the part of the individuals, institutions and organizations participating in exchanges. Among such preparations the learning of foreign languages is of outstanding importance. The whole experience of the Exchange of Persons Programme has confirmed and reinforced this obvious conclusion, showing that the success of an international fellowship can depend almost entirely upon the linguistic knowledge of its holder. Whether the aim of travel and study abroad is a general cultural understanding of other peoples or the more explicit acquisition of certain types of knowledge, language will always remain among the foremost problems demanding attention.

For that reason it is impossible to attach too much importance to the means by which foreign languages are taught. The actual techniques of teaching need not concern us here, for this aspect is adequately cared for by the many specialists in the field. More important from the 'exchange of persons' point of view are the means that can be used to take language instruction beyond the classroom and to allow practical expression through contact with persons from other countries. The importance of this instruction cannot be overstressed. Far too often the learning of languages in schools is directed towards examination requirements and little or no attention is paid to the learning of languages as a first step towards actually communicating with people from other lands. Any concentrated effort to work towards the latter objective is therefore of great interest.

It so happens that the three movements described in this chapter were initiated and developed in France. An important point to bear in mind is that France is one of the few countries of the world possessing a language which is internationally understood. In common with the English-speaking countries, there is less need for students in France than in many other countries to learn foreign languages for the purpose of international communication. In certain other countries two or more foreign languages are learnt as a matter of course and are essential to anyone who is anxious to establish himself in a profession or in commerce. The benefits to be gained from learning foreign languages are so obvious that individual initiative can be relied on to produce satisfactory results. In France, however, it has been found desirable to stimulate the quality of language teaching and learning by the means described here. France is, in many ways, a country particularly well suited to the development of experimental methods along these lines. All the same, the lessons that have been learnt are widely applicable among other countries wishing to supplement their normal methods of language teaching with such methods.

The International School Correspondence movement, although of great interest, does not demand lengthy comment here. It should be seen, largely, as a first step in actual communication with foreigners. As a practical exercise in expression and understanding of foreign languages and cultures, the system is admirable. But, unless it can lead to further development, it must remain relatively sterile. The effects of 'pen-friendships' are rarely enduring and, unless they can be followed up in other ways, can have only a partial influence even upon the learning of a foreign language. It is of value that a student should have the interest and incentive to express himself in writing, but even this is very far removed from the demands of personal contact.

With the other two types of movement described, the situation is somewhat different. In the linking of schools and the exchange of foreign language assistants, the possibilities of learning foreign languages through practical experience are greatly improved. But corresponding dangers arise from other directions. In both cases, and particularly the former, young and inexperienced students are thrown into a foreign milieu, which is often quite unlike their expectations. However suitable for language practice such a situation may be, it more than defeats its own ends if it arouses in the participants an enduring distaste for the countries they are visiting. This possibility throws a great responsibility upon those who are organizing such schemes. Constant care must be taken that in bringing young people of different nationalities into close contact the cause of international understanding is not prejudiced through basic cultural and social differences, which have not been previously appreciated by the participants.

The ways of overcoming these dangers lie in several directions. Firstly there is the problem of selection. Classroom brilliance in a foreign language is not necessarily a guide to a student's adaptability to the situations he will encounter abroad. Rather the whole personality of the 'exchangee' is to be taken into account.

Secondly, the importance of briefing and orientation before departure cannot be over-emphasized. Exchangees should have as clear as possible an idea of the situations they are likely to encounter and how they will be expected to behave.

Thirdly, much of the success or failure of a scheme can depend upon the practical details of organization, transport, reception, financing and other such points, which, although some of them are relatively unimportant in themselves, can have an immense impact for good or evil upon a stranger arriving in a foreign country. Many of the failures under any scheme can be readily attributed to lack of attention to one or another of these points.

It could be argued that questions such as these have no direct relationship to the problems of teaching foreign languages. This would certainly be true if foreign languages could be considered as nothing more than a classroom subject. But once they are accepted as a means of understanding between individuals and nations, the whole problem assumes very much greater proportions.

The point that is being made here is best illustrated from Unesco's experience in promoting international understanding through the exchange of manual and non-manual workers. Each year Unesco sponsors and pays for the travel of over 1,000 European workers going abroad in groups during their annual holidays. These men and women have not, in general, a very good knowledge of the languages of the countries they are visiting. But in being received and entertained by foreign workers in the same occupations, an immediate bond of common interest is established which often creates the incentive for more profound language study. Among students the facilities for language study are generally far greater than among workers. But no amount of skilled instruction will serve the desired purpose if they lack the incentive that must be based upon a genuine interest in the people and the country whose language one is studying.

INTERNATIONAL SCHOOL CORRESPONDENCE AND THE TEACHING OF MODERN LANGUAGES[1]

This is not the place to give an account of the many forerunners of the International School Correspondence movement, some of which date back several centuries. Far-seeing educators declared long ago that modern languages should not be taught in the same way as classical languages. In modern language teaching, purely theoretical teaching should be combined as much as possible with practical use of the language. When people cannot converse, written communication in the shape of an exchange of letters can and should both increase interest and constitute a particularly effective additional exercise.

The ISC movement actually originated in 1919, immediately after the first world war. In view of the material and moral support given by children in the United States to their comrades in war-devastated areas of France, Mr. de Geouffre de la Pradelle, Professor of International Law at the Faculty of Law in Paris, having just returned from a mission in the United States, thought that it would be an excellent thing to form direct and lasting ties of friendship between the children of the two countries. He confided his idea to one of his oldest friends, Mr. Ch. M. Garnier, whose duties as Inspector-General of Modern Languages and whose standing enabled him to exert a particularly strong influence on French teachers. At the same time, and in agreement with his French colleagues, Dr. Roehm set up a similar agency in the United States, at Nashville, Tennessee. Franco-American inter-school correspondence had begun.

Franco-British correspondence, instituted by Mr. Paul Mieille, followed soon after. In 1922 the movement expanded and took the name of International School Correspondence (ISC). It continued to spread very rapidly. In 1929, after barely ten years, it had developed so much that some co-ordination of the activities of the various agencies appeared indispensable 'in order to facilitate their work and provide for the educational and moral supervision of correspondence without which this international educational movement might deviate from its true and appointed course'. Under the auspices of the International Institute of Intellectual Co-operation, which was to bear all the expenses of the new institution, representatives of 10 ISC agencies established the Standing Committee of ISC which continued until the second world war, under the chairmanship of Ch. M. Garnier, to ensure

---

1. This section is condensed from the working-paper prepared for the Ceylon seminar by Paul Barrier, Secretary-General of the International Federation of Organizations for School Correspondence and Exchanges (IFOSCE) and Director of the French Agency for International School Correspondence (ISC).

the co-ordination of the various activities and the standardization of methods. In 1939 there were as many as 25 agencies affiliated to the standing committee.

After the break caused by the second world war, the agencies resumed their activities. They immediately realized that their work would again require co-ordination. The directors, at a meeting in Paris in 1946, decided to reinstate the standing committee but to extend its mandate to cover exchanges and travel of students and schoolchildren as well as exchanges of correspondence. This led to the creation of the International Federation of Organizations for School Correspondence and Exchange (IFOSCE) under the presidency of Professor Fr. Closset, Director of La Jeunesse Belge a l'Étranger (Belgian Youth Abroad). Since 1948 IFOSCE has been one of the non-governmental organizations admitted to consultative arrangements with Unesco. There are at present 34 agencies belonging to 20 nations affiliated to it; of these 17 are concerned with visits of students and schoolchildren abroad and exchange of correspondence, 3 with travel abroad only, and 14 exclusively with exchange of correspondence.

It may be useful to give a specific example, with facts and figures, of the work done by one agency, and of the assistance which it renders to the teaching of modern languages. I will take the French agency as an example, not so much because it was at the origin of the movement as because it is naturally the one that I am best acquainted with.

The first important point is that, while the agency is not established by law as a government service, it has a definitely semi-official character; for example, it has been for a long time the only service authorized by the Ministry of Education to organize, on the latter's behalf and under its supervision, exchanges of correspondence between young people in France and those in French oversea territories and countries abroad. And as these exchanges have proved themselves more and more clearly to be a new instrument for the teaching of modern languages, the public authorities, and particularly the Departments of Secondary and Primary Education, and of Technical Training, and the Ministry of French Oversea Territories have given greater and more specific moral and material support. It can be said that the French ISC agency is today, *de facto*, if not *de jure*, almost 'nationalized'.

In this capacity it appeals to teachers for their collaboration and generally obtains it. It would be truer to say that it places itself entirely at their service. By means of the two circulars which it addresses annually, at the beginning of the school year in October and at Easter, to all modern language teachers in state schools, it supplies them with up-to-date information on opportunities for exchanges and any special details relevant at a given date or to a given country. In return it expects them to include in the end-of-year reports which many of them submit to it, suggestions and comments which will help it make its activities more specific and effective.

From the agency's creation in 1919 until the end of the school year 1951-52, and despite the break caused by the second world war, the number of French boys and girls brought into contact with an equal number of pen-friends in French oversea territories and other countries abroad had risen to 1,657,242. For the last two school years, the totals were 93,400 and 100,062 respectively. These figures show a very marked increase from one year to the other—in large part due to the growing interest of the public authorities in the exchanges, which they are more and more convinced should form a normal part of education.

Exchanges are effected with the specialized agencies affiliated to IFOSCE or, in countries where no such agencies exist, with schools or exchange services direct. The exchanges in all cover 63 countries, some of them neighbouring countries, others as distant as New Zealand, Australia and Japan. The constant expansion of the system of inter-school exchanges of correspondence is a fact; every year new agencies apply for affiliation to IFOSCE and the annual reports submitted to the latter practically all testify to increasing activities.

The teaching of modern languages can have three aims, varying according to the different educational levels and types of school: to teach the use of a foreign language, written and spoken, literary and colloquial; or to further the cultural training of the pupils concerned by teaching them about foreign customs and ways of living and thinking; or, lastly, to inspire pupils with a desire to understand other peoples and to live at peace with all mankind, by helping them to acquire a truer knowledge of foreign countries.

It should at once be mentioned that these three aims are also those of International School Correspondence. The following definition of ISC's objectives is contained in the pamphlet dealing with this subject:

'The services that can be rendered by ISC are of three kinds:

'(a) *Educational*. Bilingual correspondence between pupils of different countries is a great help to foreign language teaching, because it makes the study of a foreign language more interesting and alive and helps the pupil to acquire a more colloquial vocabulary.

'For instance, a French boy has to correct any mistakes in French made by his correspondent, and he does this with far greater care than when he is correcting his own exercises. Such correspondence will also inspire him to pay more attention to his own language and make progress in it.

'Another remark often made by our correspondents is that a pupil, in correcting faulty expressions, realizes that some of them are literal translations of idioms in the foreign language, and this improves his understanding and knowledge both of that language and of his own.

'(b) *Cultural.* Exchanges of letters should help both correspondents to a better knowledge of the civilizations of their two countries. That is one of the main benefits to be derived from the study of modern languages. But is it not also the only way of preventing correspondence from quickly becoming dull? Pupils soon lose interest in details regarding the age, tastes, lessons, family situation and daily life of their correspondents; but if the teacher, while taking care not to destroy his pupils' initiative or interfere with their freedom, can suggest more lively subjects of interest to them and especially if he can persuade several pupils to correspond on the same subjects at the same time, he will be initiating real teamwork, and correspondence will become a form of study with a value and appeal that require no stressing. It means the establishment of contact with foreign civilizations and, at the same time, it leads the writer to think more carefully about the civilization of his own country and to respond to it. Here again the advantage is twofold.

'(c) *Psychological and international.* The exchange of ideas and impressions very soon leads to a feeling of comradeship and then to actual friendship. The correspondents are at an age when their affections are readily aroused and, in their imagination, they see their "pen friends" in a strange and far-off land in a particularly favourable light. And these friendships, although quickly formed, do not necessarily remain superficial. In addition to letters, pen-friends send each other post-cards, magazines, documents and also quite often presents and souvenirs. Exchange visits are often arranged. During the last war, as well as before and after it, there were many examples to prove the strength and value of such friendships.

'Those who write regularly develop orderly and methodical habits, as well as acquiring a sense of initiative and responsibility; but, above all, and this is why ISC's activities are of importance to Unesco's programme, exchanges of letters, and the visits which often follow, make an extremely valuable contribution to international understanding and peace among the nations.'

In principle, the aim of ISC is to organize direct and individual exchanges of letters between schoolchildren or students belonging to countries speaking different languages. Generally, therefore, the correspondence is bilingual. It may, however, be in one language, for ISC also encourages exchanges of letters between young people speaking the same language and belonging either to the same nation (metropolitan France and French oversea territories, for instance), or to different nations (France and French-speaking countries: Walloon Belgium, French Switzerland, French Canada, etc.). When correspondence is bilingual, the two pen-friends may start by writing each in his own language but, as soon as they feel able to do so, they write in the foreign language. First of all they write only part of their letters in the foreign language, then gradually more and, as soon as possible, they use only that language.

Except for any supervision which families may wish to exercise, the letters are the personal affair of the correspondents themselves. Teachers do not interfere unless asked to do so. That is why such exchanges provide those concerned with an opportunity to learn a foreign language in a very live way, as well as with a valuable moral training in orderliness, initiative and the shouldering of personal responsibility.

In actual fact, with a very few exceptions, such correspondence can be lasting only if the teachers take a definite interest in the letters and more or less provide the writers with ideas; many do this because they know that ISC supplies them with a powerful means of stimulating their pupils' interest and making a deeper impression with their teaching.

The letters prove to the children that the teaching of modern languages is not merely a school exercise, but leads to the practical use of a foreign language in everyday life. Thus they come to realize that the lessons have a real value and importance and open up entirely new horizons. The language written by the correspondent is not always exactly the same as that in the textbooks, which may perhaps be a little dry and academic; it is really the language as it is spoken.

Interest can be kept up only if the letters contain practical and specific information about the foreign country concerned, its general customs and the people's outlook, details of the correspondent's daily life in a town or country district, descriptions of his food, national holidays, local or family celebrations, customs and dress, agriculture or industrial products, scenery, flora and fauna, monuments and books read. Letters, postcards, newspapers and magazine cuttings, samples of local products and documents of all kinds, which keep the correspondents' curiosity constantly alert, hold their ready interest and give them pleasure, secure for them the practical knowledge of a foreign country which all teachers of modern languages aim at giving.

ISC, in procuring correspondents from many different regions for pupils of the same class, makes it possible to give a general idea of the countries whose language is being taught. For English, for example, letters are received from correspondents in various parts of Great Britain, the Commonwealth and the United States of America, and this enables the teacher to start very profitable lines of study.

Here are a few examples: the wool industry in the British Commonwealth; English cathedrals; sport in English-speaking countries; Scotland, its geographical features, history, monuments and present-day life; various types of building in the United States; the fauna of Australia and New Zealand. Natural curiosities and characteristic features of the different countries are compared: Italian, French and Canadian lakes, Norwegian fjords; prairies and steppes; various types of mountain; the large rivers of the world; agriculture and cattle-raising; industries (particularly interesting for vocational and technical schools); types of dwellings, schools and monuments; varieties of costume and food; sport; the theatre.

As the materials arrive they are displayed in the classroom. Then at any school function and particularly at prize-givings, the best and most characteristic materials are selected to form a general exhibition which parents are invited to inspect. The documents and samples received are also used to make albums and collections of illustrated papers, stamps, and even insects or plants. Some classes have managed to form small libraries of foreign books by book exchanges with correspondents. It is a good plan to have pupils sing in a foreign language and read and comment on the most interesting parts of letters received or poems to which foreign correspondents have referred.

Far from being detrimental to other subjects, this can often be of assistance in teaching them. Exhibitions and collections can very well be organized with the consent of the geography teacher. The drawing teacher finds subjects to use in foreign or national materials received; in mathematics, problems involving foreign currency and measurements, set at the request of the language teacher, are a useful preparation for travel abroad. Lastly, and perhaps most important of all, teachers of literature find that foreign correspondence is a definite help to their pupils. Wishing to give their young correspondents information on the literature of their own country, pupils feel obliged to bring their knowledge up to date. It is often in replying to questions asked by their correspondents that they learn more about their own literature.

However, it is mainly by integrating International School Correspondence into their own teaching, drawing from it certain data and explanations which circumstances make particularly vivid and topical, that teachers can create the desirable atmosphere. As one teacher wrote to us: 'From time to time, when a letter is interesting, I explain it in detail and sometimes allow it to be the subject of a whole lesson. The children write down idioms and expressions which they can use in a future letter (a few pages are reserved for this at the end of the English exercise book). Sometimes I dictate an instructive extract. For the pupils, these lessons are a real slice of life and they find them more exciting and, especially, more topical than the lessons set in their textbooks.'

The possible advantages are obvious in respect to style, vocabulary and syntax. The explanation of a word which surprises pupils because they have not met with it before, discussion of a term which may be incorrect or of a construction which does not seem quite right. Culturally, it is easier still to derive advantages from international correspondence and, if the teacher knows how to awaken the interest of his class, the progress made is far more marked. An effective method is *collective* inquiries, conducted by groups. With this aim in view, the French ISC always tries to find correspondents from all parts of a foreign country for pupils of the same class. This teamwork, which is thoroughly consonant with modern educational ideas, allows pupils themselves all the freedom and spontaneity that can be desired. However, it is obvious that small children in the beginning classes who are scarcely able to write correctly in their own language or make out an address, cannot decipher and understand a letter in a foreign language, however simple, without some assistance. Blank, uninteresting letters discourage a reply. Very soon they become less frequent and finally stop altogether, because the children say 'we can't think of anything else to say to each other'. Initial enthusiasm gives way to keen disappointment, even accompanied by a feeling of dislike for foreign children. A disappointed pupil may sometimes lose all interest, throughout his school years, in school correspondence, the foreign country concerned and the study of its language.

Age is not the only consideration. It is important to take into account a child's intellectual capacities and particularly his character. Teachers often notice that the best pupils do not necessarily make the best correspondents. One pupil with a quick mind and ability to grasp things easily will lack the necessary perseverance and regularity. On the other hand, shy children and those not particularly gifted in other ways may keep up regular correspondence. They are proud to show the letters they receive as these give them a prestige in the class they would not otherwise enjoy. The self-confidence thus acquired has an effect on their general behaviour and they become much better at languages.

In any case, the whole class should not automatically be drawn into the international school correspondence scheme. Lazy children, who are the first to lose their enthusiasm, disappoint foreigners and often give the young people of their own country a bad reputation abroad.

That is one reason why the French agency advises teachers to enter their pupils in three different stages: the most promising pupils at the beginning of the school year, in October; average pupils in January or February; and those that seem the least gifted at the beginning of the Easter term. Moreover, pupils should not be allowed to correspond unless they have proved, by their efforts and progress, that they are fitted to take part in an activity which should be regarded by them as a sort of reward and a selection for special responsibilities.

Should correspondence between children of different sexes still be forbidden, as it was twenty-five years ago? That would appear unreasonable. Some teachers who have experimented with mixed correspondence in recent years have assured us that it produces good results. Correspondence is more interesting and frequent, and the letters are more carefully written.

The ideal would be for every class to enter into correspondence with all the principal countries of the world. That is not feasible, particularly as at present the number of names of foreign correspondents sent to the agencies is contingent upon many variable factors. In organizing exchanges with a given country the age of the partners is the most important consideration. Thus Great Britain mainly supplies very young correspondents, whereas Germany sends the names of many adolescents. In addition to regular correspondence with a friend in a country whose language is being studied in class, it is desirable for pupils to have a second correspondent speaking the same language but living in a country with which exchanges are slower and more difficult.

Further, in order that pupils may acquire a fuller knowledge of various civilizations, it is important for them, in addition to their bilingual correspondence, to conduct unilingual correspondence with young people whose language is not much studied in their country, or with members of their own national community, especially in the case of very large countries like the United States of America, or groups of countries like the British Commonwealth or the French Union. Such correspondence, which has no linguistic advantages for one of the partners, is valuable mainly from the point of view of forming friendships and gathering information.

There is one recommendation of primary importance: correspondents should write *legibly*. Experience has shown that national handwritings in Roman script are not exactly the same, but the course of the correspondence is jeopardized if the partner has difficulty in reading letters and still more so if he is unable to decipher the sender's name and address.

How often should correspondents write? It is often said that interest dies if too long a time is allowed to elapse between letters. On the other hand, international school correspondence should not take up time reserved for school work. A letter from each correspondent once a fortnight would appear to be the happy medium.

There is another danger: delay in answering letters. See that pupils reply to their correspondents quickly. If a foreign correspondent fails to write, the pupil who is kept waiting should send him a friendly reminder. In case of complete failure to obtain a reply, apply to the appropriate agency for another correspondent. Owing to the slowness of sea communications with distant countries, air mail often has to be used; it is expensive, but with many countries it is the only way of ensuring that letters are exchanged frequently enough to sustain interest.

Pupils' attention should also be drawn to the fact that the difference between school holidays in various parts of the world is a constant hindrance to correspondence. Schools throughout the southern hemisphere are closed when those in the northern hemisphere are at their busiest. Hence pupils should write to their correspondent's private addresses and not to their schools.

Should beginners try to write part of their letters in the foreign language, or insert an increasing number of foreign sentences in letters drafted in their own language? Educators who attach primary importance to purity of language consider that an English or German schoolboy will learn far more French by reading a well-written and fairly long letter in French than by composing three or four laborious sentences himself. Psychologists, on the other hand, point out that children of 11 or 12 derive much amusement from the mistakes of their young foreign friends, taking a great deal of pains to correct and explain them and that this system of correcting each other's letters is a successful and absorbing form of 'active education'. At all events, the proportion of each letter written in a foreign language should gradually be increased. It is a good idea to write that part of the letter on a separate sheet which the partner can return with corrections. However, in expressing his inmost feelings and thoughts. each correspondent instinctively uses his own language and it is better so.

Let us not forget that correspondence should never become a 'school exercise'. Every teacher quickly realizes what sort of letter most appeals to his pupils. It is essential that letters should be amusing and interesting, kindling the flame of the children's enthusiasm.

It should not be forgotten how much exchanges of photographs can encourage friendship in its early stages. With the help of his imagination, a child sees or thinks he sees his correspondent doing the things he has described; he is no longer just a name, but a person and to some extent a friend. There should of course be no allusion to such controversial matters as politics and religion. It is impossible to over-emphasize the importance of the reference to this point contained in ISC's rules.

While postcards are a pleasant proof of friendly feeling and provide necessary illustrations, they cannot replace letters. The lazy habit of sending more and more postcards and fewer and fewer letters would soon destroy the feeling of comradeship and the enthusiasm which make the correspondence worth while and ensure its continuity. This does not of course apply to picture postcards with written comments; these are not just vague greetings dashed off in a hurry. On the contrary, if the comments are written with forethought, they form an appropriate part of the exchange of information and impressions which is one of the main attractions of real correspondence.

There can be no question of making it compulsory for pupils to communicate to their fellow-pupils all the letters they receive, any more than they can be made to write joint letters. Pupils volunteer to bring along their letters and other material received, thus enabling the teacher to pick out interesting words, colloquialisms and information of all kinds for the benefit of the whole class, just as they volunteer to make their contribution to an inquiry or to some other form of teamwork. Although pupils are under no obligation to hand round their letters, when they do so the proceedings should form a part of the regular activities of the class. Many teachers set aside the last part of a certain lesson for them; this form of teaching, where the pupils themselves supply the materials, is, if properly understood, by no means the least interesting and effective.

It is certainly no small thing to have learnt by experience that we must teach children to rid themselves of the feeling, so common that it would seem almost hereditary, that foreigners are necessarily either peculiar or hostile. However, that is a somewhat negative achievement; we can and should go much further and aim far higher. It is not even enough to become familiar with the way of life in a foreign country, with the manner in which people organize their existence, what they eat, their favourite games, what they produce, or their beauty spots; it is essential also to understand their feelings and way of thinking.

Just as friendship springs from interest in a pen-friend's private life, his joys and sorrows and those of his family, so the spirit of international understanding will grow if we can interest our young people in a foreign country's joys and sorrows, in its efforts to overcome difficulties and in its spiritual life.

THE LINKING OF SCHOOLS[1]

The linking of schools (in French, *appariement d'écoles*; in German *Partnerschule*) is the system whereby two schools in different countries agree to exchange groups of pupils under the guidance of teachers. This system was devised and carried into effect between France and Great Britain at the close of the first world war and resumed immediately after the liberation of France at the end of the second world war.

Under the linking of schools system, relations are established between schools for the purpose of exchanging groups of pupils under the guidance of teachers, either during the holidays or during the school year (third term). Pupils in the linked schools previously exchange group correspondence on themes suggested by the teachers. Pupils benefiting from the exchange system are accommodated by the families of their opposite numbers (or in rare cases as boarders in the school) and the teachers by their colleagues in the other country. The teachers' duty is to accompany the children during the journey, to place them in the families of their correspondents, to keep a discreet watch over them and to deal with any little difficulties that may arise. They also accompany the pupils on their group outings—visits to monuments, factories, theatres, concerts and so on. When the exchanges are arranged during the school term, the teachers accompanying the group are required to give lessons in class to the foreign children, even completely replacing the foreign colleague if the exchange is simultaneous, while the pupils go to school with their foreign schoolmates. On an average the groups exchanged comprise about ten boys or girls—in some cases the groups are mixed—between 13 and 17 years of age, the usual age being 15 or 16. But many schools form far larger groups, especially when exchanges take place during the holidays. The teacher responsible is then assisted by a colleague from his own school, who does not necessarily teach languages but may teach some other branch of the humanities (history, geography or French literature, for instance). The language teachers and heads of schools are responsible for deciding the date and duration of exchanges. These generally last from a

---

1. This section is based on the working-paper prepared for the Ceylon seminar by M. le Recteur Audra, Director of the Office National des Universités et Écoles Françaises.

fortnight to a month, but may last longer; there have been exchanges lasting for two months or even a whole term.

The business of the Office National des Universités et Écoles Françaises is to put French schools in contact with similar schools abroad, to provide them with all the information and advice they may need for the purpose of arranging the exchange (group tickets, insurance, etc.) and to explain any small points on which misunderstandings might arise between linked schools. In order to carry out the latter part of its work, the Office keeps in close touch with official bodies in other countries. It receives reports from teachers who have arranged exchanges of pupils, and also their complaints, and deals with the Directorate for Secondary Education on their behalf with a view to obtaining decisions that will make their work easier and give them the necessary encouragement.

This type of exchange was first arranged between French and British schools. Since 1951 it has been extended to German schools. During the summer of 1952 a certain number of French and Spanish schools expressed the desire to be put into direct contact with each other; two linkages were arranged, and there is every reason to expect that there will soon be many more. Then, early in 1953, a large number of applications for linkages were received from the Italian Ministry of Education.

Schools anxious to arrange an exchange with a foreign school apply to the competent service in their country (in France to the Office National des Universités; in Great Britain to the Central Bureau for Educational Visits and Exchanges; in Germany to the Kulturministerium in each particular *Land*, which passes on the applications to a central organization which, for the time being, is the Directorate for Cultural Affairs in Mainz). These services pass on applications for linkages from schools in their country to the Office des Universités. Each application is accompanied by a form giving all the necessary particulars regarding the applicant school: total number of pupils, number and age of the pupils learning French, number of pupils likely to take part in an exchange, names of the teachers responsible; character of the locality (agricultural, industrial, commercial) and social background of the pupils. The Office des Universités then makes inquiries among French schools that seem to be similar to those from which applications have been received. When these schools (which have filled in the same forms as the foreign schools) have signified their agreement, the schools with which they are to be linked are informed through the same channel and requested to give their agreement as well. When they do so the linkage is declared settled and the head of the school which has been the last to give its agreement immediately gets into touch with his counterpart abroad, as does also the language teacher who will be responsible for the linkage. Enquiries continue until the linkage is settled. In some cases schools which for various reasons are very difficult to arrange for are put on a waiting list.

Preparations for the Exchange

The language teacher starts making arrangements for the linkage as soon as the two schools concerned have concluded an agreement. This operation must take account of the pupils' social background, age, religion, tastes and so on, with a view to the ensuing correspondence and exchange. The date of the exchange is decided in the initial stage of the correspondence between heads of schools and teachers. From then on the teacher is very busy with preparations for the exchange, which take up most of his spare time; during lessons, he also has to see that the correspondence between pupils is proceeding satisfactorily (in addition to correspondence, all kinds of documents are exchanged). He has a great deal of business to attend to, including recruitment of pupils, talks with families and formalities connected with the purchase of railway tickets at reduced rates, getting passports and visas, etc. At least a whole school year is needed for the organization of a really successful exchange of pupils.

Exchanges during Term

When all arrangements have been made according to schedule, the group of pupils leaves with the teacher to live for a while in the foreign country. A teacher of English at a Paris *lycée*, who accompanied her pupils to Edinburgh for three years running, writes as follows: 'We are entirely satisfied with this system of exchanges for six to seven or even eight weeks with a group of ten to twelve pupils, divided up between different families and classes and accompanied by their teachers, who are also on an exchange basis, reside in town and teach every day in the school. Experience has shown that the children derive twice as much benefit from having contact with both the family and the school. The fullness of school and family life abroad leaves no time for boredom or homesickness. The presence of the teacher is a support to the children; it relieves the parents of anxiety and it also makes for an easy settlement of minor problems that would assume exaggerated proportions if the children were left to themselves in a country where they do not yet feel at home with the language. Besides, the teachers themselves have a very real need for frequent contacts with the country whose language and civilization they teach and undoubtedly derive great profit from their return to the country, not as mere tourists, but to work and to live the everyday life of a British teacher. The children make far greater progress in English, in general culture and also in development of character, than do those who merely go abroad for a holiday.'

The pupils go to school but they are not obliged to attend all the lessons. As a rule the teacher in the host school suggests a curriculum from which they choose what they like, or else they ask of their own accord to attend the lessons in which they are specially interested. For instance, a British group which was received by the Lycée Henri IV in Paris divided its time between French lessons (7 to 11 lessons a week for a month), Latin and mathematics and the teachers expressed satisfaction with their work in these subjects. They found the most difficulty in adapting themselves to history and geography lessons. Quite often pupils who are exchanged work harder in the foreign school than they do in their own.

Exchanges during School Holidays

Naturally no lessons are attended during such exchanges. Apart from group outings under the guidance of their own and foreign teachers, the pupils' whole time is spent with the families of their schoolfellows, who make plans for each day's activities. The cultural outings include visits to museums, libraries and historical and artistic centres of interest (with explanations by teachers or archaeologists), theatres and concerts of classical music (with a preparatory talk). The children are taken to see plays in towns which have a municipal theatre. Schools in the Paris area receiving foreign pupils set aside one or two days for a tour of Paris with an evening at the Comédie Française. Sometimes a company of amateurs gives a performance of a classical play or recitals of folk songs and dances. Guided visits are also arranged to important sites such as dams, port installations and to industrial plants, such as textile mills, steel works and factories where musical instruments are made, mines, model farms, stock-farms, etc.

Regional Linkages

So far we have been concerned with the simplest form of linkages, between one school and another. But some linkages, such as the 'twinning' of towns, are arranged as part of a rapprochement having a political bearing that goes beyond their scholastic interest. The most striking post-war example of 'twinned' towns is afforded by two small provincial towns—the French prefecture of Blois and the English country town of Lewes. Not only are pupils exchanged each year, but the prefect, mayors and deputy mayors of Blois visit their counterparts in Lewes. The moving spirits behind these exchanges are two language teachers. Periodically, each sends the other a letter on life in his town and country, for publication in the local newspaper, so that the population in each town is given first-hand information on what is going on on the other side of the Channel.

The Bordeaux-Bristol exchange is an instance of a regional linkage. Exchanges are made between the two universities and also between the secondary and continuation schools of the Académie of Bordeaux on the one hand, and the corresponding schools in the Bristol area on the other. Over 500 schoolchildren are exchanged each year and this provides an occasion for official friendship celebrations between the two cities and neighbouring towns. Similar relations were established in 1932 between the Académie of Lille and South Yorkshire and were resumed immediately after the second world war.

Prerequisites for the Success of a Linkage

If a linkage is to be successful, long and careful material and psychological preparation is required. The necessary contacts between the two schools should be made as early as October, if possible. Both groups should be of the same size and the pupils of the same age. The teacher, supported by his headmaster, is responsible for the preparation. He has to be constantly originating and directing activities, keeping up the pupils' interest and enthusiasm, winning over the parents who are sometimes unwilling to part from their children or reluctant to welcome a foreign child and do not always understand the need for sending their children abroad.

As these linkages involve extra expense for such demonstrations of international friendship as receptions, excursions, and so on, the teacher, together with his headmaster, should seek financial assistance from municipalities, parents' associations, old pupils and other sources.

No matter how great their devotion and enthusiasm, they must have their travel and correspondence expenses reimbursed, and there should be official recognition of the educational and international importance of the work they are doing.

Advantages of Linkages

The advantages of the linkage system will necessarily be most clearly apparent in the academic field, particularly in connexion with the learning of a foreign language. On this point, the reports of the teachers accompanying children are all the more interesting because the teachers know their pupils before they leave, keep an eye on them during their visit and teach them again on their return. Needless to say, the improvement is proportionate to the pupils' previous knowledge of the foreign language and to their ability, though there have been some pleasant surprises with children who had previously shown little aptitude for languages. The teachers notice that the best pupils make spectacular progress; the less gifted get used to hearing the language so that they can understand everything in about ten days, and all learn expressions that are different from the literary and often old-fashioned vocabulary found in textbooks, besides gaining an ability to speak with greater fluency and a better pronunciation. Lastly, the foreign language becomes a fact associated with human activity instead of a bookish exercise. On his return, a pupil who has taken part in an exchange shows greater interest and industry. He feels obliged to distinguish himself and in his eagerness carries his friends along with him. Language classes where some of the pupils have been exchanged are better and livelier than the others. Lastly, the pupils' outlook on the world broadens and this leads directly to the subject of the advantages of the system from the point of view of international understanding. In this respect a few quotations from teachers' reports may prove enlightening.

A teacher of English at the boys' *lycée* at Saint-Germain-en-Laye writes: 'Our French boys made full use of the opportunity they were afforded for improving their English and for getting to know a civilization which is different from ours much better than they could from a textbook. They were able to form a good idea, at first hand, of the country they were visiting and the families they were living with.' The headmaster of the boys' *lycée* at Limoges remarks: 'The visits are very carefully prepared and are of great benefit to all concerned, whether masters or pupils. On their return to France, the pupils asked to go back to England. They all improved their pronunciation and are now as fond of English as they are of their English friend and his family and the little town where they lived.' A teacher of German at the boys' *lycée* at Versailles thinks that 'the exchange system helps to broaden the pupils' outlook and makes for mutual tolerance; its value extends beyond the very real linguistic benefit it affords, which in itself would be enough to recommend it to pupils and their families.' A teacher of German at a boys' *lycée* in Lyons expresses the same opinion: 'Besides, our aim is not merely to teach a language, but to educate, to enable the children to get to know a foreign country, under its many and varied aspects, and to bring them into contact with its people.' A teacher of German in the *lycees* at Besançon likewise states: 'From the remarks that reach me about our visit I have grounds for thinking that it has had a lasting influence on the children in both countries. I shall wait to see whether the next few weeks bear out this judgment. The children, whether German or French, seem interested in any foreign problem discussed in their hearing: their outlook has been considerably broadened. We (my German colleague and I) have at all events the satisfaction of having carried out a work in which there were no underlying motives of selfishness, financial gain or prestige, but which was purely and simply the outcome of our desire to co-operate. We can therefore be sure that our effort, though humble and on a small scale, has some human value and is therefore a work for peace.' 'If I were asked what lesson could be drawn from this brief experience', writes a teacher of German at the boys' *lycée* at Fontainebleau, 'I would say that such activities not only help us in our teaching of languages but also have a considerable influence from the purely human point of view. Our boys have come to realize the vanity of egocentrism. In expanding their mental horizon, they have broadened their sympathies. They have shaken off restricting prejudices. They have grown aware of their place in the human community, but they have never understood so well the meaning of their homeland as when they came back to it.' A member of the staff, with a degree in English, at the boys' *lycée* at Clermont-Ferrand, concludes: 'Of all the benefits that the boys may have derived from their visit, the greatest is not linguistic progress; it is on a different plane—that of friendship. Between these boys who were together for almost a month, some in France and others in England, there has sprung up a genuine friendship, made easier by similarities in age. This friendship between young people, brought together in different places and circumstances, is, in my opinion, something lasting that will not disappear with distance and time.' A teacher of German at the Collège Classique at Lannion, says: 'From the outset the boys were all with Germans and forced to make use of their knowledge of the language. I can truly say that they coped creditably with this difficult situation and that they very quickly and with hardly any trouble adapted themselves to these new surroundings. From the beginning there was perfect understanding between the German and French pupils and the ice was very soon broken. Contacts were established and real friendships were formed which I trust will be firm and lasting.' A teacher of English at a *lycée* at Bordeaux stresses the cultural benefits of visits abroad. 'They provide a genuine international education, both for the children exchanged and for the parents with whom they stay. Both acquire a deeper and wider understanding from this contact with a different civilization from the one they are used to and which they automatically regarded as the best. Over five hundred new families on both sides of the Channel were brought into touch with each other. Exchanges are no longer regarded as exceptional, nor a trip abroad as an adventure. The success of our undertaking is not to be measured purely or chiefly in quantitative terms; it has built up an atmosphere which must be preserved at all costs.' In conclusion there is the opinion expressed by a teacher of English at the boys' *lycée* of Versailles: 'From the point of view of general development, which is even more important than the learning of languages in any sound scale of values, our exchanges are particularly useful. Many families of pupils who were exchanged a few years ago have not lost sight of each other. About a quarter of the exchanges were renewals of old ones. Some parents wanted their children to get to know other families, but relations with the previous families have remained excellent except in a very few instances. When brought into contact with a different civilization and outlook, the pupil acquires a keener awareness and greater depth and maturity of character. When he already has some bent and can throw off his national prejudices to a certain extent, he returns home with some realization of the relativeness of values.'

FOREIGN LANGUAGE ASSISTANTS AND THE TEACHING OF MODERN LANGUAGES[1]

The employment of foreign language assistants has increased to a remarkable extent since the last war, particularly in British and French schools. Principals and teachers alike acknowledge their services to modern language teaching. Numbers of future teachers have also been enabled through this system to make long stays in the country whose language they are going to teach. In addition, by arousing among their pupils an interest in the country which they represent, and by taking part in school exchanges, 'linkages' and club activities, they serve as a bond between French and foreign school children. International understanding cannot fail to benefit from their increased employment. Foreign assistants are employed in France in establishments for primary education (primary teachers' training colleges), secondary education (*lycées* and *collèges*) and technical education (*École Normale Supérieure de*

---

[1]. This section is taken from the working-paper with the same title prepared for the Ceylon seminar by M. le Recteur Audra, Director of the Office National des Universités et Écoles Françaises.

l'Enseignement Technique, École Centrale des Arts et Manufactures, etc.). The growing importance of a working knowledge of modern languages has also led a good many higher educational establishments to make use of their services—the Institut Agronomique, École de l'Air, École des Ponts et Chaussées, and so on.

The information given below is based on nearly 50 years' experience, and on ministerial circulars, instructions to assistants, and the hundreds of reports received each year by the Office National.

These reports come primarily from the principals of French and British schools, but they are often reports made by foreign assistants in France and by French assistants in Great Britain. They vary in quality but some of them are as noteworthy from the human angle (the discovery of a country and a mentality hitherto unknown) as from the educational point of view.

The introduction of foreign language assistants into *lycées* and *collèges* was a logical outcome of the great reform of 1902, when the direct method was instituted for the teaching of modern languages. The ministerial instructions issued on 15 February 1904, which bear the mark of the leading light in the reform, Émile Hovelacque, are still the 'bible' to which all may refer to discover the underlying idea and the way in which the services of foreign language assistants should be used. There have been slight alterations in regard to the status of assistants and to the lines on which they carry out their teaching duties, but the essentials remain unchanged. The young foreigner is no longer expected to enforce the use of his native tongue amid the din of recreation time in the playground, and the 12 hours of conversation lessons each week are fitted into the regular school hours and given in the school building in the same way as the regular lessons. But the assistant is still asked to take a leading part in the activities of a club where the pupils not only speak the foreign language exclusively, in an atmosphere created by prints, posters or other illustrations decorating the walls, but also have opportunities of attending plays or films, shows, concerts or gramophone recitals, and exhibitions of documents, travel picture-books, photographs, or various articles sent from the foreign country, such as dolls in local costume, utensils, pottery, sculpture, and so on, likely to interest the French pupils and to help create an atmosphere.

The employment of foreign assistants naturally gave rise to the need for special agreements with each country whose language is taught in the schools. Agreements were thus concluded with Great Britain, Germany, Spain and Italy.

The agreements concluded with England and Wales in 1905, and with Scotland in 1906, are still in force, despite some slight changes in the ways in which their provisions are applied, which were agreed between the Ministry of Education in London and the Scottish Education Department in Edinburgh with a view to adapting them to new circumstances. The assistants are chosen by the Ministries concerned after consultation with candidates. The exchange of assistants between England and Scotland on the one hand and France on the other is continuing and expanding most successfully, as is shown by the number of assistants sent. During the academic year 1952–53 there were 505 French assistants in England and 61 in Scotland, while there were 340 English and 60 Scottish assistants in French schools. The various Commonwealth countries also send their share. Although no special agreement has been concluded with the Canadian, Australian, New Zealand and South African Governments on this subject, French diplomatic representatives in those countries centralize candidatures, and a regular flow has come into being which enables French pupils to establish direct contact with qualified representatives of Commonwealth countries overseas. From time to time students from some other country, such as the British West Indies or Cyprus, are received and open the eyes of their French pupils to a new aspect of the territories in the British Commonwealth.

With Northern Ireland the exchanges, which are necessarily few, are arranged through the Ministry of Education in London, which forwards the suggestions of the Ministry of Education in Belfast.

As regards the Republic of Ireland, the Ministry of Foreign Affairs in Dublin has stated that the educational system in that country was, broadly speaking, similar to that obtaining in private schools in France, and that it would doubtless be difficult to organize exchanges as with other countries. This explains the small number of Irish assistants in French schools, who are received in a purely private capacity.

Since the last war the Institute of International Education in New York has centralized candidatures for the 40 assistants' posts reserved every year for Americans by the Office des Universités. A selection board chooses the 40 candidates in New York, and forwards particulars of a few more, in case some drop out.

English language assistants come, therefore, from a wide variety of countries, and it is interesting to note that every year some principals express a preference for assistants from a particular place. One may ask particularly for an Englishman with an Oxford accent, while another prefers a Scotsman, and yet another an American. Some are more eclectic and ask the Director of the Office des Universités to send them an assistant from a different country every year. Thus some establishments have received Canadians, Australians, Englishmen, Scotsmen, Irishmen, South Africans, Americans and New Zealanders.

Agreements similar to the Anglo-French agreement were signed with Prussia in 1905, with Saxony and Austria in 1907, with Bavaria and Hesse in 1912. The exchanges for which they provided were interrupted by the 1914 war and were not resumed until 1929, when new agreements were concluded with Austria and Germany, whose various States then chose the Akademischer Austauschdienst in Berlin to act as their agent.

The second world war caused another breakdown in exchanges between France and these two German-speaking countries. During the year 1939-40 German and Austrian assistants were replaced by Swiss and, after the cessation of hostilities, by German refugees and Saarlanders. The regular exchange of assistants with Germany and Austria was not resumed on its former basis until the beginning of 1947 (Austria) and October 1949 (Germany), while a few posts were reserved, as a reciprocity measure, for Switzerland and a larger number for the Saar.

From 1929 to 1930 the Office des Universités was responsible in France for proposing to the Ministry of Education the assignment of the German language assistants whose names were submitted to it by the Berlin Austauschdienst and the Kulturministerium in Vienna; similarly, these two organs were responsible in Germany and Austria for the allocation of French candidates whose particulars were forwarded by the Office des Universités.

Since the last war, and up to 1953, the procedure for the appointment of German language assistants in France has remained the same, with this difference that the foreign governments concerned submitted their lists of candidates for approval to the French High Commissions in Germany, the Saar and Austria, which then forwarded them to the Office des Universités. As for the past two years the employment of French assistants in Germany has no longer been limited to the former French zone of occupation but has extended to the whole of Western Germany, the Akademischer Austauschdienst in Bonn and not the General Directorate of Cultural Affairs in Mainz will henceforth be responsible for submitting lists of German candidates and for allocating French candidates.

The names of all German candidatures must be submitted to the competent Kulturministerium in Germany, which forwards them to the Austauschdienst before 1 January every year for the following October term. In the same way the names of all French candidatures must be addressed to the Office des Universités by the same date. Their submission so long in advance enables appointments to be made before the summer vacation, so that candidates can be informed in good time of the decision taken with regard to them.

Appointments of Swiss assistants in France and of French assistants in Switzerland are arranged by direct negotiation between the Office des Universités and the Universities of Basle and Zürich.

An agreement with Italy was concluded in 1912 but remained inoperative. No Italian language assistants were appointed in France until 1947; at that time there were 6 men and 5 women assistants, that is, 11 posts. In 1948, there were 15 men and 12 women, or 27 posts. In 1949 this figure rose to 28, and in 1950 to 29. Since that date the total has not changed. No French assistants were appointed in Italy until 1949. There were then 8 men and 4 women. In 1950, there were 10 men and 5 women. This number remained constant in 1951. In 1952 2 new posts for men and 3 for women were created.

An agreement for exchanges with Spain, similar to the Anglo-French agreement, was signed by the French and Spanish Ministers of Education in 1913. Like that concluded with Italy, however, it was not put into operation. In 1945, 17 Spanish assistants were appointed. This number rose to 44 in 1946, 46 in 1947, 63 in 1949, 66 in 1950, 74 in 1951 and 88 in 1952. There are no French language assistants in Spain.

There is no agreement with Russia. Mention should, however, be made of 10 posts for Russian language assistants created in France in 1950 and all at present occupied by refugees.

Finally, one Arabic language assistant holds a post in Paris.

Questions relating to assistants, which were at first dealt with by the Musée Pédagogique, have since 1928 been the responsibility of the Office des Universités which, on behalf of the Ministry of Education, corresponds with the various French and foreign authorities on all matters appertaining to exchanges of assistants in France.

For this purpose the Office des Universités asks Directors of Education, in December of each year, to let it know the number of men and women assistants in the various modern languages whom the different establishments in their district (*lycées, collèges*, teachers' training colleges and technical colleges) wish to employ during the coming school year, together with the special requirements of each establishment.

The Office des Universités informs foreign authorities of the number of posts it will be possible to offer to their nationals.

On the receipt of candidates' files, the Office des Universités sends them to the establishments where posts are available, having due regard to the wishes of the establishments concerned, the number of posts allowed by the budget, and the qualifications and wishes of the candidates. It then submits its suggestions for approval by the Minister, who signs the appointments.

The status of foreign language assistants is described in a pamphlet recently published by the Ministry of Education, which is a synthesis of previous instructions and supersedes all earlier texts on the subject.

An assistant appointed by the Minister of Education on the proposal of the Director of the Office des Universités is a young teacher or student responsible for conversation lessons which are intended to help pupils to acquire fluency in the foreign languages they are learning. For administrative purposes, he has the status of a resident master in a secondary school or technical school, or that of a trainee in a teachers' training college. He is paid at the same rate.

On the whole, language assistants declare themselves satisfied with the reception given them on their arrival. The principal of the establishment meets them at the station himself or sends a member of his staff. A tea or luncheon party is given in their honour. They are introduced to the vice-principal, the bursar, the resident masters who are to be their constant companions, and the teachers with whom they will have to co-operate and who arrange for their conversation lessons and for their regular classes to fit in with one another as harmoniously as possible.

The assistant generally lives on the school premises, and there again his position as a foreign guest entitles him to a comfortable, well-lit room, with adequate heating in winter, where he can feel at home and work at his ease. He takes his meals with the resident masters. As the latter are of about the same age as himself and likewise still really students, there are constant occasions for friendly contact. The school cannot always provide the assistant with a room, in which case he has to find quarters elsewhere at its expense. Some prefer this arrangement, as it leaves them freer to go out in the evenings.

The various clubs in the town provide the assistant with opportunities to meet people and extend his acquaintance with French life. Some join music clubs which are glad to welcome their talent, others sports clubs, through which they are able, when playing in matches, to visit a number of French towns with their team. One assistant, an exceptionally good Rugby player, was given the freedom of a French city in recognition of his prowess. The social aspect of the exchange of assistants is not the least important. These young foreigners, who intend to teach French in their country later on, take away pleasant impressions of their stay in France which do a great deal to foster a friendly feeling between the two countries.

The conversation lessons given by the assistant are intended not only to help pupils to acquire fluency in a foreign language but also to acquaint them with the life, customs, traditions and outlook of the people whose tongue they are learning. To illustrate these informal talks the assistant therefore brings all kinds of documents that he has collected himself or that have been supplied to him by the cultural department of his embassy. These may be newspapers, reviews, illustrated books, postcards, prints, tourist folders, illustrated catalogues, records, films, songs—anything, in short, that is likely to impart a live interest to the conversations The assistant uses them to arouse his pupils' attention, to entertain them and awaken in them a desire to know more about the foreign country and ultimately to visit it.

Assistants do all they can to make their conversation lessons as pleasant as possible. By creating an atmosphere of informality, the assistant aims at giving his pupils the impression that they are actually in his country—transported thither perhaps by some words, a picture or a song—so that they entertain a friendly feeling towards it and gradually develop a sense of international understanding which will in the long run banish the hatreds of former days.

On the other hand, the foreign assistant can attend the classes in French literature, philosophy and history given in the establishment to which he is attached. It is pleasant to note from young assistants' reports that they have much appreciated the instruction given by French teachers. Those appointed to small towns too far from the nearest university to allow of their taking courses there, found first-class teaching on the spot that enabled them to perfect their knowledge of French literature and culture.

Mention should be made of the advantages of the allocation of foreign assistants to non-university towns. Holders of fellowships appointed to some French universities too often associate with their compatriots and see less of French life than do assistants appointed to establishments in small provincial towns. It often happens that the latter, after expressing anxiety at being sent to a place they have not even heard of, soon discover the advantage of being the only person to speak their mother tongue and say that they make more progress than if they had stayed in Paris. In this way they also learn more of a side of French life that is not unimportant and of which they would doubtless have remained unaware if their horizon had been bounded by St. Germain-des-Prés and the Boulevard St. Michel.

Then again, their presence throughout the school year in parts of France where foreign visitors are never seen, unless travelling on conducted tours, helps to remove some of the prejudices that may still prevail—as they have from time immemorial—against peoples speaking another language. The friendships formed between the assistant and some families in the district are often continued after the assistant leaves and are a definite contribution towards international understanding.

Whether appointed to an English, Welsh, Northern Irish or Scottish school, the French assistant has the same status. The various Ministries—the Ministry of Education in the case of England and Wales, the Scottish Education Department in the case of Scotland or the Ministry of Education in the case of Northern Ireland—always adopt the same attitude and consult one another beforehand about any minor changes in the application of the Anglo-French agreement of 1905 and the Franco-Scottish agreement of 1906.

The Office des Universités keeps all the files of candidates and arranges the necessary interviews between candidates and the representatives of the organizations responsible for assistants.

Just as in England and Scotland candidates are examined by a commission on which a representative of the Office des Universités is invited to serve, so in France candidates are convened for a similar interview during which they are questioned on their studies, tastes and special aptitudes, and receive information and advice about the work they will have to carry out. In January and February each year British inspectors visit university centres in France to interview candidates for this purpose, together with a representative of the Office des Universités. This interview is a British tradition, as a headmaster never appoints a teacher before having a talk with him about the post which he might be offered. He wants to make sure for himself that the new staff member has not only the requisite academic qualifications but also a personality that will command obedience and respect from pupils.

In addition to these interviews, candidates attend lectures given for their guidance by the English professors in all faculties. There was some question of organizing a special course in London for French assistants, but the idea had to be dropped owing to practical and financial difficulties. There is no point in giving a lengthy account of the way in which English schools are run. The assistants will soon see for themselves. Young Frenchmen should, however, be given some idea of what they will find and what is expected of them. In this connexion, perusal of a few reports written by headmasters and assistants sheds valuable light on the way assistants have carried out their work and gives their fellows an inkling in advance of what to do and what not to do.

After the interviews the files are sent to the Ministry of Education, which distributes them according to the needs of the service and the applications received from headmasters and with as much regard for the wishes expressed by candidates as is compatible with the report on the interview and the candidate's qualifications.

The headmaster writes direct to the candidate offering him a post in his school, and as soon as the agreement is concluded between the two parties, the Ministry of Education is informed and sends the official notification of appointment. The Ministry of Labour is then notified and issues the labour permit. Once he has received these two documents the assistant can take up his post. He first asks the headmaster to help him find accommodation. The annual allowance of £272 covers the assistant's entire expenses. It is paid in 10 monthly instalments which, since 1952, have been exempt from income tax, the only deduction being the contribution to the National Insurance Scheme.

In theory, the 12 hours which form the maximum working week in both Great Britain and France are spent in giving conversation lessons to small classes of not more than twelve pupils. However, in British schools with their traditional independence, where the headmaster is the supreme authority like the captain of a ship, the assistants are given a great variety of tasks. They are often asked to help coach certain pupils for their French examinations. Furthermore, the tradition of British schools is such that it would be ungracious of the assistant not to take part in the corporate life of the school where there is more of a community sense than in French *lycées*. He cannot take 'French leave' after periods or keep aloof from the various school activities. He attends matches with the rest of the school. On special school occasions he may contribute a French item, e.g. scenes from Molière, Labiche, Marivaux, Courteline and so on. He organizes exhibitions of books, prints and posters and does everything in his power to give his pupils a better knowledge of France. It is a pleasure to be able to state that French assistants, following the lead of their British colleagues, have shown initiative and enthusiasm in their contributions to school activities.

One of the best proofs of the good work done by assistants in improving international relations is afforded by the use of German assistants in France over the past few years. Ten were appointed in 1949 with the consent of principals of schools. The principals were satisfied with their work and the assistants themselves were pleased with the reception they were given. The following year the Ministry appointed 45. In 1952–53 there were 92 out of a total of 146 German-speaking assistants, the others being Austrian, Swiss or Saarlanders.

Principals of schools appreciate the teaching ability of German assistants and their capacity for hard work. In a girls' *lycée*, where six of the teachers had been deported during the war and three did not return, the German assistant succeeded in winning the sympathy of the entire staff of the *lycée* and of pupils and their families. Most of the assistants' reports reflect very real feelings of sympathy and at times a remarkable clear-sightedness. Several state that their year as assistant is the best they have ever spent, and one (in 1952) undertakes, on behalf of her colleagues, to reveal France's true character to young Germans and to make them love France: 'I am better able than before', she writes, 'to communicate to my pupils my love for the French language, France and the French people, and to do something useful for our two peoples.'

In France, the important part played by foreign assistants in the teaching of modern languages, and still more in the development of international relations between schools, is recognized by the various divisions (primary, secondary and technical) of the Ministry of Education. The wants of all the schools which have applied for assistants have still not been supplied, but this is only for budgetary reasons. It is to be hoped that further funds will be available in the near future. It should be mentioned that in 1953–54 30 new posts were created in France by the Directorate of Secondary Education and that, for the first time, 12 British, German, Italian or Spanish assistants are being appointed to *lycées* and *collèges* in North Africa.

In addition, an interest is now being taken in the employment of assistants even in non-European countries. The Protestant Board of Greater Montreal has appointed six French assistants in secondary schools for the academic year 1953–54.

CHAPTER XI
TEACHING MODERN LANGUAGES TO ADULT MIGRANTS

Among the countries which, since the second world war, have had the highest immigration figures—Argentina, Australia, Brazil, Canada, Israel, the United States—two, Australia and Israel, have been particularly affected by the impact of mass migration and have at the same time shown themselves specially active in their efforts, by teaching their national language under modern methods, to assimilate the waves of new citizens they have attracted to their shores.

'Governmental action on a national scale aimed at setting up an organization and providing materials and finance is, it is believed, a fairly new conception', observed the authors of the study describing the Australian experiment which appears in condensed form below. And they continue, 'It is, however, one which is in keeping with the development of the world's social conscience—the great migrations of the world have flowed largely uncontrolled and without integrated official effort until comparatively recent years. Often the immigrant was left to fend for himself in his country of adoption and many immigrants were, in the past, subject to some sort of exploitation in their new land—by employers, by workmates, officials and traders. The immigrant who is unable to speak the language of his new country is at a disadvantage in all his dealings. He lacks information, local knowledge, knowledge of regulations or the social forces to which they give expression, knowledge of the reasons why his new environment is as it is. His economic and social stability is frequently threatened because of ignorance of the new language. Moreover conditions are so different from those of his homeland that if the skills and habits of his past are used without adaptation in his new environment, success is very doubtful. Without official intervention and help success may be achieved, but only at great effort over a long period of time, when a trial and error process will produce, with perseverance, the desired result.

'Lack of skill in the new language is more often than not the cause of the loss of effort, time and happiness. For the lot of the immigrant is in fact a hard one, with the problems of physical, linguistic, and social and economic adaptation pressing for solution.

'And it is not merely the national of the new country who is in a position to exploit a newcomer—his own fellow-countryman who has previously made his adaptation to the new land is in a better position than anyone to appeal to the new arrivals in their mother tongue because he has the linguistic skills combined with the local knowledge. He can explain the unknown factors in the new environment to the newcomer but he can explain them as he sees fit—and therein lies the danger.

'The recognition, however, of the vulnerability of the immigrant has prompted socially conscious persons to press for his protection, and it is recognized that his primary need is for the tool of information—the new language. With the acquirement of skill in the language comes the possibility of acquiring information and with information comes more intelligent decisions and possibilities of choice. Finally, at a later stage, come wider opportunities of social intercourse, of social co-operation, and perhaps assimilation and integration into the new community.'

It is, of course, not surprising that both Australia and Israel should have made language learning the essential prerequisite for aculturation. That is the obvious and sensible method. What is surprising, and what particularly interested the participants at the Ceylon seminar, is that, proceeding independently as they did to solve a problem which for them was quite new, these two countries should have arrived at roughly the same basic conclusions regarding language teaching methods.

This is the more surprising since conditions of immigration were very different in the two countries. Australia had originally been founded by migrants and had had its population regularly supplemented by immigration for a century and more. Up until the outbreak of the second world war, its population, native-born or immigrant, had remained remarkably homogeneous, with 80 per cent of the total stemming from ancestors who once inhabited the British Isles. Immigration from this quarter was resumed after 1945, but migrants of British or Irish stock in the most recent wave no longer constituted more than a minority of the whole; they were far outnumbered now by displaced persons or immigrants of Slav or Germanic stock and by immigrants from countries of southern Europe such as Italy and Greece. Between 1947 and 1952 over 300,000 non-British migrants arrived in Australia. Most of them knew no English and they found themselves in a country which, because of its geographical isolation and its almost complete linguistic unity, has perhaps less of the linguistic tolerances that are to be found in other countries. When these non-English-speaking immigrants reached Australia during the post-war years most of them had jobs waiting for them, or found employment fairly quickly, so that dispersion, often to remote farms or sheep-stations, was rapid and little time was spent in reception centres. This in turn meant that the time available for language instruction through actual contact hours with a teacher was relatively short and explains why it was necessary at first to organize pre-embarkation and shipboard instruction in English, (replaced more recently by a network of continuation classes), and also why a fairly elaborate mechanism of radio and correspondence courses had to be devised. It may also explain why the Australian system, when compared with the one in vogue in Israel, seems more rigid, with somewhat less scope allowed to the individual teacher and greater stress on uniform methods and textbooks.

Israel, on the other hand, shows the pattern of a homeland revived nearly two thousand years after the Dispersion. Already under the Mandatory Government immigration had been considerable, but after the establishment of the new state in 1948 figures shot up to between 150,000 and 250,000 a year for the next few years. These immigrants, though coming from countries with civilizations as different as the United Kingdom and the Yemen, India and Rumania, had at least the common bond of religion and in part at least of a single cultural tradition. Though pre-embarkation and shipboard training might be lacking, the migrant to Israel enjoyed the advantage on landing in his new country of patriotic stimulation and a high emotional motivation. The size of the country and the sheer weight of immigration into Israel also usually forced the immigrant into a reception centre with a strongly communalized atmosphere, where he could count on remaining for a considerable time. Here, or possibly in some other community which would become his permanent home, the bulk of his language instruction took place. In Israel, in the field of language teaching to migrants, the emphasis is always therefore on the community or the group.

What then, in spite of these differences in the pattern of immigration, is the common methodological ground in language teaching which both Australia or Israel seem to have found?

First, the multilingual nature of the migrant intake literally imposed the direct method as the only possible one. This method was occasionally modified in practice in the case of unilingual groups of migrants bound for Australia and receiving language instruction in their country of origin or on shipboard. Such groups have also sometimes been taught by bilingual teachers (in both countries) after landing. But as a general rule the strictest kind of direct method teaching prevailed.

The forced adoption of this method, taken together with the time factor, compelled a rigid economy in the vocabulary and in the structures taught. These had to be streamlined and all non-essentials had to be weeded out from courses that could not afford to be conducted in a leisurely or academic fashion.

The approach used was invariably the oral-aural one recommended by most contemporary language teaching methodologists. The participant from Israel[1] described to the Ceylon seminar how—even in classes he conducted for well-educated immigrants who had already had experiences of their own in learning foreign languages by traditional methods—he would insist in the early stages of instruction that notebooks, grammars and dictionaries be banished from the classroom and that his pupils devote all their time to listening and speaking.

To bring pupils forward as rapidly as possible in their ability to speak and understand the national language, great emphasis was laid in both countries on drill, and particularly on drill in carefully graded structure patterns from the living language. Drill sessions properly conducted by energetic and imaginative teachers seem to have proved much more effective than the old-fashioned system of memorizing long lists of unrelated words and phrases. The fact that the language of instruction was also the language being taught made it necessary to postpone formal grammar or complicated grammatical explanations to a much later stage, and there seems to be no evidence that this postponement did any particular harm.

In the selection and grading of structures and, indeed, in many of the pedagogical principles observed in both countries, much was undoubtedly learned from recent teaching in the United Kingdom and in the United States. On the whole, Australian directives tended to be influenced by the methods devised at the Institute of Education at London University for teaching English as a second language, while in Israel a good deal seems to have been learned from the United States Army Special Training Programme and from the doctrines expounded since the last war at American universities such as Cornell, Georgetown and Michigan. Differences between American and British practice do not seem to have been important enough to have created any really material divergence between the techniques followed in Australia and these followed in Israel.

Lastly, there was the problem of the teachers. Both in Australia and in Israel it was discovered that a new species of instructor must be trained for the new job and also that language teachers with secondary school experience were not always best equipped for the new job. The discussion of these methods and of their

---

1. Mr. Judah Shuval, Director Ulpan Ben-Yehuda in Jerusalem.

application, together with an outline of some of the administrative problems that confronted these two nations, form the subject of the two sections that follow.

Unlike Australia or Israel, Canada has not sought to devise special techniques for the teaching of either of the two official languages, English or French, to new Canadians. Though the Federal Government pays half the cost of language classes for immigrants and furnishes all textbooks and teaching materials free, the choice of method is a provincial responsibility. It appears that all the English-speaking provinces with the exception of British Columbia have elected to use the Basic English series, 'Learning the English Language', prepared by Language Research Inc. of Cambridge, Massachusetts. A French series with a similar methodological slant, 'Je parle français', prepared by M. René Gauthier, is in use in the Province of Quebec.

The short section which ends this chapter deals therefore not with language teaching methods in Canada but gives a brief description of the linguistic and cultural pattern prevailing in that country. It should not be forgotten that the process of aculturation and the problems of language do not come to an end with the migrant's first year or two in his new homeland. 'New' countries, moved generally by local political and cultural factors, have adopted different patterns of cultural and linguistic assimilation ranging all the way from the most rigid application of the melting-pot policy to others leading to a more elastic and diversified national grouping. Australia and Israel adequately represent the unitary tendency in its current form, Canada the formula of unity in diversity. The author of the Canadian paper expressed the relevance of this problem succinctly in a footnote to his original essay, 'As the solution of the problem of languages in relation to *national* understanding must often precede the solution of the more complex problem involving *international* understanding, it was thought that this factual account of developments in a nation of multicultural and multilingual origins could not fail to be of interest.'

ISRAEL[1]

The political revival of the people of Israel in their own country is inextricably tied up with the revival of their ancient Hebrew language. Since the second destruction of the Temple and during

---

1. This section is based on the working-paper 'On Teaching Hebrew to the Nation; Aims, Projects, Educational Institutions, Methods, with Special Reference to the Problem of the Immigrants', prepared for the Ceylon seminar through the good offices of the Israel National Commission for Unesco.

generations of long exile, the language was cut off from its roots; it ceased to be a living language spoken by the mass community, and shrivelled into an inadequate medium used mainly in holy books and prayers, until it seemed as though the language would never be used again.

The new pioneering settlers of our generation, coming from different countries and speaking different languages, adopted the ancient Hebrew language not owing to any compulsion or outside pressure but owing to an inward necessity to shake off the dust of exile and renew their national life: almost intuitively, the pioneers went back to the ancient Hebrew language, the language of their forefathers. The language became adaptable to the new creative spirit in the country, discarded obsolete forms and adopted a new one, and within one generation changed from an archaic bookish language, rhetorical and involved in style, to a simple living language, realistic and precise, with a name for every object and a suitable expression for every action. The Hebrew language, which had already been one of the official languages during the Mandatory Government, with the establishment of the State became the language of the Knesset (parliament), the press, the theatre and radio, society and the family.

The life and force of a language is to be determined not only by its innate qualities, its wealth of vocabulary and its ability to give a precise expression for each object and action but also by its wide usage and popularity among the masses and all sectors of society. From this point of view the Hebrew language, since the beginning of its revival, has been struggling continually against the invading waves of foreign expressions which have remained deeply inculcated in the hearts of very many among the new population. No wonder that the older community considers it one of its main tasks to absorb the new immigrants not only economically but spiritually, culturally and linguistically, and to introduce their brother immigrants into Hebrew-speaking circles.

The Department of Culture of the Va'ad Leumi, the Jewish Agency, the General Federation of Jewish Workers and other public organizations exerted much effort during a long period for the development of a network of evening classes for immigrants according to their social group and intellectual standards. Hebrew teachers and learned men were enlisted for this collective activity which achieved the following results: over 60,000 adults, men and women, acquired the rudiments of the language through the evening classes of the Va'ad Leumi alone during a period of 13 years prior to the establishment of the State. Thousands more studied within the framework of the General Federation of Jewish Workers. Up to the establishment of the State, the Jewish population in the country numbered about 600,000 of whom 400,000 were adults and most of whom knew the language and led an entirely Hebrew life under the Mandatory Government.

The establishment of the State of Israel on 15 May 1948 marked the beginning of mass immigration into the country. The amazing historical process of the transfer of entire communities from exile began and continued on a scale unheard of in the history of Israel. During a period of four years over 650,000 immigrants came to the country, a number exceeding that of the total former population. With the joy of the old community at the ingathering of their dispersed brothers there grew the danger of foreign elements penetrating into the language, the fear that the immigrants would divide themselves into their own communities according to the language they spoke, that a Babel of languages and idioms would destroy originality and creativeness in the country. It is obvious therefore, that the teaching of Hebrew to immigrants became a matter of emergency. The Government, the Jewish Agency, the General Federation of Jewish Workers and all responsible public institutions in the country realized the urgency of teaching immigrants the fundamentals of the Hebrew language and culture, for their assimilation. The Ministry of Education and Culture opened a special department whose task was to weave a network of classes for immigrants all over the country. Financial and organizational assistance was also given to local authorities and public institutions for any activities related to the teaching of the language and the training of language teachers.

Classes were soon opened everywhere, in towns and villages, in immigrant camps and settlements. Qualified and unqualified teachers, philologists and students were all drawn into the project and, although the pedagogical forces were insufficient and financial possibilities were limited, extensive work was achieved in the field during a period of four years. Thousands of new immigrants filled classrooms in the evenings and learnt the rudiments of the language. Many were the difficulties in the way of the immigrants. Shortage of teachers, shortage of books, difficulties in mental adjustment of the widely different types of immigrants, and, in addition, lack of a unified curriculum—all these greatly hampered the work of teaching. In spite of this, however, achievements were satisfactory. At least 120,000 adults went through these classes during the period 1948–52 and were assimilated linguistically into the life of the country. During this teaching process clearer lines emerged and improvements were gradually introduced in the methods used for teaching immigrants with different backgrounds and different intellectual standards. Regular centres for the teaching of adults were established; one of the most important among them was the *ulpan* ('place for study') which grew to be well known both in the country and abroad for its structure and system and which contributed greatly to the promotion of the language among the people.

With the establishment of the State of Israel, thousands of educated men and women arrived in Israel from different countries. The greater part were members of the liberal professions—engineers, lawyers, teachers, doctors, economists, accountants, artists, technicians, etc., who could have assisted in the development of the country and at the same time would have solved the problem of their employment but for their lack of Hebrew.

The Government of Israel and the Jewish Agency soon realized that the absorption of immigrants would not be complete unless full assistance were given in the teaching of the national language for the benefit both of the immigrants and the country. It was also realized that the regular classes held for immigrants by the Government, local authorities and various public organizations, could not meet the urgent requirements of the educated immigrants owing to: the broad general character of the studies conducted in these classes (the limited number of hours, lessons given in the evenings after a hard day's work, and the prolonged period of study); the heterogeneous character of the students as regards their cultural background and education, the difficulty of dividing the students into suitable groups, and the lack of a fixed and officially approved curriculum.

Subsequently the idea was conceived that certain units should be formed for the instruction of these men of the liberal professions, units based on the following principles: students would be free of any worries connected with their own livelihood and that of their families, enabling them to concentrate entirely on the study of the language; the courses would be intensive and suited to students with a secondary and university education. Thus, by the joint effort of the Ministry of Education and Culture and the Jewish Agency, the *ulpanim* came into being, and successfully disseminated the Hebrew language among thousands of educated immigrants who, in a comparatively short period, were entirely assimilated into the life of the country. The first *ulpan*, called 'Etzion', was opened in Jerusalem in September 1949, after which other *ulpanim* were opened in various parts of the country (Nahriya, Kiryat, Motzkin, Har Cana'an, Pardessia etc.).

The Absorption Department of the Jewish Agency provided the buildings (both class buildings and lodgings) for the students, while the Department for the Teaching of the Language of the Ministry of Education and Culture provided the teachers and the necessary equipment. The students settled down in these buildings, receiving full board and lodging and all personal services during their course of study, with the proviso that all expenses thus incurred would be reimbursed by the student to the Jewish Agency after the termination of his studies and after securing employment. The *ulpan* course lasted five months, and composed 600 hours of lessons and private study.

Students were accepted into the *ulpanim* according to their intellectual abilities. Their cultural background and knowledge of Hebrew were examined by a special committee composed of representatives of the Department for the Teaching of the Language and of the *ulpan* section of the Jewish Agency. Three basic classes were established in each *ulpan:* Class A for beginners, Class B for advanced students and Class C for qualifying students. In the larger *ulpanim*, classes were subdivided with a view to rendering them as homogeneous as possible for intensive study. The number of students in a class was 20 to 25. The enthusiasm of the teachers in their important work of teaching the language to the new 'intelligentsia' in the country, and the serious approach of the students themselves to the study of the language, together, brought about excellent results.

The chief object of the *ulpan* was to lead the student into articulation and out of his reticence, to encourage him to express in Hebrew all his wishes and requests, and to reply simply and directly to any question put to him, as well as to enter into the field of his profession by a gradual acquisition of the language. The *ulpan* student acquired all these through the systematic lessons given in class, through the Hebrew spirit pervading the institute throughout the hours of the day, and through the encouragement and assistance he obtained wherever he turned during his stay in the *ulpan*. Within two months he acquired about 1,000–1,200 basic words (chosen by experts and inspectors of the department and based on their research). After another three months he doubled his active vocabulary and left the *ulpan* with a sufficient treasury of words to serve him in his first independent steps.

At the same time the student also acquired some knowledge of reading and writing: he learnt to read advanced texts (with vowelling) and intermediate texts (without vowelling); to write letters, invitations and notes of an elementary kind making only a few spelling mistakes.

With the realization that, apart from learning the language, it was most important that the immigrants should imbibe the culture of the country and participate in its problems, an important place was allocated in the *ulpan* for cultural club activities, held on special evenings: community singing, discussions and popular talks on life in Israel (information about the country, its economy, government institutions, society, etc.), walks and trips to historical places, visits to museums and exhibitions, group attendance at theatres and concerts, etc. The students were divided into groups which assembled for meetings, selected committees and, together with the pedagogic director, the administrative director and the staff of teachers, planned the course of studies of the *ulpan*, its projects and activities. The *ulpan* student thus lived continually in an active atmosphere of Hebrew culture.

As the ultimate purpose of the *ulpan* was to prepare the student for work and life in the country, a terminal course was given at the end (usually an additional month added to the five-month course), with the help of various Government offices. These lessons enabled the immigrant to resume his profession qualified in the Hebrew language. For example, an intensive course was given to groups of accountants who had special lessons in correspondence and accountancy terminology; lawyers were trained in Hebrew and grew familiar with the basic legal and economic terminology. The student thus acquired, while qualifying, specific knowledge which helped him to practise his former profession.

The success of the *ulpanim* is due not only to the good planning of the teaching and the training, to the intensive lessons, the careful division of students into homogeneous groups, and to the readiness of the students to give all their time and energy to their studies; but also to the efficient teaching methods used in the course—'methods', in the plural, for it is impossible to give one uniform method as being the one used in all the *ulpanim* and by all the teachers. It would be more helpful to explain the fundamental principles of the *ulpanim* and the various teaching techniques adapted to the students according to their mentality, ability and tendencies.

The foremost principle, which is the foundation of all adult language teaching, is the principle of the natural or direct method, i.e. the teaching of the fundamentals of the language without making use of a methodical and regular translation into another language. From the very first day the teacher addresses his pupils in Hebrew, and gets acquainted with them by mentioning names, surnames, pronouns (I, you, he) mimicking, pointing and using gestures and actions and only in exceptional cases will he translate into another language. Despite the preliminary difficulties which the student has to overcome, he becomes acquainted with every word he hears from his teacher and learns to use it immediately without having to introduce another language between the sound of the word and its meaning.

The language material is chosen according to the two following principles:

Actuality. During the first phase of the course only such words and phrases as are most topical and used in everyday life, concerning objects surrounding the student, are chosen from the rich vocabulary of the language. As the student's knowledge of the language extends so the range of subjects introduced to him widens.

Use of material. Every word or idiom introduced to the student is first absorbed passively by him, but the teacher does not desist until the knowledge becomes active and the student can use it in conversation. The adult immigrant who goes back to school has an urgent and practical object before him—to *listen* to Hebrew and express freely whatever he feels and thinks. The teachers' efforts are directed to achieving this object; to bringing into play to the utmost all the intellectual faculties of the student, especially his auditory and vocal organs. The student listens and absorbs the new words and sounds issuing clearly from the lips of the teacher; he creates an association between the syllables and the meaning of the words, and is then taught to use them actively, first by pure imitation and later freely and independently.

Many teaching methods are used for achieving this object: talks on various subjects, dramatizations of certain situations, conversation with constant exercise and repetition, singly and in unison. Exercise and repetition in unison is considered by many teachers as the most beneficial method of learning to speak Hebrew freely. Apart from the mnemo-technical factor there is a most useful psychological factor. By speaking in chorus the student emancipates himself from linguistic and social inhibitions, overcomes his shyness and does not hesitate to pronounce words in a language still foreign to him.

Another good exercise is the use of new words in sentences. The student is required to construct sentences by making use of new words which eventually become engraved in his mind. The teachers are instructed to pay special attention during all lessons to the pronunciation of words and to encourage the students to rid themselves of their foreign accent. Community singing holds an important place in these courses. The words of the songs are explained and through singing them they are eventually learnt by heart; new words are thus added to the students' vocabulary.

The Hebrew *ulpan*, within its framework of intensive and uniform studies, has been an important experiment in methods of teaching adults. It has also served as a model for the creation of subsidiary institutions for the teaching of the language to adults, amongst which the first is the work-*ulpan*. The *ulpanim* described above are intended specially for the members of the liberal professions among immigrants who can stay in a boarding school for a period of five to six months and who can give themselves over entirely to an intensive study of the Hebrew language so as to become assimilated to the people of the country. These immigrants are usually about 35-45 years old and during their studies are free from the burden of earning a livelihood. Their board and lodging fees are either paid in advance or in instalments after they enter employment in the country. But amongst the immigrants who apply to the *ulpanim* are many younger persons, from 20 to 35, most of whom have no means of livelihood but wish to enter some form of manual employment. Thus the idea was conceived of establishing in the agricultural settlements special *ulpanim* socially and culturally suitable for such young immigrants. These *ulpanim* were established on the basis of work and study together, that is the students worked half a day in the agricultural settlement in which they were lodged and half the day they studied. Work-*ulpanim* for younger people were opened in collective settlements all over the country. It should be stressed that the initiators of the work-*ulpanim* (the Jewish Agency, the Ministry of Education and Culture and the representatives of collective settlements) consider the employment of the students not only as a means of covering the cost of their studies and board but also as an important social and educational project, for during their six months of study the students of the work-*ulpan* acquire not only a knowledge of the living language and Hebrew culture, but find themselves throughout the day and evening in a natural Hebrew atmosphere. While living in the collective settlement the new immigrants become attached to the new farming life, they study while they work and by working they become absorbed into the life of the country.

During the three-year period 1949-52 over 5,000 immigrants with secondary school or university qualifications passed through the *ulpanim* or the work-*ulpanim* and joined the circle of the working intelligentsia in the country. However, the greater part of the immigrants in their thousands and tens of thousands could not enter *ulpanim* owing to their employment, soon after coming to the country, in part-time or full-time jobs. With the worries of earning a livelihood and supporting a family, even those immigrants who saw the necessity of learning the language could give only a part of their leisure hours in the evening to study. For such immigrants a network of popular classes was started—the 'popular *ulpan*', consisting of four to five hours of intensive study usually in the evenings during five days of the week and, in all, 20 to 25 hours of study during the week. The whole course takes six or seven months. The teaching methods of the other *ulpanim* were adopted except that in the popular *ulpan*, whose students had a hard day's work behind them, the study was necessarily less intensive.

The popular *ulpan* differs from the *ulpan* in the type of student that frequents it. While the *ulpan* is intended mainly for professional men or for persons with at least a secondary school education, the popular *ulpan* is open to all types of immigrants who wish to learn the language. The only condition they must accept on joining is to attend the course during the 20 hours a week and for a period of from six to seven months.

The popular *ulpan* may be said to be half-way between the *ulpan* and the more extensive popular lessons given in the *ulpanit* (plural, *ulpaniot*). To the bulk of the immigrants who can spare but a few hours of their time for study, the opportunity is given of attending various popular courses divided into two types:

The *ulpanit* (a small *ulpan*) consisting of one class studying ten hours a week (four sessions of two and a half hours each), the whole course lasts 10 months.

The second type, the popular *ulpanit*, consisting of one class of four and a half hours a week (held three times a week), the whole course lasting 20 months.

These classes are open to the widest circles and give an opportunity to every immigrant and citizen in the country to make use of his free time and learn the language. Although lessons in these classes are not intensive and do not have the advantage of the methodical regularity and the continuity of the *ulpan* or the popular *ulpan*, yet the students achieve satisfactory results. The *ulpaniot* and popular *ulpaniot* are the most popular educational institutions in both town and village, and thousands of new immigrants, as well as some of the older inhabitants of the country who have not acquired a satisfactory knowledge of Hebrew, attend these classes in which they make good progress.

The pressure and urgency of the work to be done with regard to the teaching of the language to the newcomers did not allow much time to be spent drawing up a regular curriculum. The teachers, especially the better ones amongst them, realized the aim of the project and did their best to achieve it: they enabled students to speak Hebrew adequately, to have some knowledge of grammar, to read a newspaper and write a short composition. However, the details of the curriculum were not fixed and there were almost as many curricula as there were good teachers. The expansion of this network of teaching institutions which drew into the project many young and inexperienced teachers, and the realization of the importance of forming regular and uniform principles for mass education of immigrants and others, necessitated the working out of a fixed and regular curriculum which served as a guide to the teachers in their work.

The Department for the Teaching of the Language of the Ministry of Education and Culture appointed preparatory committees for the purpose, and in September 1952 the draft of an official curriculum was issued to all adult institutions dealing with adult education.

The ultimate aim of the student and the underlying principle of the curriculum were defined as follows:

'An immigrant issuing from one of the educational institutions of the Department for the Teaching of the Language will have acquired a satisfactory standard of knowledge of the Hebrew language and its culture. This knowledge will qualify him to become a good citizen of Israel.'

In other words, the teaching of the living language is the main purpose of the curriculum. But, together with the acquisition of the language and through it, a means of access into the culture and environment of Israel (without which his assimilation is not complete) is given to the immigrant, who is usually entirely ignorant of them.

This principle expanded the already broad education programme even further and forced teachers to give more attention to lessons in citizenship.

The following are the details of the curriculum:

Speaking. Active knowledge of words and idioms sufficient to hold a conversation on an everyday topic (in a supplement to the curriculum, a list of 1,500 basic words, chosen and arranged by a group of teachers and inspectors and proposed as the minimum language material needed by the student, was distributed to teachers); ability to give a simple talk on life in Israel and its community; ability to understand a talk.

Reading. Fluent reading of printed matter of a vowelled and non-vowelled text (material from a daily paper, and easy prose); reading of cursive but non-complicated writing (invitations, notices, letters, etc.).

Writing. Clear and simple writing; noting impressions and experiences (summaries, letters, reports, notes, etc.) in a clear and simple style.

Grammar. General knowledge of the formation and use of the language.

Literature. Knowledge of some classical writers through reading selections from their works.

Scriptures. General knowledge of the stories of the Torah and the earlier prophets; some chapters from the Books of the Prophets.

Legends. Selected chapters from the legends of the Wise.

Knowledge of the country. General knowledge of the different zones of the country and its inhabitants, the economy and problems of the country.

History of Israel. General knowledge of the important eras in national

history with special stress on the ties of the nation to its land.
Citizenship. Knowledge of the different Government institutions, the Zionist Organization and public organizations; the basic law of the State, types of settlements, Government economy, educational and cultural institutions, feasts and customs of Israel.
Singing. Knowledge of selected folk, feast and national songs.
The time allocated in each term to the various subjects was divided as follows:

Subject	Term A	Term B	Term C	Term D
	%	%	%	%
Hebrew language (speaking, reading, writing, spelling, grammar)	81	45	30	25
Bible	7[1]	8	12	12
Traditional legends	4[1]	5	5	5
Literature	—	5	8	10
Knowledge of the country	Included in language	7[2]	10	10
History of Israel	—	10[2]	12	15
Citizenship	—	12[2]	15	15
Singing	8	8	8	8

1. Stories told by the teacher.
2. Subjects related to topics of conversation held in the language lessons.

The knowledge to be acquired has been fixed at a minimum compulsory for all types of educational institutions for adults —*ulpanim* and *ulpaniot*—approved by the Government. The difference between the institutions does not therefore lie in the amount of knowledge acquired and the material included in the curriculum, but in the intensiveness and consequently the comparative length of the course.

The above curriculum was adapted to the different institutions as follows:

Institution	Hours per week	Length of course months	Average hours in entire course
Ulpan	30	5	600
Work-*ulpan*	24	6	580
Popular *ulpan*	20	7	560
Ulpanit	10	10	420
Popular *ulpanit*	4½	20	400

A student who terminates a five-month course in an *ulpan* or a ten-month course in an *ulpanit* should acquire the same standard of knowledge. Certain differences in the achievements of the two types should be expected, however, owing to the special teaching conditions of each type and the intellectual and social standard of the students.

In the *ulpan* there are 600 hours in a complete course; the number of hours decreases in the other institutions to 400 in the popular *ulpanit*. It is obvious therefore that the *ulpan*, through more exercise and repetition, inculcates a solider and completer knowledge of the different subjects. On the other hand the longer period spent in the 'extensive' type of institutions has proved of invaluable help in acquiring the language, for the student's constant dealings with friends, work and family afford him many opportunities to absorb and digest what he learns. It can therefore be assumed that the results reached in all the types of institutions are more or less the same.

Each course is divided into four terms: at the end of each term there are examinations which qualify the student to be promoted to the next term. At the end of the four terms the student receives a government certificate of proficiency. An adult may, if necessary, stop his course of study at the end of a term and receive an official certificate stating that he has terminated that particular term. Should he wish to resume his studies in any of the courses opened in his neighbourhood he will be allowed to join the relevant term of the course according to his certificate.

This uniformity in curriculum, with its division into terms and its proficiency examinations, has been introduced so as to give the maximum opportunity to every adult immigrant in any time and place. The new curriculum was introduced into educational institutions for adults at the beginning of the academic year 1952-53. Its principles and the methods of carrying it out were explained to teachers in seminars held all over the country by the Department for the Teaching of the Language.

The new curriculum has necessitated the publication of new school books for adults arranged according to its general lines and introducing the vocabulary of basic words included in the programme. The Department for the Teaching of the Language has accordingly set out to compile a new book on fundamental education for adults based on the principles of the curriculum. This book will be ready by the next academic year and will assist the teachers in their instruction of adults. The Department has also begun issuing a series of education and reading publications on the different subjects included in the curriculum (the Bible, knowledge of the country, singing, etc.) which will serve as reading material for the students and a guide to the teachers.

Furthermore, the weekly publication *Prozdor*, which was first issued by the Ministry of Education and Culture three years ago and intended for new immigrants learning Hebrew, has proved of considerable assistance to teachers. The publication is vowelled and its style is clear and simple. At the end of each column a translation of difficult words and idioms is given in languages with which the immigrant is familiar. Another publication that has proved useful to the teacher is the daily *Omer*, which is issued by the General Federation of Jewish Workers. This publication too is vowelled and intended mainly for new immigrants. Both publications encourage public spirit and the sense of citizenship as well as helping to teach the immigrant the language.

AUSTRALIA[1]

The size of the problem facing the Australian authorities can be gauged from the fact that between 1947 and 1952 over 300,000 non-British migrants arrived in Australia. Most of those newcomers knew little or no English. Their assimilation—their acceptance by the Australian community—depended very largely on their knowledge of English. The Australian community, isolated as it is geographically, has less of the linguistic tolerances which are customary in countries where several language minorities exist or where land boundaries represent language boundaries too. The Australian speaks only English (except in certain limited areas) and, moreover, over the whole country the English spoken is of remarkable regularity of vocabulary, pronunciation and intonation.

To meet the situation, the Commonwealth Government set up in the Department of Immigration an assimilation division with the responsibility for organizing activities aimed to assist the eventual assimilation of newcomers, both British and alien.

One of these activities is the provision for language instruction, free of charge. The Commonwealth Office of Education provides the technical services—advice on teaching methods, textbooks, posters, etc. The day-to-day administration is handled by the State Education Departments for each of the States of the Commonwealth.

In any consideration of method in language teaching it is desirable not to overlook the factors outside those of purely

---

1. This section is based on the working-paper 'The Linguistic and Cultural Assimilation of Migrants in Australia', prepared for the Ceylon seminar through the good offices of the Australian National Advisory Committee for Unesco, in the Migrant Education Section of the Commonwealth Office of Education under the technical direction of Mr. B. A. Pittman. The editorial notes are based on the more recent information embodied in 'Review of Migrant Education in Australia', *Education News*, vol. 4, no. 6, December 1953.

methodological reasoning which can and should affect the actual method developed. In discussions of method in language teaching in secondary schools (at least in the Western world), it is customary to accept as the unique pattern the school building with its hours, timetable, holidays, compulsory attendance, division into classes, fixed number of years in which to achieve a matriculation standard, training of teachers for the specific aims of the school system, etc.

In the description of migrant education in Australia which follows, most of the teaching was however done within a framework which was dissimilar in the extreme to that regarded as normal in the teaching of languages. The main features which differentiated migrant education from more usual types of language instruction are set out below.

The paramount influences on method must be the aims of the instruction and the time in which those aims have to be achieved. When the Australian Government decided to implement a programme for the teaching of English to those new Australians who did not speak English, it was obvious that inability to speak and understand spoken English was a major barrier which would condemn the newcomer either to isolation or to refuge in a smaller unit, a 'national' group within the community. Consequently, the English language teaching activities were seen as a means of providing the skills for immediate communication between the newcomer and the existing community—a very different matter from the teaching of a foreign language, say, French, to Australian children living in a purely English-speaking environment. Newcomers urgently needed the language to become useful employees, to become good colleagues, to understand their environment, to become known to and by Australians. To meet this situation the aims of the instruction were laid down in this order:

To understand spoken English; to speak reasonably correct English; to read English; to write English.

Within the restricted time available a very strong tendency developed for the first two aims to dominate more and more over the skills of literacy in language. Sometimes they became almost the unique object of instruction. This is not surprising since the European saw so much in his surroundings to puzzle and confuse him that he realized that if he could talk to Australians he could solve many of his queries. In turn, the student's opinion became a pressure on teachers to provide for the dominant needs.

In the early stages of the immigration scheme the teaching of English was concentrated almost exclusively in two or three reception centres. It was in these centres where the pressures of restricted time were felt most severely (throughout 1949 and 1950 the adult new Australians at reception centres had an average of fewer than three weeks with $2^{1}/_{2}$ hours instruction daily, during which an attempt was made to lay a basis for learning English). Here the needs of the newcomer to master the tongue of his new environment were most clearly and constantly felt both by the new Australian and by his teacher. It was in the reception centres therefore that the main effort for the improvement in techniques was made. The need of the student became the inspiration to the teacher to analyse, recast and streamline his teaching to produce the most effective results in the shortest possible time.

The rigorous time-limit imposed in the early stages of migrant education had other implications for method—it meant that the period allowed for 'subconscious auditory assimilation'[1] of linguistic material, for instance, was cut down drastically and finally almost eliminated in the classroom.

Although the situation described above no longer exists at the time of writing, the influence of the early period still persists and the search for effective techniques still goes on. The main media now relied upon for teaching English are evening continuation classes all over Australia (administered and staffed by the State Education Departments), three radio sessions which are a regular week-end feature, and a correspondence course which caters for students unable to attend classes.

The numbers of students dealt with, as well as the time available for teaching them, had an influence on the methods developed in these formative years. It was common for newcomers to arrive at the rate of 10,000 to 20,000 a month during the years 1950–51 and a strong tendency developed to adopt methods which could in any emergency lend themselves to mass teaching and mass practice. With some 16,000 students attending 1,200 evening continuation classes, the bulk of teaching is now done in classroom situations and with smaller classes than is usual in normal daytime class instruction.

Another matter of importance to method in secondary school language teaching is that of motivation, and a successful secondary school teacher has to watch very carefully that he maintains the students' interest in the foreign language that he is teaching. Motivation needs, it would seem, a constant series of short-term interests (to maintain the strength of motives in the adolescent to learn a foreign tongue) as well as long-term interests. For this reason the personality gifts of the teacher rank very high in successful teaching. In addition he may use quite a battery of *realia* and aids to help in the maintenance of motivation. It is not too much to say that successful instruction in secondary language

---

[1] H. E. Palmer, *The Scientific Study and Teaching of Languages*, Yonkers-on-Hudson, N.Y., World Book Company, 1917.

teaching is very frequently connected with this matter of student motivation rather than with the organization of the material to be taught.

In the teaching of English to new Australians, however, motivation to learn English was usually sufficiently powerful in the new English-speaking environment to permit the neglect of some of the means of stimulating interest necessary in secondary school language teaching with children. It was therefore possible to cut away a great deal of material and to attempt to streamline the entire programme, with linguistic aims as the overriding consideration. The emphasis passed in our programme from the means of motivation to the linguistic material, and the material to be taught became the primary concern of the technical staff.

Another influence on the teaching programme and its methods throughout the entire history of the migrant education scheme is that students attended and still attend classes voluntarily. *There is no compulsion to learn English* and, as learning a language to even a relatively simple stage of skill involves a good deal of effort on the part of the student, there was a continual need to 'sell' the material to the students, especially with advanced classes. This involved thought and action by teachers, administrators and technicians. The methods and material used had to be adjusted closely to fit not only the long-term but also the short-term needs of the student, including his immediate domestic, social and vocational needs. In general, too, the student wanted to speak English in class as much as possible. He had a strong feeling that he required (as indeed he did) copious practice and this permitted the introduction of more techniques based on chorus responses than would seem to be the case in other educational institutions dealing with language teaching.

Methods developed in Australia in migrant education should be seen in relation to the administrative framework in which they were developed. To summarize, the features of that framework were the very short period allowed for instruction, voluntary attendance by students, the high student-teacher ratio (at least in the formative years) and the strong motivation in the adult student to acquire the linguistic skills.

It is necessary before considering in detail the methods adopted and recommended in migrant education in Australia to make some brief reference to the complexity of the material to be taught. Language teaching involves sets of related problems so complex and involved that some guidance to the teacher is necessary at every stage. The individual teacher is rarely in a position to spare the time for the organization of the material he desires to teach. In the past, teachers' ideas on language instruction have suffered from over-simplification, and the dead hand of tradition has lain heavily on the practitioner. However, with the development of linguistic science and especially with its application to the classroom, it is possible to formulate a set of principles which, while linguistically sound generally, can be applied to a problem of method. The work done by the Institute of Education, London, on English as a foreign language, by Ogden and Richards, by Fries in Michigan, are significant of the new trend—the immediate application to the classroom of the results of linguistic science.

What is to be taught? What words? What phrases? What collocations? What sentences? What intonation patterns? How are they to be taught? How are they to be practised, revised in the classroom, revised in supplementary reading? Even if we know what words are necessary, our problem is not solved, because the 'heavy duty' words of English are over-burdened with meanings, with semantic varieties. *Of* has 63 meanings listed in the Oxford Dictionary. The Thorndyke count showed 544 different semantic values for the word *set*. Which of the semantic varieties of the essential words are to be selected for teaching? And having made the necessary selection of matter, a problem of greater difficulty emerges—in what order is the material to be taught? Even when that problem is dealt with (however empirically) others emerge. With Professor Pattison[1] of the London Institute of Education, Australian experience confirms that the main difficulty in the teaching of a language is not the learning of vocabulary at all but the provision of a method or means to make the vocabulary 'operative'.

Unlike a subject such as mathematics, where the very logic of the subject provides much of its own order of presentation of new material and no teacher would lightly depart from the progression of theorems already established, in language teaching the instructor must be capable of the most rigid control of words and patterns—and even intonation, if he is to present his material efficiently in the new language. Translation can be and is used to make up for deficiencies in the ordering of material.

Considerations of the frequency of the words to be taught could not be overlooked. In the short period available for instruction it was essential that the student be taught the indispensable word. As is well known, the structure and mechanism of English is such that a group of very common monosyllables supply the links between the words of meaning and in any frequency count these 'heavy duty' monosyllabic words dominate numerically and provide as it were the background of English into which meaning

---

1. B. Pattison, *Address on Inauguration into Chair of English Language Teaching*, University of London, 27 November 1950.

is fitted or, if you prefer it, the mortar which binds the bricks together.

These 'structural' words are words such as: *a, the, I, he, she, it, was, is, are, did, does, do, at, of, in, to, by, his, her, their, your, this, that*. A glance at this list will show that they are not words which can be taught with the same ease as *cup, saucer, hat*. You cannot pick up any object and teach 'structural' words—they just don't lend themselves to that sort of treatment. They cannot be taught in isolation. In order to be taught effectively they would have to be incorporated into a phrase or a sentence. Their incorporation into phrases would do violence to other considerations, e.g. the English verb would not achieve its normal frequency, and there seems to be no alternative but the incorporation of these words into sentences and the teaching of the whole sentence as the unit of instruction.

Whatever may be the merits of translation as a method (and they appear very doubtful) or as an auxiliary of a method, the fact remains that translatory teaching was early realized to be totally unsuitable to the teaching of English to new Australians. The reasons were not far to seek and were, in the first place, administrative rather than methodological. Classes of 40 could and did contain students of many nationalities (sometimes as many as 16 nationalities) and this fact precluded any use of translation into the mother tongue of the student. The loss of the time devoted to translation, had it been adopted under these conditions, would have been disastrous, and the lessons would have become boring in the extreme to the majority of students. On purely linguistic grounds the most powerful argument against translation as a constant teaching medium was that the semantic varieties of common English words cannot be translated by single words of mother tongues without the safeguards of lengthy periods of study in which to explore meanings.

There is a very sharp lesson for every language teacher in Palmer's semantic analysis of the English word *here* and its equivalent in French. Apart from its 'core' meaning of *ici* it is translated by *voici* or *écoutez* when elliptical, on occasions by *tenez* by *ça* in *ça et là* (*here and there*), by *jusqu'ici* (up to here) and in its collocations *here, there and everywhere* by *partout*. And these are only a few of the main uses. There is a strong tendency for the actual creation of errors by unguarded translation. After all, a teacher who tells students, say, that the French for *on* is *sur* should not be surprised if the student subsequently translates *on my left* as *sur ma gauche* when he should say *à ma gauche* or *on Tuesday* as *sur mardi* unless the teacher has given almost as much weight in his teaching to the exceptions to his own generalization as to the original translation itself. With the change of emphasis from the structural in a sound language course, extreme care must be taken with the common structurals. They are heavy duty words, and when used in different ways their translation changes in another tongue. It would seem that the main semantic varieties would have to be thoroughly catalogued and taught separately—and if this has to be done there is much to be said for their presentation in situations which will clarify the various meanings without recourse to translation. But even when mis-translation is not likely, there is a serious objection to its habitual use. The intervention of a second language between the thought and its spoken expression is a formidable bar to fluency—an unnecessary bar, for the skilful teacher who teaches in situation can train his students to form a direct association between thought and speech.

Nor was it possible for administrative reasons to use translation in the very much more acceptable way that it was used in some of the courses developed under the U.S. Army Special Training Programme 1942–45. The student in these courses could be informed in his native tongue at the end of the lesson or at the end of the week what had been taught, and could be given information on the linguistic background to the teaching material with special reference to and comparison with the students' tongues.

There is no doubt that a teacher who has a knowledge both of the students' tongues and of the language to be taught will, other things being equal, be the more effective teacher; but his main claim will rest on the degrees of emphasis with which he teaches various grammatical facts in anticipation of the errors which will arise owing to the structure, semantics, pronunciation and intonation of his students' native languages. He will be in a stronger position to discriminate between the individual idiosyncrasies in his students' errors from observing the more general ones. He should be quicker to devise remedial drills at all stages.

Linguists capable of uniting effective teaching methods with the necessary theoretical knowledge were not available for the staffs of the reception centres. Consequently there remained no option but to use English, the language to be taught, as the actual teaching language too in the generality of cases. If translation is unsuitable and the language to be taught has to be the medium of instruction, the method will clearly be a 'direct' one. In view of time limitations it would be impossible to expect success by an 'uncontrolled' direct method. It was necessary that the steps in the presentation of the words and sentences of the new tongue in the classroom be so closely organized and integrated that no student could claim with justice that the language was incomprehensible.

In the early experiments insufficient control of sentences and vocabulary in the classroom did cause this complaint and indeed the inexperienced teacher still gives rise to difficulties of his own making.

With persistence and effort, however, the teacher can acquire the necessary skill in the control of his material and while it is impossible to say that all phases of the scheme of the teaching of English to new Australians are in the hands of persons able and willing to control their speech, there is a sincere effort to clarify the students' problems in comprehension by controlling the structure taught and used in teaching.

Basic English textbooks were used both in the language teaching in the pre-embarkation stage in Europe and in shipboard education because it was felt that it provided, especially in the early stages, a very sound approach to problems. Whatever its excellencies, and they are many, Basic is based on an 'island' vocabulary which was not entirely suited to use with students who were to be plunged almost immediately on arrival in Australia into the linguistic jumble of an English-speaking community. By its limitations of vocabulary, which are also its pride, Basic English was unsuitable for use as an introduction to a community which certainly did not restrict its vocabulary.

Grammar has an essential role to play in any scheme of language teaching. The question to be resolved is the nature and place of that role. It is common in secondary school language work to bring to the classroom grammatical notions and vocabulary. As a result one of the commonest complaints of language teachers is that students do not know the grammar of their own tongue properly before beginning the study of a second. It is not too much to say that it is unlikely that the criticism will ever be answered, since 'grammar' for the native speaker is a very different matter from grammar for the foreigner in any tongue. The aim of the one is the correction of common errors in the native speaker and the aim of the other is the diametrically opposed one of the analysis of the basic mechanism of the language—a mechanism which the native born speaker has at his command on arrival at school.

The role played by grammar in the Australian scheme was confined to its exhaustive study prior to the compilation of the syllabus and the application of these findings in the syllabus. English grammar was studied with Jespersen, Palmer, de Saussure, Sturtevart, Bodmer, Curme, Nesfield, Fowler and a host of others. Grammar largely dictated the logical ordering of the syllabus, provided much of the material on which structures were grouped and was a touchstone for final reference. But grammar and its terminology were banished from the classroom. There is no point in telling Ukrainian peasants that *the* and *a* were 'articles' when the entire concept of the 'article' is missing from their own tongue. In the methods recommended to the teacher of migrants in Australia the basic tenet is that the creation of language habits is the aim—not linguistic analysis. Analysis can only have a legitimate place in the few classes composed of persons with higher education and considerable linguistic experience. The need was felt for a syllabus aimed at the structural difficulties of students, with which could be linked as closely as possible the immediate social and vocational needs of students.

Considerable difficulty has been experienced in reconciling several apparently irreconcilable and contradictory tendencies into a syllabus graded on purely structural lines. There was the demand on the one hand for speech formulas to fit social and vocational needs of the students (indeed, class attendance depended to a great extent on its supply); on the other hand there was the need for a form of instruction which would introduce the linguistically ungifted by gradual and well-graded steps to the new language. There was the classroom difficulty of having students of extremely varying degrees of linguistic ability, and the quite different difficulty, in well-graded classes, presented by students of a variety of nationalities whose native languages were structurally very diverse and whose difficulties in English had to be approached from widely differing points of view. Those students whose languages differed most markedly from English were the Slavonic group who required instruction and concentrated drills on many structural points that could be quickly absorbed by other groups, e.g. German, Italian and Dutch.

Part I of a recommended syllabus was produced and published in 1951 by the Commonwealth Office of Education for the guidance of instructors and teachers of English to new Australians. Parts II and III followed in 1952.[1] These syllabuses were the concerted effort of experienced instructors and combined the order and methods they had employed and found successful in the classroom. They presupposed the practice of 'situational' teaching, i.e. the presentation of structures to be taught in a situation with concrete illustrations, followed by drill situations in which persons and objects mentioned were actually present and in which the students responded in speech to the situation in front of them.

The syllabuses also assumed that the teacher could not or preferred not to make use of the students' languages and give explanations of usage. Therefore the situation had to be self-explanatory, and

---

1. These have now been revised and incorporated in one special issue of *English, a New Language*, vol. 4, no. 1 (September 1953), Sydney, Office of Education.

while each one dealt with a grammatical structure, the rule involved was not to be presented as such but was to be made self-evident and to be practised by the students until its use became habitual. It is obvious that the progression from structure to structure must follow a logical development with regard to difficulty and to the relation of structures as well as to frequency of usage; the question of suitability for situational teaching had also to be considered.

As an example, the patterns *I can go, I must go, I will go,* follow the same structural form in English. The first two (with *can* and *must*) have the same form in other languages, whereas the third (the future tense) is different except in German and Dutch. Therefore, in the syllabus, *can* was taught first (on the score of frequency and immediate need), *must* next, and then the future form. Again, for two different reasons, the present continuous tense was taught before the present of habit. Firstly, in a situation moving before the students' eyes, the present continuous form (*I am going,* etc.) was the correct one to use, secondly it followed logically from the first few units of the syllabus, in which the present tense of the verb *to be* had been taught. The verb *to have* was taught at a fairly wide interval after the verb *to be,* because it had been found that Slavonic students confused *to be* and *to have* on account of their lack in the Slav languages.

Since at this stage the greatest number of students were women who were being accomodated in camps while awaiting homes with their husbands, this syllabus made use of a vocabulary that was considered essential for women. At the same time the grammatical progression was fixed for any type of student—male or female. It was only necessary to change the vocabulary and the suggested situations to suit the syllabus to any group of people. For example, the feminine situation illustrated by the formula: *there's a sheet on the bed,* could quite easily be changed to a masculine one illustrated by: *there's a hammer on the bench.*

In its final form the syllabus was divided into three columns. Column A was concerned with the strict logical progression of grammatical structures from which there was to be no departure. Column B contained social formulas that departed in some respects from the order of Column A but was linked as closely as possible. It also contained some grammatical structures that were so necessary in intercourse in the community that they were incorporated—but only in their simplest form—in this column. Teachers were expected to drill them more intensively in connexion with Column A at a later stage. Column C contained suggestions for combining previously learned structures in revisionary drills.

The elementary syllabus in a tentative form was sent out for a trial period to experienced instructors, whose comments were incorporated in the published version. Part I—the elementary syllabus—stopped at a point where it was felt that students would have a fairly adequate speech mechanism to cope with normal situations.

In Parts II and III most of the common structures of the English language were dealt with. They were graded from the point of view of logical progression and of difficulty. The principle of frequency of usage compelled to some extent a delay in introducing certain comparatively simple structures. It must be admitted too that there was a little criticism of the delay in introducing some more difficult structures which teachers felt to be essential to their students' needs. Parts II and III continued the Column A of Part I, but here the resemblance ended. Columns B and C were replaced by Columns D, E and F. Column D was concerned with oral and written composition. It consisted of suggestions for the treatment of semantic varieties of verbs and prepositions, and for practice in word order and the use of tenses and various common collocations.

Column E contained forms of English for social use and suggested various common formulas to fit common situations. Column F consisted of word mechanisms, i.e. examples of word formations that are typically English and which might help the student in his manipulation of the vocabulary of the language, e.g. the formation of various types of compound nouns or of adjectives. These were not intended to be taught as word lists, but were given as suggestions for development in oral expression fitting the interests of students.

It was found impracticable to fix the order of the units in Columns D, E and F, though, as far as possible, they were linked with the structural units of Column A, but the teacher was advised to select those units which best fitted the needs of his class.

While the elementary syllabus dealt mainly with the spoken language, Parts II and III linked the spoken with the literary and written languages. It was felt that this syllabus taken as a whole showed a distinct advance especially in the gradual introduction of forms that were likely to prove stumbling blocks to students, e.g. the articles and the tenses.

The constant demand for a textbook was answered in July 1948 by the appearance of the first edition of *English for Newcomers to Australia*, and in January 1951 the second edition. The latter was a much enlarged version of the first and included presentation of structures, exercises, substitution tables, verb series, pronunciation drills and reading material. The introduction of structures was somewhat hasty in many cases, the vocabulary largely uncontrolled and in the more advanced section there was an overuse of grammatical terminology, but it had attractions for the student, especially the student conditioned to a 'reading' approach to a foreign tongue.

In 1952 appeared the third edition, which was based on the three syllabuses. It consisted of a student's book and a teacher's book, the latter including tried suggestions for the presentation of the units in situation and for drilling the structures.

The order and speed of introduction of many units was somewhat different from that of the syllabus, as the composition of classes was rapidly changing, the preponderance of Slavonic students having given way to German, Italian and Dutch. However, the needs of the former as well as those of some other groups, e.g. Lebanese, were not neglected.

The form of the textbook shows considerable compression, as space and expense were a consideration. There were no illustrations, which, in any case, are hardly necessary in 'situational' teaching, but exercises were fairly profuse—this in answer to the problem of the teacher who might be faced with two or even three groups at different standards of attainment. Though the textbook was not aimed at the student who had already attained considerable proficiency in English, it was found by most teachers that even the elementary stages provided him with acceptable remedial drills for the errors of advanced students.

Having arrived at the point where it is decided that translation will not be employed, that the sentence will be the unit of instruction and that new words will be introduced in sentences, how is the material to be taught in the classroom? First it will have to be *presented* and secondly it will have to be *drilled*.

Presentation is the part of teaching where the student role is listening and watching. The teacher is active—and describes his activity in English. It is essential that presentation should be clear, unhurried, and carefully controlled. The situation should be decided in advance and some thought given to the gestures and objects to be used by the teacher to present with conviction and clarity. The teacher may repeat his action and his words two or three times at quickening speeds, he may write the formula on the blackboard and the class may then repeat the sentence also.

With a slow class a second presentation with different objects may be advisable. Suppose, for example, it is desired to teach *between*, known objects are taken and the presentation might be: *The plate is between the knife and the fork* the objects being clearly visible to all and the teacher indicates them as he mentions them or if the class were men—more interested in tools than in knives and forks—the presentation might be: *The hammer is between the chisel and the saw.* It is the structural word which is being taught not the names of the objects—they can be changed at will always provided they are known, for new content words must not be introduced until the structure is quite familiar.

As any reader of Palmer's works knows, substitution is regarded as the best basis for fluency exercises and substitution was recommended and used as the second stage in the teaching process of each semantic unit. It is not too much to say that a language teacher who neglects substitution as a classroom exercise is depriving himself of his most powerful weapon if the teaching is based on sentence patterns for the pattern remains a single instance unless it is 'universalized'. (It must be said, to the credit of the old 'grammatical' approach, that this quality of universality was one of its real advantages.) That is to say, if a sentence pattern such as *There is a cup on the table*, was to be taught, substitution of *cup* by, say, *plate, knife, fork, hammer, chisel, peg, box of matches* should be practised and it was found that, if the teacher procured the actual objects, very rapid and effective drills could be done in chorus by the class in response to the manipulation of the objects by the teacher. It is important to realize that the class repeats the whole sentence, not merely the new word. The particular value of substitution as a teaching device lies in the fact that the framework of the sentence is unaltered. This throws the repetitive mechanism in the correct place—on to the structure of the sentence. While the content 'words' are being changed the framework received the amount of repetition which it needs and deserves, for it is the framework and *not* the 'content' word which is being taught.

In order to give the student the maximum practice in the structure of his new language and in order to give practice in rhythm and intonation, the concept of the 'drill situation' became the one which finally dominated the last stage of teaching process recommended for new Australians. This means in practice that repetition from material written on a blackboard is replaced by repetition in response to a rapidly changing situation controlled by the teacher. It was found possible to produce a drill situation to fit any structure, elementary, intermediate, or advanced, and the principles governing the selection of the situation were that the objects used should be easily procurable and easily manipulated, and that the situation could be so organized that the student could do a great portion of all the speech done in class, either in chorus or individually—the teacher's role being reduced to organizing the situation and controlling student reaction by gesture or movement of some kind rather than by the interrogative form of question-answer technique.

An advantage which has proved in practice to be a valuable

quality of good drill situations is the speed with which revision can be done. Drills should be varied when revised, i.e. the structure should be constant while the meaning is new, otherwise the structure taught may remain too closely tied in the student's mind with the presentation in the teaching situation which he first saw and repeated—that is to say, a student might legitimately and regularly use a structure like *there's a cup on the table, there's a fork on the table, there's a plate on the table*, and not realize that he could use basically the same structure in *there's a man at the door, there's someone on the air*.

English has a stress and intonation peculiar to itself as have, of course, most of the languages of the globe, but English is peculiar in that stress and intonation probably play more part in the comprehension than in most languages. In most languages the weakening of the unstressed syllables does not seem to be as marked as in English. The ə sound to which all but a few vowels are reduced in English when unstressed constitutes so characteristic a feature of the language that misconception and misunderstanding can occur when the rhythm and the weakening of this sound are not incorporated in the speech of the student. Nor do many languages have the same degree of stress on the main syllables as English. Briefly, it would be true to say that in English we emphasize more but we also weaken more than in most other tongues. This quality of English is very rarely appreciated when the student is dealing with isolated words, but when the sentence is the unit of teaching and care is taken with the rhythmic pattern of that sentence, then the rhythm becomes familiar to the student from the first and considerable time can be saved in the acquisition of fluency. Rhythm can become an ally of the teacher and a very powerful one, for it is a very much more primitive matter than some of the other qualities of languages which may have to be learned through the intellect. A strong argument for the teaching of English in sentence patterns is the emphasis which rhythm acquires in this type of teaching.

Attention to rhythmic speech has been found a valuable aid in classes of disparate standards. Generally the more advanced students have learned English in Europe or from reading or have picked it up in the community and, while their command of the language may be fairly adequate for practical purposes, they have acquired so many defects of speech that they are very willing to join in chorus drills with the elementary students in an effort to remedy faults of pronunciation, rhythm and intonation. Many of them, indeed, are forcibly struck by the discovery of the differences between their own language and English and the fact that the transference of old speech habits to the new language has been the cause of most of their speech peculiarities.

It might be possible in a course aimed solely at the ability to read in English to exclude altogether considerations of intonation. However, intonation plays a very great part in meaning in spoken English and is often indicative of the speaker's state of mind and, as our students have to deal immediately with Australians both in social and official situations, it was necessary not to overlook the social implications behind our melody of speech. So few speakers are aware of the actual mechanics of intonation they habitually employ, and so little exact information about it is available in a popular form that would appeal to teachers whose special interests are not linguistic, that this aspect of English has not been as adequately treated as it might be. It is accepted, however, that the teacher's intonation should be controlled to the same extent as the grammatical structures he uses, that the intonation patterns practised should be limited to those most frequently used and to those whose implications are the most neutral, and that the simplest forms should be drilled before variations and complexities—especially those of an emotional nature—are introduced. In teaching with substitution on a structural pattern, students are given considerable practice in intonation when the same tone is adhered to in every sentence of the substitution table. Teachers who have attended schools conducted for teachers of new Australians have been given simplified information on this subject and the textbook, *English for Newcomers to Australia*, gives advice about the patterns to employ in the classroom.

Pronunciation—so seriously regarded by foreign learners of a language—has always received the attention it deserves. For the reception centres charts were prepared containing lists of words to drill specific vowel sounds and teachers were urged to give concentrated drills on those sounds which gave difficulty, particularly those which did not occur in the learner's own language and those which he confused in speaking, e.g. the consonants θ, f and final $\textit{ʒ}$; the vowels i and I, $æ$ and e.

In the third edition of the textbook, pronunciation drills were based on knowledge of the sound systems of the major linguistic groups to be found in classes, and lists were arranged to draw the teacher's attention to errors due to differences between the languages, e.g. sounds which were peculiar to English, or which were used in different positions in words or in different groupings from those of the student's language or in which spelling was likely to mislead. Drills were, in short, to be aimed at perfecting those sounds which students generally confused in speech, with a consequent confusion of meaning. All advice to teachers with regard to the actual mechanics of speech has been based on a comparison of languages and the prime needs of students to understand and to make themselves easily understood.

Although the teaching of the English language was the major aim in the Australian experiment with our newcomers, a subsidiary but important activity was the teaching of background material and the provision of general information on Australia. It was found necessary, owing to the difficulties of the partly known language, to concentrate on the practical aspects of everyday life first (such matters as postage, coinage, clothing, food prices could be dealt with on a very restricted vocabulary provided always that the concrete materials were actually present). It was even possible in the first week at a reception centre with an elementary class to deal simply with certain Australian resources —metals lent themselves to adequate treatment with samples of ore or metal and a large-scale map. Even figures of output can be included in this type of instruction.

Posters were prepared, and sent to all teachers, about the everyday matters of Australian life—the beach, food, banks, police, fauna and flora, tools, etc. and the posters could be used several times with sentence structures of varying difficulty. For example, a picture of a platypus in a very elementary class could be used for this type of talk:

'This is a platypus. This is a picture of a platypus. This is the head of the platypus and that is the tail. These are the four feet of the platypus. This is the tail of the platypus. The platypus has a head, a body and a tail. It has two eyes; it has four feet and it has a coat—a fine coat.' A few days later it might be possible to deal with the same picture somewhat in the following manner:

'There's a platypus in the water. It's swimming. It's looking for food. That's its nest in the bank of the river. The coat of the platypus is soft and valuable. You must not kill platypuses. They are not dangerous. They cannot bite you, they cannot fly, they can walk and they can swim. They like swimming better than walking.'

Later again, when the present of habit is taught, the same picture could be used for more advanced talks:

'This is a platypus. It's an Australian animal. It's a funny animal. It has a beak like a duck, it swims like a fish, it lays eggs like a hen and it eats worms, tadpoles, and shrimps. It lives in the banks of streams right from Queensland to South Australia. It is a mammal. You mustn't kill platypuses.'

Thus information could be linked with sentence structure in the teaching points of language which had been covered. These talks are usually short but if the control is good, the teaching is a rewarding experience as students appreciate the fact that they are getting information in English after a few days' instruction.

As instruction progressed, the major industries of Australia could be covered. Posters were produced to cover the wool, metal, steel, gold industries and in such a way as to be readily linked with common sentence structures. When the past tense was taught, the historical background of Australia could be covered. It was found that the approach most appreciated by newcomers was that which showed historical forces making the Australian character today. A syllabus of suggested topics of proved interest to newcomers was prepared and circulated amongst teachers in Reception Centres and, in May 1952, a Bulletin was issued by the Commonwealth Office of Education for teachers of English classes.

The main form migrant education activity takes at the present time (March 1953)[1] is the evening continuation class. Staffed by State school teachers administered by the States meeting in schoolrooms up and down the length and breadth of Australia, nearly seventeen thousand students meet to learn English in 1,250 classes—the student-teacher ratio is about 14 : 1 which appears quite reasonable for language classes. These lessons are provided free of charge to the newcomer and a very sincere effort is made by most teachers to do the best they can for their evening students. The numbers of students attending is on the increase and the teacher in many localities is acting as a link between the newcomer and the community in which he finds himself. The methodological problem, however, is by no means simple, for small isolated classes usually contain students of very different standards of achievement in English.

In order to provide some guidance to the teacher of evening continuation classes, who as a rule is a primary teacher with no special training in language teaching, a bi-monthly bulletin *English... A New Language* is published by the Commonwealth Office of Education and distributed to all teachers of classes of new Australians. In addition two or three-day vacation seminars are yearly organized in all States to give teachers an opportunity to see demonstrations, to discuss their common problems and to provide an opportunity to view English as a foreign language.[2] Experience has shown that the teacher who has for years taught 'English' as a subject to the native born speaker of the language has to revise his classroom technique completely in order to teach the language effectively to foreigners.

In the preparation of material for teaching English by radio, vigorous limitations have been imposed on vocabulary, since every

---

1. According to information published in December 1953, there were at that time 1,263 continuation classes with a total enrolment of 14,924.
2. A more recent development is the provision of regional schools of one evening's duration.

word used must be taught clearly by sound effect, or given accurate meaning through the situation. Although a booklet is produced each month to accompany the broadcasts,[1] it is felt that they must be self-sufficient, without recourse to a visual aid. The aim of the elementary course has therefore been to incorporate a minimum of words into a maximum number of sentence patterns. In general the structural approach described above has been used in all the media of instruction. The sentence remains the unit of instruction, and substitution of the noun is the common form of teaching both in the elementary and in the advanced sessions. It proved impossible to use translation as practised by the BBC, for the simple reason that too many languages were involved, but the almost insuperable task of teaching English by radio without translation has been attempted with considerable success.

The choice of situation has been the all important element in the radio teaching since upon that depended the comprehension and absorption of both the structure to be taught and a proportion of the vocabulary. Since the structures cannot, in the early lessons at any rate, be either translated or explained, their meaning and use must be self-evident—a natural and clear-cut element of the situation as it is presented or evolved. Hence the choice of a domestic setting for all the situations, as the normal life of the home, mails, telephone calls, gardening, odd jobs, shopping, etc. may be regarded as the highest common factor in the experience of all Western nationalities. Over and above this, a further service has been demanded of the situations and has influenced their handling. The programmes are addressed to foreign language speakers within an English-speaking community. The situations have therefore been used to define and illuminate the Australian version of the westernized domestic scene.

The particular audience addressed has influenced the type of session in one further respect. Our sessions are aimed at a large and extraordinarily varied group of people, including the educated and the uneducated, the technician, the professional and the labourer ... but almost certainly containing only a very small percentage of people who would under anything but the overwhelming force of circumstances have become language students. Considerable effort therefore has been expended to make the sessions as lively and attractive and as easy to listen to as possible, and to treat the language difficulties of the foreigner with tact and humour. The presence of a foreigner—Paul—on the programme,

---

1. According to the latest information, three lessons are broadcast each week, elementary, intermediate and advanced; the elementary course lasts for 52 weeks, divided into two sessions of six months' duration each, broadcast concurrently. The booklet now has a circulation of 18,000.

in spite of the very obvious disadvantage of giving an imperfect example to the listener, is due to the non-translatory character of the sessions. The making and correcting of an error is the simplest method of demonstrating certain difficulties of the language.

Of special value is the opportunity given for audience participation in the section called 'Say It With Paul', when the listeners have the satisfaction of identifying themselves with Paul by practising the structures and substitution tables with the new Australian performer as he repeats the required words and sentences after one of the Australian performers.

The advanced Sunday programme is treated in a very similar manner to the elementary sessions but is based on a wider range of structures and vocabulary, and a correspondingly wider choice of characterizations and Australian scenes.

A correspondence course, prepared by the Commonwealth Office of Education, of 24 lessons is sent to any new Australian who desires to learn English and is unable to attend evening classes. In December 1952, 10,029 students were 'actively on course' and 143 tutors were engaged on the correction of papers and guiding of their students. The course follows the methodological ideas common to all aspects of our teaching—there is rigid vocabulary control with a vocational and social bias, sentence patterns incorporate the structural words, and no translation is employed. The course is adjusted to its medium in that it is copiously and carefully illustrated.

The difficulty of conveying English pronunciation by the written word has so far proved insuperable. The student is expected to get the help of a workmate or acquaintance to overcome this obstacle. The radio lessons provide some help also.

At first sight the close co-ordination of radio and correspondence might appear both desirable and possible. In fact, however, the correspondence course did not lend itself to radio treatment and the radio course in turn proved unsuited to explanation on paper. The difficulty lay not in any gross divergence on the sentence patterns chosen and taught but in the selection of the *content* words in the sentence—in the radio course, for example, *the bell of the bicycle* may be chosen because the sound will supply the meaning, while in the correspondence course the sentence chosen might well be 'The handle of the cup is broken' as it lends itself more easily to illustration. It may be possible to co-ordinate more closely the correspondence with the radio course. Up to the present, this has not been attempted, but the point will be borne in mind as the correspondence and radio courses are being revised.

How much of the methods in teaching English developed and adjusted to suit migrant education in Australia have relevance to the more usual conditions elsewhere under which languages are usually taught? It would seem that some policies and factors affecting the choice of the linguistic material have no relevance at all. The use of vocabulary of value at daily work would be obviously unsound in secondary school language teaching to children. The tendency to develop drill situations which can be used with large numbers of students has also little general value, because only the strong motivation of the adult new Australian permits the successful employment of this technique without a disciplinary problem. A great deal of linguistic material of social value incorporated very early in a syllabus written for persons in an English-speaking environment, could be regarded and incorporated in the structural syllabus instead of doing violence to the logical progression of sentence structure as is now the case. These are obvious changes which would have to be made, as they are local adjustments to linguistic material to suit a local situation. On the other hand, can the methods be modified, can the situations chosen for use with schoolchildren make use of a more intrinsically interesting vocabulary, and can they be explored in a more leisurely manner? As the time factor is not vital, the subject chosen need not be so closely linked with the practical or material aims of making a living or of forming social contacts. Is there time to make the link between the oral and literary aims without departing at all from the oral approach?

The main question would appear to revolve around the oral aim and the overwhelming emphasis given to oral work in the early stages in Australia. This could be a matter for discussion and opinion but it is significant that no linguist of repute recommends any other course than a sound oral command of a foreign language to precede the literate skills. It is doubtful, however, whether language teachers are in complete agreement with the linguists on this matter and it would seem that, in secondary teaching of language, the written form and skills relating to it receive a prominence probably more than their due.

In language teaching insufficient attention has been given to the teaching of intonation. This is absolutely necessary in an environment where the language being learned is generally spoken, but many teachers debate its importance for children who may never leave their own country. To be convinced that it is possible —though only by means of concentrated study and specifically directed drills—one need only study the works of Jones, Palmer, Osborne and Ward, and Klienghardt and others, or observe the improvement brought about in the speech of foreigners who have undergone a practical course of graded and directed material. It is probable that increased knowledge of the subject both with regard to their own language and to others may give it greater importance in the eyes of teachers.

Furthermore it would seem that the change in emphasis from the 'content' word to the 'structural' word, from the isolated word to the sentence pattern, is now generally accepted by advanced teachers and spells the end of vocabulary lists in class teaching, of the purely grammatical approach and finally, by implication, of translation itself, especially in the elementary stages, as a major classroom technique.

There are also other points which have emerged only too clearly from the experiences in Australia—the paramount necessity for the preliminary organization of the linguistic material before teaching begins, *for the compative analysis of structures of the language to be taught and the native language of the student*, and the bending of methods to fit the needs of the student.[1] Consideration of method can most profitably begin when aims and administrative framework have been fixed.

CANADA[2]

It must be remembered that Canada is today still a mosaic of several races, languages and nationalities. History has brought it many diversified waves of immigration, from the very ancient Amerindian stocks to the displaced persons of 1946-53. Peoples of every continent have flowed in across our borders. When the *Winnipeg Free Press* wishes a 'happy new year' to its readers, it does so in 67 languages. How can so heterogeneous a mass learn to become a unified nation?

The answer of the United States of America to a comparable problem has been a unilingual and highly patriotic system of education. The Canadian solution has been more complex. There were as many Canadians, per capita, in 1939, who had their roots only recently torn from European soil, as there were Americans in the same category. The older native-born occidental stock, however, was not of one linguistic tradition, but of two. In 1941 the Federal census showed 5,715,904 persons or 49.7 per cent of the population of British origin (two parts English to one each of Scotch and Irish) and 3,483,038 persons or 30.3 per cent of French origin. The latter have been in Canada for upwards of

---

1. To meet this need, a series of comparative studies of English and certain European languages has been undertaken. The first of these, dealing with the likely difficulties of Italian students, appeared in January 1953.
2. This section is condensed from the working-paper 'Canada's Language problem in Education', prepared for the Ceylon seminar by Dr. Watson Kirkconnell, President of Acadia University, Wolfville, Nova Scotia.

twelve generations and are largely the descendants of a few thousand French colonists who settled here three-and-a-half centuries ago and have multiplied without the help of further immigration. They have naturally tended to regard themselves as the original and authentic Canadians. From such roots has been nourished a distinctly French-Canadian culture, far more humanistic and less secular in spirit then the France from which it was severed by war two centuries ago. Needless to say, it differs greatly from the largely Protestant Anglo-Canadian tradition, whose foundations were laid by loyalist refugees from the American Revolution of 1775–83 and built upon by millions of immigrants from the British Isles in the nineteenth and twentieth centuries. In the nineteenth century these newcomers were chiefly Scotch and Irish; since 1900 British immigration has been predominantly English. Because of the peaceful interpenetration of American influences by press, radio, cinema and television, this part of the Canadian population has taken on many of the traits of its American neighbours.

The point to be emphasized is that Canadian culture is basically bi-focal, with very sharp differences between the Anglo-Canadian and the French-Canadian traditions. The difference is not ethnological. A French-Canadian of Norman origin may be physically closer to the common Nordic type of East England than a dark-haired Welsh-Canadian, a dark Scotch-Canadian from Argyllshire, or an Irish-Canadian from Donegal. The cleavage between French-Canadian and Anglo-Canadian is a cultural difference largely compounded of language, religion and community experience.

It is this fundamental duality of Canadian life that has given its people a philosophy of life quite different from that of the United States of America. For a time, it must be admitted, there was a desire on the part of the Anglo-Saxons to crush out of existence the language and traditions of the conquered French. The famous *Report* of Lord Durham, following the insurrection of 1837, was explicit in recommending assimilation. Another thirty years made it clear, however, that that policy was a mistaken one; and the British North America Act of 1867 guaranteed autonomy in language and education to both national elements in perpetuity. André Siegfried may have characterized the modern resultant as 'mutual toleration without cordiality'; but at least the dual character of the nation has been conceded by both sides as a fact of Canadian life. Apart from this basic bicultural problem, the chief linguistic and cultural issue in Canada affects the 'new Canadians'.

The integration into our national life of over 2 million Canadians of non-British, non-French, overseas extraction has been a larger but by no means intractable issue. The major groups of these, in order of magnitude, are the Germans, Ukrainians, Jews, Poles, Netherlanders, Italians, Norwegians, Swedes, Russians, Magyars, Danes, Slovaks, Icelanders, Croatians, Finns, Serbs, Lithuanians, Greeks and Bulgarians. The majority of these are now Canadian-born, the descendants of the first wave of European immigration in the 1901-14 period. A second wave followed in 1919-29 and a third since 1946; but neither of these was comparable in size to the first.

It is a mistake to assume that Canada has adopted a mere Balkanization of its population by permitting each of these linguistic groups to be educated in Canadian schools in its own tongue. All Canadian schools must be conducted in either English or French, and in grades above a certain level the second national language is normally introduced into the curriculum. No other tongue is recognized by the State as the language of instruction; and even 'block settlements' are gradually permeated by the assimilative powers of the national school system in one of the two national languages.

The chief difference from the United States of America lies in the hospitality of the national consciousness to ancestral cultural activities as a secondary phase of communal life. 'Canadianization' is regarded as a natural and more or less inevitable process, but the preservation of an affectionate pride in one's ancestral traditions is not regarded as inimical to that major evolution of a national life. On the contrary, there is a growing sense that a man is a better Canadian if he can reinforce his Canadianism with the culture resources of an ancestral (non-English and non-French) culture.

In this the trail had already been blazed by the Highland Scotch in Nova Scotia. Here at St. Ann, on Cape Breton Island, is a Gaelic college, where large numbers register each summer for courses in Gaelic language and literature, bag-pipe playing and Highland dancing. All year round courses in handicrafts turn out vast quantities of tartan cloth in the authentic clan sets, from the sale of which the college is largely sustained. Every August sees a three-day Highland 'Mod' or rally of the clans, with competitions in dancing, piping and Highland sports. Each year, one clan is chosen for special honour and the titular head of that clan in Scotland is invited as a special guest. The Premier of Nova Scotia, the Hon. August L. Macdonald, will commonly welcome the distinguished visitor in eloquent Gaelic. Yet all of these Nova Scotians are likewise fervent Canadians.

An exact parallel is to be found among the Canadian Icelanders, who settled in 1875–85 in a tract called 'New Iceland' on the wide shores of Lake Winnipeg and are now completely integrated into Canadian life. A Jon Bjarnason Academy in Winnipeg still gives instruction in Icelandic at the secondary school level and a fund of $200,000, collected by the Canadian Icelanders among themselves, has been used to endow a chair of Icelandic literature in the University of Manitoba, in conjunction with one of the best Icelandic libraries in the world. Each year a special festival is held at Cimli on 2 August, on the west shore of Lake Winnipeg, and there are competitions in Icelandic sports and the reading of new original Icelandic poems written for the occasion. The climax of the day is the crowning of some Icelandic-Canadian maid or matron as *Fjallkona* or 'Maid of the Mountain'.

Comparable activities may be found in many other nationality groups, such as the Ukrainians and the Greeks.

Special significance attaches, however, to group activities into which the general public—chiefly Anglo-Canadian—enters with interest and enthusiasm. Such are the handicraft and folk music festivals, to which the late John Murray Gibbon gave so much organizing ability and financial support. The Winnipeg public took the lead in choir festivals and folk dancing festivals, in which nationality groups in costume took part with grace and effectiveness. The Polish community, first in Winnipeg and later in Toronto as well, has inaugurated an annual spring-time ball, 'Wiosna w pelsos', at one of the big hotels, at which lieutenant-governors and judges are proud to be present, and at which Polish national dances in glittering costume constitute the 'floor show'. In the normal schools and public schools of western Canada, an attempt is made on special occasions to give the children of each national origin a ground for self-respect and for the respect of their fellows by giving each group, through pageantry or ritual, a chance to proclaim the worth and dignity of its contribution to civilization. The University of Toronto Press publishes annually a biographical and critical survey of all books published the previous year in Canada not only in English and French but in all the other languages as well. It is in keeping with this attitude that the Canadian census, unlike the American, carefully records the racial origin of every man, woman and child in the country. There is no attempt to cut away the roots of the past. On the contrary, we try to engraft a Canadian loyalty on each old stock, on the theory that both graft and stock will have more vigorous life in consequence.

An interesting interlude may be noted in the prairie regions in the early years of the twentieth century. The influx of European immigrants had been so heavy that for a time the ministers of education felt that the supply of trained teachers in the English tradition was quite inadequate, and so, for nearly two decades, permission was given to teach the work of the elementary grades in the language of the majority (German, Ukrainian, etc.) in any prairie community. Once the onset of World War I had cut off the heavy stream of uneducated immigrant children, the provincial departments of education promptly terminated the use of languages other than English for instructional purposes in the lower grades. For nearly forty years English has been the greatest single factor making for the unification of the polyglot settlements of the west.

One survival of the earlier chapter lies in the place occupied by some modern languages in our high school and university system. Icelandic, for example, was early recognized as a valid foreign language in the high schools of Manitoba and is still accepted for matriculation at the University of Manitoba. In that same university, the Ukrainian language is the active concern of a two-man department and this largest of our Slavic communities also takes pride in the work done by similar professors in Saskatoon, Vancouver and Toronto.

As has already been noted, virtually all secondary schools in Canada have at least one foreign language on the curriculum. For university matriculation in many provinces, Latin and one modern language will normally be required; but in such a province as Manitoba the requirement is simply one foreign language, ancient or modern, and Latin is very frequently the language chosen. The general fact of Canada's broad bilingual background has tended, however, to make French the first foreign language in an Anglo-Canadian school and English the first foreign language in a French-Canadian school. In fact, one may correctly object that neither French nor English is, properly speaking, a 'foreign language' in this country at all. Both are national languages.

The French-Canadian, thinking in terms of economic advantage on a continent overwhelmingly Anglo-Saxon on the industrial side, takes the study of English more seriously than his Anglo-Canadian fellow citizen does the study of French. Thus in the French schools of Quebec, the study of English commonly begins in Grade V. In the English schools of the other provinces, however, the study of French hardly ever begins before Grade VII and frequently not until Grade IX. The result of this different emphasis comes out in the decennial census of the Federal Government. While 50 per cent of the French-Canadian population is reported as effectively bilingual, only five per cent of the Anglo-Canadian population is so reported.

CHAPTER XII
SPECIAL PROBLEMS OF LANGUAGE

This final chapter presents a number of short papers dealing with special modern language teaching 'situations' encountered in different parts of the world. Ceylon has the problem of expanding the use of Sinhalese and Tamil as languages of instruction and of integrating both with English, which has been described by a citizen of that country as 'not a foreign language but a foster language'. Further north, but in the same continent, Pakistan, with its Urdu-speaking western half and Bengali-speaking eastern half, seeks to modernize and expand the teaching of Arabic which is its direct link with the Islamic world. The Mexican experiment of teaching Spanish to monolingual native Indians *through* the vernacular has been selected because the Mexican problem is in many ways typical of a situation that prevails in a number of Latin-American countries. Finally, an excursion has been made into Africa which is the cradle of a whole host of language teaching problems of the future. The Trust Territory of Somaliland provides the pattern of a country with a widespread spoken vernacular just emerging into the status of a written language, and which nevertheless carries on its education in two foreign world languages, one of the West and the other of the East.

As an introduction to these studies, the editors have reprinted 'The Jigsaw Pattern of the World's Languages', an article written by Dr. Felix Walter, the Unesco Representative at the Ceylon seminar, for the special language number of *Unesco Courier*.[1]

THE JIGSAW PATTERN OF THE WORLD'S LANGUAGES

We live in a world that seems to be becoming increasingly aware of the problems of language. That is probably because our generation bumps its nose against the barrier of language more often and more violently than our ancestors did. How could it be otherwise in an age that has made travel so swift and devised ways of communication that are almost instantaneous?

---
1. January 1954.

But it is all very provoking to the human ego. We can devise atom bombs to wipe out half the world or jet planes to girdle it, but, so far as the tangle of language is concerned, we are still in the era of the Tower of Babel. Actually the situation is much worse than that: we have slipped back and are continuing to slip back. Linguists say that there are approximately 3,000 languages spoken in the world to-day, and they don't pretend they have finished counting.

What really aggravates the situation is not that many completely different tongues are spoken by groups of a few thousand, or even a few hundred, in the interior of New Guinea, or in the jungles of Amazonia or in the heart of Africa. What counts far more is that the thrust and drive of new nationalisms are constantly setting up new national languages with full official status. There is nothing iniquitous about this; a distinctive language is a very natural though not an essential attribute of sovereignty, and it is clearly silly and a waste of time to scold the Irish, for instance, for reviving their ancient tongue or the Indonesians for adopting Bahasa in preference to a European language of wide diffusion.

It is no wonder, though, that there is an increasing desire to solve what is a world problem, once and for all, by radical means. One drawback is that the reformers offer so many different paneceas. Some advocate that we should all learn one of the languages already widely spoken in many parts of the world. Unfortunately the identity of language X nearly always depends on the nationality of the advocate. The British and the Americans naturally see great inherent advantages in English.

French-speaking people are persuaded that French has certain intrinsic merits which give their language a prior claim. Speakers of Arabic or Chinese or Russian or Spanish can think up equally good arguments without any difficulty at all.

If the choice is to be one of the so-called artificial languages, then which one? Is it to be Esperanto, which has the advantage of an undoubted head start over the rivals, or one of the rivals themselves with claims to being even more scientific and even more simplified?

The ultimate solution may well lie in one of these suggestions, or it may be of a different nature altogether, but if the solution is to be effective, it must be adopted on a world-wide basis and arrived at by general consent. That will be extraordinarily difficult, and will depend in the long run on the decisions arrived at by governments and by the peoples on whom governments depend. That suggests that a first and very necessary step in the solution of the world problem of the diversity of languages is for people everywhere to try to understand the extent and nature of that problem. Only then can they properly come to grips with it.

It is a convenience to linguists to group languages into 'families' but this should not lead ordinary people astray. Thus the English-speaking person who imagines it should be easy to learn Dutch or Danish, because they also are 'Germanic 'languages, may be disappointed. Languages, like members of human families, have a habit of drifting away from one another.

It is this instable or dynamic characteristic of languages, coupled with the fact that languages are often the playthings of political and economic forces, which now favour and now retard their expansion, that makes a language map and the general language situation so changeable. The picture today is not at all what it was even a generation ago. A generation hence it will probably be quite different again. To grasp this fact one has only to survey the continents briefly one by one.

Europe makes a good starting-point for such a survey, because in Europe the number of official national languages has just about doubled in the space of a generation. This is due to a number of causes. When the Russian and Austro-Hungarian empires collapsed as a result of the first world war they were succeeded by a number of smaller sovereign units or by new regimes that took a more liberal view of the aspirations of linguistic minorities. Languages like Slovene, Slovak, Czech, Lithuanian, Lettish, Estonian, White Russian and Ukrainian ceased being just picturesque survivals, achieved full national or regional status, became official languages of instruction in the schools.

In Western Europe, not all at once, but certainly since the second world war, there has also developed an increasingly liberal attitude towards the languages of minority groups. People who now want to talk Frisian or Breton or Basque, and to have their children learn these languages, are not in most countries any longer looked on as anti-national agitators. Governments now go out of their way to give such language groups an equitable status in the community and to make reasonable linguistic concessions to them. Even Switzerland, already saddled with the problem of three national languages, judged it advisable a few years ago to admit a fourth language, Romansh, on a sort of junior partnership basis. Totting up the balance sheet for Europe, the debit side shows a great increase in the actual number of official languages, the credit side a decided improvement in the attitude towards minority languages. This may be more important than it seems, for nations, like individuals, cannot hope to assess the language problem sensibly unless they divest themselves of prejudice.

A somewhat similar process has been going on in the Americas. Ostensibly the language pattern is simple, with the original European colonizing nations providing either English, French,

Portuguese or Spanish (with Danish in Greenland and Dutch in Surinam and the West Indies) as the official language or languages for every one of the 22 countries between Baffin Land and the Antarctic. But a closer look reveals a rather more complex weave. Mass immigration has helped to complicate matters, especially nowadays when the doctrine of the melting pot with its insistence on linguistic and cultural uniformity is nowhere applied as strictly and as illiberally as previously.

Canada is a good example of the language patterns produced by immigration. When Louis XV lost New France, 60,000 French-speaking Canadians changed their allegiance. Their descendents now constitute a durable linguistic block of 3.5 millions. But there are many other second languages in Canada besides English or French. A schoolboy in Winnipeg may study Icelandic as his first foreign language, while a farmer in Cape Breton may tune in to broadcasts in his ancestral Gaelic. Newspapers and books are published in Ukrainian and Finnish, in Polish and Italian and thousands speak these languages in their homes and pass them on to their children.[1]

In the United States the extension of the teaching of Spanish in the elementary schools of the south-western States, of French in those of Louisiana,[2] and the opportunity now given in many big city schools of learning Hebrew or Polish shows, among many other examples, that a similar line is being followed. No race has been more affected by this liberalizing trend than the American Indian. It is now at last realized that language is a vital and inseparable part of the cultural fabric, and that the Indian who has not been detribalized should not be deprived of his language.

This knowledge has had even more important consequences in Mexico and in Central and South America, where the populations speaking pre-Columbian mother tongues can be counted in millions rather than in hundreds of thousands. The former country, after centuries of unsuccessful efforts to turn Nahuas, Tarascans and Mayans into monolingual Spanish speakers, has set up most enlightened programmes for tackling the problem of illiteracy in the native language first, leaving instruction in the national language to a subsequent stage. Further south still, an increasingly progressive language policy bids fair to bring back languages such as Quechua and Aymará into useful circulation.

A few significant dates, grouped closely together, serve to set the pattern for Asia. The independence of the Philippines was proclaimed in 1946, of Burma, Ceylon, India and Pakistan in 1947, of Israel in 1948, of Indonesia in 1949, Cambodia, Laos and

---

1. See Chapter XI.
2. See Chapter IX.

Viet-Nam have joined the procession subsequently. These political events have inevitably meant greatly enhanced status for Burmese and for Hebrew, for Singhalese and Tamil, for Bahasa and Tagolog, for Cambodian, Laotian and Vietnamese, for Urdu and its close cousin Hindi, to say nothing of the 14 officially recognized regional languages of the new Republic of India and all the regional languages of the other nations which have recently attained or recovered their independence.

In the meantime, north of the Himalayas, great progress seems to have been made in endowing the complex of languages in central and northern Asia with alphabets and also with new dignity and status. What is bewildering in the new Asia linguistically is that it seems to consist more and more of a series of Switzerlands on a gigantic scale.

Let us take the case of a boy or girl just starting school somewhere in Bombay State. The case is typical enough of many other states both in and outside India. The pupil will at home probably speak either Gujerati or Marathi. His or her first task will be to learn the other state language, whichever it may be, going on then to Hindi, the new federal language, and only after that tackling one of the world link-languages. It may seem a desperate situation, but no continent is attacking its language problems with greater vigour. Teachers are recruited in Syria to teach Arabic as a living link-language to the Bengali-speakers of East Pakistan; chairs of Chinese are endowed in the great universities of India; Indonesia sends future teachers of English to study this world language in Australia—its nearest English-speaking neighbour.

Though geographically far removed from one another, Africa and Oceania present similar patterns of linguistic diversity and these patterns seem to be shifting and changing in much the same way. The dominant tongues, for official and generally for educational purposes as well, are still the languages of the European countries that hold political authority. More and more, however, the tendency to use the local vernacular, at least in primary education, is spreading. But in areas where languages change completely almost from village to village, this otherwise sensible course cannot be followed, and in such cases the teaching of the European language must be regarded as the only alternative.

Another way round the obstacle is to use a lingua franca, and these have a considerable vogue in both Africa and Oceania. Nationalism, particularly local nationalism, is a factor that must be reckoned with here too; it has a characteristically stubborn way of preventing all-wise authorities from imposing one dialect in preference to others and thus 'simplifying the language problem in the interest of the native'.

What the immediate future holds for these areas must depend in a large measure on political developments during the next quarter century, and a great burgeoning of new official languages on the Asian model is well within the bounds of probability.

This very hasty scamper across the continents has been undertaken mainly to help the reader catch a glimpse of the outline at least of the shadowy forest of language, a forest which like the one in Shakespeare's *Macbeth* is threateningly on the move and never stationary. Anyone who wants to take a closer look at the individual trees of this forest would be well advised to consult a recent Unesco publication, *The Use of Vernacular Languages in Education*,[1] which, in addition to much detailed information, gives, as an annex, a useful tentative classification of the world's languages.

There remains the question of the so-called link-languages, those languages which are widely distributed over the earth's surface or at least spoken by many millions of men and women. Estimates of the actual diffusion of such languages vary greatly, but the list of the 13 languages spoken by 50 million people or over which Professor Mario Pei of Columbia University gives in his stimulating book, *The Story of Language*,[2] is probably accurate enough for the layman. His list runs as follows:

Chinese (all dialects), 450 million; English, 250 million; Hindi-Urdu, 160 million; Russian, 140 million; Spanish, 110 million; German, 100 million; Japanese, 80 million; French, 75 million; Malay, 60 million; Bengali, 60 million; Portuguese, 55 million; Italian, 55 million; Arabic, 50 million.

There is, of course, no guarantee that the same 13 languages will appear in the same order 50 years from now, or even that such lists, drawn up in the not too remote future, will necessarily show Western languages in such an advantageous position. In any case, people who speak a world-language as their mother tongue should recognize their good luck but refrain from being arrogant about it. Above all they should refrain from attributing their wide diffusion to the intrinsic merits of the language in question. All languages, be they those of 'primitive' or 'civilized' communities, adequately express the concepts of the culture from which they spring and of the people or peoples who use them. All lead the learner by the straightest and surest road, perhaps by the only road, to a knowledge and true understanding of other cultures and other peoples.

Nor can one distinguish between 'beautiful' languages and 'ugly' languages without falling into the same absurdity. To people speaking a language with few gutturals or none at all, German may

---

1. Unesco, Paris, 1953.
2. George Allen & Unwin, London, 1952.

appear 'harsh' and Arabic even 'harsher', but are they 'harsh' to those who speak German or Arabic? Assuredly not.

That wise old man Voltaire went straight to the heart of the problem in his philosophical tale *L'Ingénu*, for when the Abbé de Saint Yves asked the ingenuous Huron which language he preferred, Huron, English or French, that simple American Indian replied, 'Huron, of course'. Our own language is always the best—for us. All the more reason for not imposing it on others.

THE LANGUAGE PROBLEM IN CEYLON[1]

For roughly twenty centuries education in Ceylon was concentrated in the Buddhist temples. Our ancient kings made extensive land grants to the temples to enable the clergy, who were learned men, to devote themselves to the twin tasks of furthering religion and of promoting education. The curriculum of these schools comprised language, literature, grammar, history, logic, medicine, astrology and kindred subjects. These temple schools flourished throughout those long centuries, and our greatest contribution to literature was made by them. Our greatest poets and writers were products of these schools. Language teaching occupied such an honourable place in the curriculum that it was considered a great distinction to know several languages. Our greatest poet, Sri Rahula, had the title 'Shadbasha Parameshwara' conferred on him by the king. This title meant 'one who was proficient in six languages'—no mean distinction for a scholar of the fourteenth century when countries in the world seemed so far apart. These schools attached to temples and known as *pirivenas* continue to this day under different conditions. The State gives them annual grants of money. Their curriculum has been extended to include English, mathematics, general science, etc.

In the early sixteenth century the Portuguese came to rule the maritime provinces of Ceylon. Under them education suffered a setback. They were keener on making converts to their faith than on promoting the general welfare of the inhabitants.

The Dutch, who succeeded the Portuguese in the maritime provinces, were more enlightened rulers. Among other reforms, they encouraged education and started Sinhalese schools. However, they had to give way to the English in 1795.

The early English Governors realized the importance of creating a class of public servants well acquainted with both English and Sinhalese or English and Tamil, to help them in the administration.

---
1. This note is abstracted from a paper read before the Ceylon seminar by Mr. D. A. Wijayasingha, Assistant Director of Education and leader of the Ceylon delegation at the seminar.

They started English, Sinhalese and Tamil schools in different parts of the country, chiefly in Colombo and Jaffna. The curriculum was chiefly confined to the three R's. This system of schools was extended to the hill country after the Kandyan kingdom was ceded to the British by the treaty of 1815.

A century later, by 1940, Ceylon had gained a substantial measure of self-government in internal affairs. There was a popular demand for a system of education better suited to the needs and aspirations of the people. A special committee reported on the subject, and it was decreed in 1945 that: all education in government schools should be free; all assisted schools should join this free system; education should be compulsory from the ages of five to fourteen; education in the primary schools should be in the mother tongue with English as a compulsory second language, and the mother tongue medium should progressively be extended in the schools; a third language or a second national language was also recommended.

This, then, is the background to the language problem in Ceylon today. The position obtaining at present is that a Sinhalese child is educated through Sinhalese up to Standard VI, and a Tamil child in Tamil up to the same level. Both begin to learn English in Standard III or the fourth year.

The switch-over to the mother tongue has brought educationists face to face with various language problems. The scheme which I have outlined recognizes: the need for a widely popular foreign language in a world daily growing smaller, while at the same time preserving our own national outlook; the need to assist the pupils to acquire skills in understanding, speech, reading and writing to meet their daily environmental stituations.

Our problems are these:

Lack of sufficiently qualified teachers. This the Training Colleges are endeavouring to overcome. However, we cannot say that the problem will be solved for some years—we began with the initial handicap of starting the scheme before the teachers were trained. We need teachers who are fully equipped to teach at least two if not three languages.

An equally serious problem is the non-availability of Sinhalese textbooks in all the three media. Although several new textbooks have been published, yet the supply is small and their quality not quite up to standard. Connected with textbooks is the question of vocabularies. These should be prepared by competent language teachers keeping in mind the various age groups and the interests and needs of pupils of those age groups.

We need men thoroughly conversant with language problems to assist our nine Education Officers in the provinces. These specialists could act as guides to the inspectors and direct research work in the training colleges. They could also help in preparing handbooks to teachers at various levels of teaching.

In all these problems the economic factor militates against success. Our schoolgoing population, excluding the adults in the temple schools, night schools and adult classes, totals 1,490,293 (figure as at May 1951). When this number is broken up into the different age-groups, from the 1st standard to the higher school certificate form, it can be seen that the production of textbooks is not economical.

Finally we are faced with a three-fold problem which we are still debating: how far is it wise to get a child to learn a third language? at what stage should the third language be started? how far should we go with the teaching of the third language?

THE TEACHING OF ARABIC IN PAKISTAN[1]

Arabic is one of the most important and widely spoken languages of the world. It is the language of the Holy Qur'ān and the Sunna, the two fountain heads of Islam. A Muslim should read the Qur'ān in his daily, weekly and 'Īdain ('Īd al-Fitr and 'Īd al-'Adḥā) prayers. Salāt Janāza or the funeral prayer over a Muslim must also be said in Arabic. Short chapters of the Qur'ān must be committed to memory by every Muslim boy or girl and by grown-up converts all over the world for saying prayers, even though he or she may not understand a single syllable of them. Before a Muslim child begins to learn his mother tongue in Pakistan, he has to learn the Islamic doctrine of unity in Arabic, namely—the sentence which in English runs: 'There is no God but Allāh. Muḥammed is His Prophet.' These very words should again be on every adult's lips before he or she dies. 'Love Arabic for three reasons', said the Prophet, 'for I am an Arab, the Qur'ān is in Arabic, and the language of the Heaven is also Arabic.' Therefore, we Muslims do not look upon Arabic as a foreign language as we do English, French, German, etc. which are taught in Pakistan for scientific and cultural purposes only.

Arabic is a language of literature, administration and commerce in the Middle Eastern countries and is studied by Muslims with special interest in the Indo-Pakistan subcontinent where there are institutions in no way inferior to those of Arabic-speaking countries in point of teaching the Qur'ān and the Sunna.

[1]. This account of the teaching of Arabic as a link-language with the rest of the Islamic world was prepared at the request of the Secretariat of Unesco by Dr. Serajul Haque, Head of the Department of Arabic and Islamic Studies, University of Dacca, Pakistan. Though there are prominent Arabic scholars and work of similar nature in West Pakistan, this account is limited to East Pakistan.

Prior to the establishment of Pakistan, the idea of teaching Arabic in order to create a cultural link between the Muslims of India and those of Arabic-speaking countries did not occur to anybody. The following quotations from the Report of the Education Commission (India) of 1882 will reveal briefly the ways and purposes of teaching Arabic during the Muslim period as well as under British rule: 'After the Mussulman conquest, the mosque became in India, as in other countries of Islam, a centre of instruction and of literary activity. Education, among Muhammadans and Hindus alike, is based upon religion, and was supported by endowments and bequests in *pios usus*. The East India Company found the four ancient methods still at work in the instruction given by the Brahmans to their disciples; in the *tols* or seats of Sanskrit learning, in the *maktabs* and *madrasahs* or the schools and colleges of Muhammadans, and in a large number of village schools which also existed. These village schools give an elementary education to the trading classes and to the children of petty landholders and well-to-do families among the cultivators.' But, 'on the 12th August, 1765, Shah Alam made over to the East India Company the formal grant of *Dewani* (Collection of Government revenue). This grant effected no change in the political conditions of the Mussulmans; the official language, according to the treaty, continued to be Persian, and fiscal and judicial administration was carried on in accordance with Muslim law. Realizing the need for an institution which would train officers qualified in Muslim law, Warren Hastings in 1781, established the Calcutta Madrasah', which was then called the Muhammadan College of Bengal and was run at the expense of the State. For more than half a century this Calcutta Madrasah served its original purposes of teaching Muslim boys Arabic, Persian and the Muslim law from the original sources in Arabic and also supplied officers for the courts of justice and other Government offices. But, in 1835, when the English system of education was inaugurated in India and, two years later, when Persian was replaced by English, the Calcutta Madrasah ceased to serve its original purpose. Since then, this Calcutta Madrasah (or Muhammadan College) remained as the so-called 'seat of learning' on an orthodox basis without having any provision in its syllabi for teaching Hadīth and Tafsīr. It was thoroughly defective from both the secular and the religious points of view. For a long time, history, geography, and even the mother tongue of the students (Bengali) were not taught there. Logic and classical metaphysics formed the main subjects of study. In the course of time, more madrasahs, both Government and state-aided, were established and changes in syllabuses were effected, adding two-year title courses in Hadīth, Tafsīr, Fiqh, etc. with a view to educating *Ulamā*, or Muslim divines. Several committees were set up for further re-organization of the system and to bring it in line with the general system of education under the Calcutta University, but to no avail. The same course is being followed even now in East Pakistan, with slight modification and with the addition of English and Persian as optional subjects.

On the partition of Bengal on 14 August 1947, all the teachers of the Calcutta Madrasah opted for East Bengal. They came over to East Bengal along with the precious library of the Madrasah Āliyah, Calcutta. The madrasah is now called Madrasah Āliyah, Dacca, and is under the management of the Madrasah Education Board, East Pakistan.

There exists in East Pakistan a large number of junior and senior madrasahs under this old scheme which catered to the needs of 40,000 pupils in 1948. The number of madrasahs under the scheme increased considerably in spite of continued political unrest and the economic depression of the last decade.

After they pass out from madrasahs with the highest degree, the students wander about for their livelihood. Since they do not know English, they are unfitted to serve as Arabic teachers in the English high schools. Of course, some of them enter the university after having passed the matriculation examination with English and mathematics only, and obtain B.A. and M.A. degrees to qualify themselves for Government service. Others become Muhammadan marriage registrars, imāms of mosques or teachers of madrasahs under the old scheme from which they received their education. But the majority remain unemployed.

The well-to-do and the intelligentsia seldom send their sons or wards to these institutions. But 'the poorest section of the people', says the Report of the East Bengal System Reconstruction Committee, 1952, 'flock to these institutions, those who can hardly afford to meet their own expeness, much less to pay any fees, while the teachers have practically to depend upon the charity of the people for their paltry wages which are often irregularly paid.' The medium of instruction in these madrasahs is Urdu (which is not the mother tongue of the people in East Bengal) from the secondary stage.

The English system of education was introduced in 1835 and the Muslims kept themselves aloof from it and were consequently deprived of all Government offices. Though oriental subjects were taught in the schools and colleges, and Arabic was an optional subject with Persian, Sanskrit, Pali, etc., it did not for a long time receive the attention it deserved.

Thanks to the Aligarh movement started by the late Sir Sayyid

Ahmad Khan during the late seventies of the nineteenth century, the Muslims took to English education in earnest. From that time Muslim boys have been studying Arabic along with other secular subjects taught under the English system of education, and by 1953 there were 16,000 offering Arabic as their matriculation subject. After passing the matriculation examination with Arabic, the students generally take up modern subjects and only a few are left who continue Arabic in the university, where the medium of instruction is English.

At the beginning of the present century a fresh attempt was made, by the late Shamsul 'Ulama Mawlana Abu Nasr Waheed, to reorganize the old madrasah system of education and, with that object in view, he visited the renowned Jami 'ah al-Azhar of Cairo, and seats of learning in Syria, Palestine and Turkey, as well as Oriental institutes in Europe, particularly those of Berlin and Vienna and the École Nationale des Langues Orientales Vivantes of Paris. On his return to India in 1907, he prepared a reformed scheme of education in the light of the experiences gathered abroad, in order to revise the courses of studies in the madrasah system of education. Committee after committee was formed and public leaders like Nawwab Sir Salimullah, G.C.I.E., Nawwab Nawwab Ali Choudhury, and Nawwab Sir Sayyid Shams al-Huda helped him in the matter. Finally, in May 1913, the Bengal Government appointed the Dacca University Committee with Sir Robert Nathan as the president. The committee 'recommended that a Department of Islamic Studies should form an integral part of the Dacca University, combining with instruction in secular subjects taught in a university'. Accordingly, the reformed scheme of madrasah education came into force during the session 1915-16, and was first introduced into the old scheme (Govt. Senior Madrasahs) at Dacca, Chittagong and Hoogly. The old scheme (Government) junior madrasahs at Rajshahi, along with five other aided senior madrasahs and a large number of non-Government junior madrasahs, also came under this scheme. The Calcutta Madrasah did not accept the scheme and remained aloof, as did a number of junior and senior madrasahs in Bengal.

The reformed scheme madrasah education has, however, achieved its object of attracting students to higher education. It has further developed Islamic education on modern scientific lines and co-ordinated Islamic education with modern university education. By 1948 there were 85,000 pupils from East Pakistan in these new scheme madrasahs.

After passing the high madrasah examination, the majority of the students of this scheme come to the university and take up general subjects. Some of them, having additional mathematics in their high madrasah examination, go in for science. Only about 200 students every year enter the Islamic intermediate colleges and pursue the Islamic studies group.

Besides the three systems of education mentioned above, in which Arabic forms a subject of study, we have in East Pakistan another system of madrasah education known as the 'Darsi Nizāmī Course, after the name of Mulla Nizamuddin of Lucknow. This was introduced in Bengal in the beginning of the eighteenth century by Mowlana Adbdul 'Alī (Known as 'Bahr al-Ulūm' or Ocean of Learning), son of Mullab Nizamuddin of Lucknow. This system follows a course of studies which gives prominence to Arabic logic, metaphysics and Muslim law. The famous Dār al-'Ulūm of Deoband (India), follows a course similar to Darsi Nizamī, laying greater stress on Hadīth and Tafsīr. A number of madrasahs, both senior and junior, under this scheme are in existence in all the districts of East Pakistan. The number of students receiving education in these madrasahs is fairly large. They hail from very poor and conservative families. No tuition fee is charged and most of the students are offered free board and lodging. Books are also supplied to them from the madrasah libraries. This system of education is not recognized by the Government nor do the madrasah authorities like to be under them. The students and the teachers belonging to this system are conservative in their dress and manners. The graduates of these institutions generally go to the villages and earn their bread either by preaching Islam or opening a *maktab* (in the Middle East known as *Kuttāb*) to teach young boys and girls how to read the Holy Qur'ān and say their prayers. These scholars mostly depend on public charity for their livelihood. It is often said that they increase the bulk of the unemployed among the Muslims of East Pakistan, but at the same time these are the scholars who have still kept the torch of Islam burning in the remotest corners of East Pakistan.

We have seen the different systems of education in East Pakistan, where Arabic has a place in the syllabus. Recently the report of the East Bengal Educational System Reconstruction Committee has been published, and we expect that in the future we shall have only one system of education here, in which Arabic will form a compulsory subject for all Muslim students up to the secondary stage. Steps are now being taken to teach Arabic by Arabs through the direct method. Thanks to the Syrian Government, three cultural delegates have already been assigned to Karachi, Lahore and Dacca to popularize Arabic by contact with Pakistani students and teach them Arabic through the direct method. The Syrian cultural delegate in Dacca has already been able to arouse great enthusiasm for Arabic among our students. In the city of Dacca proper he has opened three centres for training Arabic teachers to teach Arabic by the direct method.

Teachers from different institutions, both Government and Government-aided, enrol in them. Under the supervision of Professor Ahmad, these teachers are given practical training in teaching Arabic to the boys in their classes by the direct method. Successful teachers are offered *sanads*, certificates issued under the signatures of the Director of Public Instruction of East Bengal and Professor Ahmad. Each course lasts for three months and the Government of East Pakistan grants facilities to enable these teachers to attend the classes. Thirty-three teachers have already obtained certificates. The trained teachers have now gone back to their own institutions and are teaching their students Arabic by the direct method.

Before partition, the universities of India taught Arabic only as a classical language, starting from Class VII of the English schools. But they never thought of teaching it as a living language with world-wide ramifications. Students therefore cared very little for it, nor could they produce any original work in Arabic which might have served to create a cultural link with Arabic-speaking countries. After partition, the University of Dacca felt the need of producing Arabic scholars who could talk and write Arabic freely and create a fraternal link with Arabic-speaking countries. In accordance with a recommendation of the Academic Council, of 22 August 1951, the Executive Council of the University of Dacca therefore resolved that a certificate course in modern Arabic be introduced as soon as possible. The head of the Department of Arabic and Islamic Studies was further requested to make the necessary arrangements for teaching the course. He prepared the draft ordinance and the syllabi relating to the course, which were passed by the Committee of Courses and Studies. The head of the department, after making the necessary arrangements to appoint a suitable Egyptian or Syrian scholar as reader at the university, further recommended that the certificate course be introduced from July 1953. The matter is now under consideration. It is expected that the Central Government will help to appoint a reader in modern Arabic as they have done in the case of other foreign languages, namely, Chinese and French. In the meantime, an elementary course in modern Arabic has been introduced in the university. In addition to all the above steps East Pakistan has formed cultural associations to popularize Arabic in Pakistan.

Such have been the various efforts, so far, in East Pakistan to teach Arabic for the purpose of creating a cultural link with the Arabic-speaking countries of the world.

SPECIAL PROBLEMS OF LANGUAGE

TEACHING SPANISH TO MEXICAN INDIANS THROUGH THE VERNACULAR[1]

The Institute for the Literacy of Monolingual Indians (Instituto de Alfabetización para Indígenas Monolingües), which comes under the Ministry of Education, is the body responsible for bringing literacy as well as a knowledge of Spanish to the Mexican Indians. It was set up in August 1945, under the terms of the law passed to launch the national campaign against illiteracy. Article 14 of this law makes definite provision for the publication of bilingual primers as a means for teaching Spanish to non-Spanish-speaking elements in the population.

A group of educators and language experts had been hoping for some time for an opportunity to experiment with new teaching methods with a view to bringing education to Indians across the barrier of language and really making them members of the national community. They were fully aware that the Mexican rural school system, in spite of its desire to reach all the people, everywhere, made no special provision for the Indians, merely lumping them together with the rest of the rural population. The result of this was that the Indians lived on year after year in the same state of cultural neglect. Those who had managed to learn Spanish were so few in number, and their Spanish was so poor, that it might really be said that the problem[2] had not even begun to be tackled.

In this respect, the efforts of the sixteenth-century missionaries were not forgotten. If they had not had to give up their work in this direction because the progress made by the natives alarmed the original Spanish conquerors, we, the Mexicans of the twentieth century, would not have had to deal with the problem of a nation split up into a linguistic mosaic—a problem that makes education infinitely more difficult and also slows down the economic and social progress of the country. For the nation has to support a population which is indeed Mexican by birth but which, because of the language barrier, constitutes a foreign element within the country.

The first sign of dissatisfaction became apparent in 1936. In that year an isolated experiment took place among a group of Tarahumara Indians in the State of Chichuahua. A little later

---

1. This study, an account of the use of the mother tongue as an initial stage in learning the national language, is an abridged version of the working-paper prepared for the Ceylon seminar by Mrs. Angélica Castro de la Fuente, Secretary to the Institute for the Literacy of Monolingual Indians. The information it contains has been revised and brought up to date by the author since the Ceylon seminar.
2. Of Mexico's 19,660,000 inhabitants according to the 1940 census, nearly 2,500,000 were registered as having an Indian mother tongue. Almost 50 per cent are reported as monolingual, that is knowing only their native Indian tongue. Over 50 languages are spoken by the Indians of Mexico, some of them by relatively large numbers of people, some of them by mere remnants of former speech communities.

a first congress of philologists and linguists was called, whose aim was to find a solution to the technical problems raised by teaching literacy in native languages. This congress selected the alphabets to be used for transcribing languages which had never yet been represented graphically. At the same time a Council for Indian Languages was set up as a permanent organization, with the task of encouraging the scientific study of native languages and cultures. This body was also asked to draw up the plan of action to be followed by the Institute for the Literacy of Monolingual Indians, originally called the Institute for Literacy among the Speakers of Indian languages. The plan as drawn up consisted of three stages.

Stage One. Selection of 10 teachers from each of the Indian language regions in the country with emphasis on: graduation from an urban or rural primary teachers' training college, native birth in the region in question, practical knowledge of the Indian language spoken in the region. Training in Mexico City, to emphasize general and local anthropology, general and local linguistics, general and specialized teaching methods, with supervised preparation of texts for a regional bilingual primer.

Stage Two. Selection of bilingual rural teachers from each of the Indian language regions. Their training, under the general supervision of the institute, at the hands of the certified teachers trained in Mexico City.

Stage Three. Teaching of literacy to Indian-speaking natives by rural teachers who would use the appropriate bilingual primer for this purpose and be guided in their work by the specially trained supervising teachers.

Work was started in the following Indian language regions: the Northern Nahua of Puebla; the Southern Nahua of Puebla and the State of Morelos; Mayan of Yucatan, Campeche and Quintana Roo; the Tarascan of the State of Michoacán; the Otomí of the Mezquital Valley in the State of Hidalgo.

These linguistic regions were chosen because, apart from the Tarascan one, they were areas where a large number of inhabitants spoke only their native language. Tarascan was included because it was thought desirable to try out the new methods in a language area where experimental work on the teaching of reading and writing through the native Indian language had been started earlier, in 1939 and 1940. This earlier experiment had had to be given up because of lack of funds. In all 50 teachers received special training and five primers were published, one for each region.

Arrangements were made, in conjunction with the regional educational authorities and with the Ministry of Education, for the selection of these teachers, their seconding, their transportation and board and lodging in Mexico City. These bilingual teachers were officially called instructors. A detailed curriculum was drawn up by the institute and specialists were recruited for each subject in the three basic fields of anthropology, linguistics and pedagogy. Contracts had to be drawn up for these specialists and the planning of their courses supervised. The anthropologists gave a complete survey of physical, social and cultural anthropology, and then the ethnologists, using material supplied by the trainees themselves and furnished in answers to questionnaires, directed studies of the cultures of each of the language groups represented by the trainees. This additional first-hand material served to supplement the information the ethnologists already had available in published form.

The methods used in the field of linguistics were rather similar. First the trainees were taught the basic facts about language and the basic methods of studying linguistics. At the same time each of the languages represented by the trainees was subjected to a thorough linguistic analysis. Some of the ethnographic data were supplied in one or another of the Indian languages and these texts could then be subjected to linguistic analysis.

The pedagogical expert, using the data supplied by the linguists and the ethnologists, and with the help of the bilingual trainees, would then proceed to construct the primers within the pedagogical framework each language called for. In order that the primers might be used by adults as well as by children, the method followed in their drafting was an eclectic one—that is to say, it was sometimes a global, natural, method and at others consisted only of common words or expressions.

As soon as the primer was drafted it was tried out under field conditions before a first edition was printed. This first edition was usually limited to 500 copies or so, in order that it could be tried out again by the bilingual instructors with the rural teachers selected under stage two. When this second test had been completed, it was time for the definitive edition; 125,000 were run off in Mayan-Spanish, 20,000 in Tarascan-Spanish and 50,000 in Otomí-Spanish.

Each linguistic region was divided off into working areas, the criterion of division being the network of roads and railways which would enable the work in each area to be properly controlled and inspected. Each area was given a number, and was placed under the supervision of one of the teachers specially trained in Mexico City, who was to act as inspector of all schools and centres set up to combat illiteracy among the Indians.

Bilingual rural teachers were selected and were then concentrated in urban centres which were easy of access and where the cost of living was not too high. Here they received intensive training. The training was given by a linguist who had completely mastered the Indian language in question and by a pedagogical expert. The rural teachers were taught elementary linguistics of a practical nature so that they would be equipped to read and write their mother tongue just as easily as they read and wrote Spanish. Their pedagogical training was largely confined to showing them how to use the primer and how to make the best use in their teaching of supplementary material. Teaching aids to supplement the primer were prepared and sent out to the teachers. Once trained, the rural teachers were redistributed in areas where Spanish-speaking Indians were fewest and where their help was therefore most needed and most likely to prove effective.

When it was discovered that there were not enough bilingual rural teachers to go round, other persons of both sexes were recruited and trained, and were officially designated as literacy workers (*alfabetizadores*). As they were not trained teachers in the first place, their special instruction was limited to using the primary and auxiliary material and to reading and writing in their Indian mother tongue. These literacy workers were able to lend a hand to the regular teachers who were not bilingual and to take over the job of teaching reading and writing to Indians who spoke only their mother tongue. Where schools already exist they do the preparatory work, and where there are none they can do a teaching job themselves. To ensure that the provisions of the law are properly carried out, there has to be constant supervision to see that the instructors, the rural teachers and the literacy workers are making proper use of the primers.

The teaching staff of the institute, working in conjunction with the specialized linguists, issues instructions for the use of the first part of the primer, which is meant to teach Indian illiterates to read and write in their native language. The institute's work is co-ordinated with that of the various educational authorities through basic directives which the institute has drawn up and which lay down the functions of all persons employed in the Indian literacy field as well as those of the various educational agencies concerned with this activity.

The institute makes a point of co-operating with local communities and does what it can to help them solve their social problems. This helps to gain the confidence of the Indian inhabitants who are then likelier to attend the literacy centres set up amongst them. It encourages sports and games in order to strengthen the spirit of co-operation and to bring school and community in closer touch with one another. It organizes competitions for the best short story or the best letter written in the native Indian language. It supplies oil lamps to villages where there is no electric light. It helps in the building of schools by mobilizing all the available local resources and bringing them together. Similarly, the institute is active in arranging for repairs to schools and to school equipment.

Each State of the Federal Republic in which primers are used is considered a separate 'project', the whole enterprise is still in an experimental stage; hence the term. Attached to each of these projects is a technical section. At first each section was directed by a linguist who was assisted by an educational expert. Now the roles have been reversed, and each section is headed by one of the bilingual native Indian teachers trained in Mexico City. This method has produced excellent results; it has been found that co-operation with the native Indian teachers is much better when they are given a larger measure of responsibility.

As its name indicates, the function of the technical section is to give all possible help and guidance to the rural teachers, the literacy workers and the instructors. The section is also responsible for getting out a fortnightly bulletin with suggestions to teachers and a monthly publication with information of a more general nature.

The original plan of action drawn up by the Council for Indian Languages has been amplified, particularly for stages 2 and 3: here practical experience has been a guide to useful modifications.

For instance, at first all primers were bilingual, but after they had been in use for a time, the need for introductory primers made itself felt. They were necessary to make the literacy teaching easier and more effective in its very first stages, when both teachers and pupils come up against the problem, for example, of the very long words that are so common in Tarascan, which is an agglutinative language, or of the nasalization signs, and pitch accents that have to be used with Otomí vowels. These introductory primers have greatly simplified the problem of teaching in the early stages.

Recently a really radical change has been made in the methods for teaching Otomí. Modifications have been made in the alphabets first prepared at the congress of philologists and linguistics, with a view to simplifying and expediting the work of the teacher and of the persons engaged in using the Indian primers in teaching to read, and also to making the transition to Spanish more gradual by introducing all the phonemes of this idiom. The Otomí alphabet in use today is very similar to that of Spanish. It differs only in the use of certain symbols which represent phonemes not found in Spanish. These pre-primers are written only in the Indian native language—two for both Tarascan and Otomí have been prepared. The first of the Otomí primers is written exclusively with phonemes which exist in both languages, Otomí and Spanish. The second introduces the Otomí phonemes which do not occur in Spanish.

There has thus been complete willingness to introduce any changes which seemed necessary to make the system more effective and workable. One problem has been a certain lack of understanding, not only on the part of the general public but on the part of some of the teachers as well. Some of them became convinced that the intention of the whole scheme was to strengthen the hold of the native Indian languages. They all very much want to learn Spanish because they feel that their continued ignorance of this language shuts them off from a fuller life and make it possible for others to exploit and deceive them. This phase of initial suspicion has now been left behind as far as the Tarascan project is concerned. In the Mezquital valley it is hoped that the introduction of the new Otomí primer will gradually dispel the reserve that is still encountered there.

Another recent innovation is the tendency to stop concentrating on literacy alone and to go in for a minimum programme of primary education. When heads of families find out that their children are being taught to read and write but not to do simple arithmetic, they are apt to conclude that the children are wasting their time and to keep them away from school. The ancillary social work, which has been described as forming a part of stage 3, is also indispensable if people are to be persuaded to form a community with the school as its centre and if the teaching is to be really effective.

The actual teaching of Spanish is begun orally, using the direct method. As soon as the pupils have gone through all the material prepared for them in their native Indian language—and this is much more than is contained in the primers, including as it does readers designed to create proper reading habits—then they pass on to a series of profusely illustrated texts prepared in Spanish. When they have tackled these, they turn to the Spanish section in the original primers.

As a matter of fact, the problem of teaching Spanish has not yet been fully solved. It has been proved indeed that the use of the native language provides a useful intermediate step. In the same way it has been shown that the child or adult who learns to read in the vernacular tongue reads the foreign language, in this case Spanish, freely and easily, the only difference being that one is comprehended and the other is not!

As an intermediate step between reading orally in the native tongue and in Spanish, printed bilingual materials are being prepared with short sentences. In Otomí, a *Book of Animals* has just come out which, besides carrying out the aims already indicated, also introduces the Otomí phonemes and digits.

To make the Indian peoples completely literate in Spanish will be a long, slow, process—for people who do not speak Spanish it is a foreign language, and it is necessary to proceed with the same scientific methods as are used for teaching English or any other language. However, since those engaged in this task are bilinguals with a quite limited general preparation, it is necessary to produce bilingual materials and a series of aids for learning Spanish.

THE LANGUAGE PROBLEM IN THE TRUST TERRITORY OF SOMALILAND UNDER ITALIAN ADMINISTRATION[1]

The language problem in the Trust Territory of Somaliland under Italian Administration is rendered difficult not only by technical but also by religious and political considerations. These have induced those responsible to adopt a cautious attitude and so avoid hasty solutions that might further complicate the situation. Since the beginning of its responsibilities in this Territory, the Italian Administration has however been fully conscious of the importance of the problem and has devoted much attention to it.

Except for the extreme south, where Swahili is also spoken, and the small town of Brava, south of Mogadishu, where they speak a Bantu dialect, the mother tongue of the indigenous population throughout the territory is Somali, one of the Cushitic languages. Owing to the social structure of the Somalis, who live grouped in tribes, the Somali language includes a number of different dialects, but these do not vary so greatly that people from the north cannot understand or be understood by their fellow-countrymen in the central or southern regions. Apart from these differences of dialect (which tend to lessen with increasing exchanges and the progress of the country towards a unified political life) we can indeed speak of one Somali language, spoken by the indigenous population of every social class and cultural level in their everyday relations.

But Somali is not a written language. It was not until 1922 that a certain Osman Yusuf, a Somali from Obbia, in the region of Mudug, the dialect of which tends to predominate over all the others and can be considered the best expression of the language, invented an alphabet of 10 vowels and 19 consonants known as the Osmanic alphabet, to represent the sounds of the language. This alphabet did not meet with success; at the time, the importance of Osman

---

[1]. This paper was originally read before the Ceylon seminar by Professor Emilio Baglioni, Director of Secondary Instruction in Somaliland. It is presented here in slightly abridged form.

Yusuf's initiative was not appreciated by his fellow-countrymen.

In 1949 a Society for the Somali Language and Literature was organized by the League of Somali Youth (the leading nationalist party) with the following aims: to collect books on the Somali language; to study the language and publish the results; to improve the script; to use the language for all social intercourse; to eliminate foreign words not strictly necessary; to agree on the most correct terms and words; to revive Somali art and literature; to encourage the use of Somali both as a cultural language and as an instrument of education to buy material necessary for the printing of books in Osmanic characters.

The Society for the Somali Language and Literature, which supports the immediate official adoption of the Osmanic alphabet, is convinced that only in this way can illiteracy be overcome and mass education attained. Recently, also, certain Somalis of the league and society mentioned above expressed their conviction that until the Somali language, oral and written, becomes the official language for teaching in primary schools, at least in the lower classes, the problem of illiteracy cannot be solved, citing as evidence the results obtained in some schools organized on their own initiative, where the pupils learn to read and write with spelling-books cyclostyled in Osmanic characters.

In these schools—and they themselves recognize the fact—the syllabus is limited to reading and writing, the literature of the Somali language being confined to folksongs, legends and proverbs; there are neither formal literary nor scientific works—not even in the form of popular manuals. But, they say, men and women, children and adults are able in a short time to read and write in the language, i.e. they possess a natural means—their mother tongue—for conducting and developing their daily relations.

Given the enthusiasm and earnestness animating the followers of this movement, the majority of whose members are of the younger generation, it might therefore seem easy to solve the problem. But the social and political interests of Somaliland do not begin and end with the league and the society—even though these represent a young and audacious intellectual elite, they are not *all* Somaliland.

Confronting this movement with all the weight of its ancient tradition is the religious and juridical Muslim world which, through its preachers, wise men and cadis, forms the basis and support of the whole economic, social and religious structure of the territory. For obvious reasons, though their knowledge of Arabic is often somewhat limited, these preachers and cadis are misoneists, and hostile to the diffusion of Somali as a written language; they consider Arabic the only proper medium for

expressing not only religious feelings but all other features of the life of the Somali people, both in the territory and abroad. An exception is made, of course, for the use of other languages, especially Italian, which is recognized as an instrument of education and a means for contact with the outside world and Western civilization in particular.

If other means of opposition, such as those deriving from differences in dialect associated with tribal rivalry, which are gradually dying down, may be set aside, the attitude of these influential bodies, held in respect and consideration by the population and representing a dominant social class which fulfils essential functions, cannot be ignored by those responsible for guiding the territory smoothly towards independence and a higher form of civilization. Hence, when in April 1950 the Italian administration had to face the problem of education, the question was: *which* language, besides Italian, should be chosen as an instrument for education—Somali of Arabic?

There are undoubtedly good reasons in favour of Somali; but there are also serious religious, social and political reasons for going carefully. The Italian administration, before making a decision, therefore held a 'referendum' of the heads and notables of the territory, to provide data on which to base its policy in solving the language problem. The referendum was in favour of Arabic. The Advisory Council of the United Nations, meeting on 17 May and 30 August 1950 took the same view. At the same time, the Advisory Council agreed with the Italian administration that the possibility of making Somali a written language should be studied. The Territorial Assembly, the representative organ that is being converted from an advisory to a legislative body, was in favour of adopting Arabic instead of Somali.

It is well to make clear, however, that the Italian administration's caution in dealing with this difficult problem does not mean that it is against the spread of Somali as a written language. On the contrary, it has encouraged and facilitated every experiment attempted in this field, either privately or by officials of the Italian administration itself. Mention may be made of the facilities given by the Italian administration for the publication of Professor Maino's works; the two experimental primary school courses organized in the Government schools at Mogadishu and directed by an Italian teacher with the help of Osman Yusuf's son; the studies and lectures on this subject by Professor Moreno, who, under the auspices of the Italian administration, has started the publication in serial form of a Somali grammar and has given lectures on the matter at the Social and Cultural Institute in Mogadishu. The *Corriere della Somalia*, the unofficial local daily newspaper, has not only published articles on the problem, but has gone so far as to do so in Somali, using Roman characters. Lastly, special bonuses have been introduced for Italian teachers who devote themselves to the study of Somali.

On the other hand, it must not be overlooked that the hostility manifested in official indigenous circles has been strengthened by those who think that the adoption of Somali in Osmanic characters will isolate the country both from the Islamic and Western worlds. At the Eleventh Session of the Trusteeship Council in July 1952, while discussing the 1951 report of the Italian Administration in Somaliland to the United Nations, the representative of the United Kingdom very properly remarked that the task of creating educational institutions among the Somalis was one to dishearten the most optimistic Administrators.

The administration has sought the opinion of experts who have visited the territory on behalf of the United Nations and Unesco. In the report of the Technical Assistance Commission which visited the country in 1952, for instance, the education expert, after acknowledging the interest the Italian administration had taken in the solution of the problem through the measures mentioned above and also through such audio-visual aids as radio transmissions and documentary films in Somali, expressed his opinion that the Somali language was the best instrument for mass education and stated that he was therefore favourably inclined to its transcription, as being a possible instrument for education in the primary schools—at least in the lower classes.[1]

The expert sent by Unesco, who visited the territory from the beginning of February to the end of April 1953, in his report also acknowledges the lively interest of the Italian administration in the problem and agrees with its responsible organs that the solution should be to adopt Somali as the means of education in the lower classes of the primary schools. He writes however: 'As a citizen of a country where teaching is always conducted in the local language, I considered it necessary to find, as soon as possible, the way of introducing the teaching of Somali as a written language. The study *in loco* of the problem has shown me that this solution would be premature and inapplicable';[2] and he states (page 84) that there are so many considerations of a political and religious nature that the question cannot easily be resolved.

It has been necessary to mention all this to make clear the situation in which the Administration finds itself and to explain its attitude; it has been well aware, from the outset, of the importance

---
1. Appendix C of the report, page 213.
2. Page 13.

of the problem but has at the same time felt that it cannot be solved on a purely technical, linguistic and pedagogical basis.

There is another and no less difficult side of the problem. On the assumption that, when the situation is ripe, Somali, oral and written, will be adopted as the language for teaching in the lower classes of the primary schools, what alphabet should be used?

Besides the Osmanic alphabet, already mentioned, other attempts have been made to transcribe the sounds of Somali in other characters. The attempt to transcribe the language in Arabic characters is not of much importance, because certain Somali vowel sounds are lacking from that alphabet, but attempts to transcribe it in Roman characters have met with remarkable success. There exists a publication by Professor Maino and some experimental transcriptions of Somali folksongs and legends, in Roman characters, made by Mr. Panza, who directs the two experimental courses in the primary schools at Mogadishu. According to the compilers of these alphabets, with some duplication of vowels and a few consonent combinations, the Roman characters can render all the sounds of the Somali language.

I recently exchanged views with the son of the inventor of the Osmanic alphabet and showed him the transcriptions made by Mr. Panza. The young Somali, though upholding the adoption of his father's alphabet, had to admit that the Roman alphabet, with the above mentioned modifications, is effective in rendering all the sounds of the Somali vowels and consonants. But this admission on the part of a tenacious champion of the Osmanic alphabet must not lead us to believe that the solution of this second aspect of the problem is in sight. Whereas the purely linguistic objections can be easily overcome, there are other reasons for opposition to the adoption of Roman characters that, whatever we may think of them, have taken deep root in the minds of the Somalis.

Besides the nationalistic reason there is also the religious reason; it is feared that the adoption of Roman characters may be the prelude to attempts to propagate the Christian religion. The Somalis cite what has happened in nearby territories (Kenya, Tanganiyka, etc.), where the adoption of Roman characters for transcribing the local language has preceded by a short time, or coincided with, the propaganda of Christian missionaries.

It is useless to point out that Muslim countries, like Turkey, have adopted the Roman characters without relinquishing the faith of their fathers. Resistance on this point is very strong, and will not be easily overcome. Although the expert of the United Nations Technical Assistance Commission and the Unesco expert have spoken in favour of Roman characters, until now only one

Somali—Mohamed Abuker Mohallum—has openly declared himself in favour of them. At the moment it is impossible to reduce the opposition, even by drawing attention to the fact that the cost of a printing-house, with Osmanic characters, as well as that of typewriters with a similar keyboard, would be altogether prohibitive.

Still, the Administration is confident that the problem of the Somali language and alphabet will in the end be solved, and in a way that meets the real needs of the population.

There is no doubt that the ever growing number of indigenous teachers appointed every year by the administration for primary education furnishes what we might call a 'natural' contribution to the solution of the problem. These Somali teachers are inclined to speak to their pupils in Somali, a fact which, while contributing to the development and enrichment of the language serves, too, gradually to extend it and make of it the natural language for teaching in the lower classes of the primary schools.

Primary education is carried on—officially—in Arabic and Italian. The oral and written study of Arabic is begun in the preparatory class and continued uninterruptedly until the fifth and last class of the primary schools. Italian is studied in the preparatory and first classes and the pupils are taught to write it only in the second class.

Arabic meets religious and juridical needs and commercial requirements, owing to the frequent business relations of the Somalis along the coast with Arabic-speaking countries of the Middle East.

Besides being the language of the State charged with the trusteeship of the territory, Italian is the language most widely spoken both along the coast and inland because of the continued relations that have been established for more than fifty years between the Somalis and Italy. Italian is, in a way, the *lingua franca* in many parts of Africa. From Tunisia to Libya, Ethiopia, Eritrea, Somaliland and, since the second world war, as far as Kenya and Tanganyika, Italian is understood and frequently spoken by a good part of the population. In Libya, Eritrea and Ethiopia, as well as in Somaliland, it is often the only Western language used by the intellectual elite to maintain contact with European civilization and culture.

All the teaching in the primary schools (and this year experiments will be made also in secondary schools) is based on the conception of an 'active school', so that, with reference in particular to the teaching of languages, the 'natural method' is followed. By following this method in the primary schools, after two months' attendance, Somali children are able to write in Italian. Experience shows too that the words traced by them in their copy-books reflect a clear meaning in their minds because they refer to concrete objects of their world and everyday life. Learned in this way, the language, although not their mother tongue, becomes a means of expressing the child's personality, a means identified with practical experience of things and facts encountered in the child's environment and of the common acts of daily life. The enrichment of the vocabulary, accompanied by a wider knowledge of the morphological and syntactic structure of the language, goes hand in hand with the enrichment of the child's mind and therefore with the complete development of his personality.

The usefulness of this method has induced the school authorities to extend it to the teaching of Arabic. Here, too, the results have been excellent. Even in the Indian schools at Mogadishu the same method is used for the teaching of Roman characters and the Italian language. Thanks to this method, it has so far been possible to overcome—at least in part—the difficulties encountered in the primary education of the Somalis, who, as we have seen, are obliged for the moment to begin their education in two foreign languages.

APPENDIX
MEMBERS OF THE SEMINAR

STAFF

Director: Professor Theodore Andersson, Director, Master of Arts in Teaching Programme, Yale University.
Unesco Representative: Dr. Felix Walter, Department of Education, Unesco.
Administrator: Colonel R. J. F. Mendis, Deputy Director of Education, Office of Education, Colombo, Ceylon.
Professional Advisers to the Director: Oberschulrat Dr. Adolf Bohlen, Münster, President of the German Modern Language Teachers Association, Director of the Landesinstitut für neue Sprachen, Münster; Professor Louis Landré, University of Paris, President of the French Modern Language Teachers Association and the International Federation of Modern Language Teachers; Miss S. Panandikar, Principal, Secondary Training College, Bombay, India.
Documents Officer: Miss M. Beckman, Department of Education, Unesco.

PARTICIPANTS FROM MEMBER STATES

Australia: Mr. J. McCusker, Officer-in-Charge of the Migrant Education Section of the Commonwealth Office of Education.
Cambodia: Mr. Vannsak Keng, Lecturer in Indo-Khmer Literature at the Lycée Sisowath, Phnom-Penh.
Canada: Miss Florence E. Bennee, Nutana Collegiate, Saskatoon, Saskatchewan, now Dean of Women, Indore Christian College, Indore, India.
Ceylon: Reverend Brother Conran, Principal, Maris Stella College, Negombo, Ceylon; Mr. E. Ediriwira, Principal, Government Central College, Hanwella, Ceylon (Representative of Government Grade I Principals' Union); Mrs. T. Janszé, Principal, St. Paul's College, Milagiriya, Bambalapitiya, Ceylon (Representative of the Ceylon Headmistresses' Association); Mrs. C. L. Motwani, Principal, Musaeus College, Colombo, Ceylon (Representative of the All-Ceylon Union of Teachers); Mr. R. Sri Pathmanathan, Lecturer in Classics, University of Ceylon, Peradeniya, Ceylon; Mr. D. A. Wijayasingha, Assistant Director of Education, Education Department, Colombo, Ceylon (Leader of the delegation).
France: Mr. Serge Denis, Inspector-General of Public Instruction (Leader of the delegation); Mr. Maurice Grangié, Director of Education,

APPENDIX

Pondicherry; Mr. C. Journot, Cultural Counsellor, French Embassy, New Delhi, India; Mr. Pierre Meile, Professor at the School of Oriental Languages, Paris.
German Federal Republic: Dr. Elisabeth Winkelmann, Lecturer in the Teacher Training Institute, Hamburg.
India: Shri A. K. Chanda, President, Board of Secondary Education, West Bengal; Professor K. N. Misra, Professor of English, Science College, Patna; Mrs. G. Parthasarathy, Professor of English, Presidency College, Madras.
Indonesia: Mr. Fr. Wachendorff, Acting Inspector of English Teaching, Ministry of Education, Djakarta.
Israel: Mr. Judah Shuval, Director, Ulpan Ben-Yehuda in Jerusalem (Adult Education Schools for Adult Immigrants).
Italy and Trust Territory of Somaliland under Italian Administration: Professor Emilio Baglioni, Director of Secondary Instruction in Somaliland.
Japan: Mr. Saburo Hoshiyama, Assistant Professor of English, Nagoya University (Leader of the delegation); Mr. Shotaro Matsukawa, Principal, Shonana High School, Fujisawa-shi.
Hashemite Kingdom of Jordan: Mr. Jiryis Qusus, Inspector of English, Ministry of Education, Amman.
Pakistan: Dr. Serajul Haque, Head of the Department of Arabic and Islamic Studies, Dacca University.
Thailand: Miss M. L. Boonlua Kunjara, Assistant Director of the Triam Udom School.
Switzerland: Mr. Gilbert Etienne, Lecturer in Hindu Art, Lahore University.
United Kingdom: Mr. J. G. Bruton, Education Officer, British Council, New Delhi; Prof. L. A. Hill, Professor designate of English Language and Literature in the University of Indonesia; Mr. R. Mackin, Education Officer (Linguistics), British Council, Pakistan; Dr. W. L. Presswood, Chairman, Council of the Modern Language Association (Leader of the delegation); Mr. S. Stevens, Director, English by Radio, British Broadcasting Corporation.
United States of America: Dr. Norman A. McQuown, Professor of Anthropology and Linguistics, University of Chicago.
Viet-Nam: Professor Nguyen Vu Thieu, Professor of Philosophy and English Grammar at the University of Hanoi.

OBSERVERS

Indian National Science Documentation Centre (INSDOC), New Delhi: Mr. A. L. Gardner (United Kingdom), Unesco Adviser in Scientific Translation.
New Education Fellowship (NEF): Miss Chitra Wickramasuriya (Ceylon), Member of the Council of the National Education Society of Ceylon, Assistant Lecturer in Education, University of Ceylon.
World Organization of the Teaching Profession: Mr. C. S. Ponnuthurai (Ceylon), General Secretary, All-Ceylon Union of Teachers.

UNESCO PUBLICATIONS: NATIONAL DISTRIBUTORS

ALGERIA
Editions de l'Empire,
28 rue Michelet,
ALGIERS.

ARGENTINA
Editorial Sudamericana, S.A.,
Alsina 500,
BUENOS AIRES.

ASSOCIATED STATES OF CAMBODIA, LAOS AND VIETNAM
Librairie Nouvelle Albert Portail,
Boîte Postale 283,
SAIGON.
Sub-depot:
Librairie Albert Portail,
14 avenue Boulloche,
PHNOM-PENH.

AUSTRALIA
Oxford University Press,
346 Little Collins St.,
MELBOURNE.

AUSTRIA
Wilhelm Frick Verlag,
27 Graben,
VIENNA I.

BELGIUM
Librairie Encyclopédique,
7, rue du Luxembourg,
BRUSSELS IV.

BOLIVIA
Libreria Selecciones,
Avenida Camacho 369,
Casilla 972,
LA PAZ.

BRAZIL
Livraria Agir Editora,
rua México 98-B,
Caixa postal 3291,
RIO DE JANEIRO.

CANADA
University of Toronto Press,
TORONTO.
Periodica Inc.,
5112 avenue Papineau,
MONTREAL 34.

CEYLON
Lake House Bookshop,
The Associated Newspapers of Ceylon Ltd., P.O. Box 244.
COLOMBO I.

CHILE
Libreria Lope de Vega,
Calle Estado 54,
SANTIAGO DE CHILE.

COLOMBIA
Emilio Royo Martin,
Carrera 9a, No. 1791,
BOGOTA.

COSTA RICA
Trejos Hermanos,
Apartado 1313,
SAN JOSE.

CUBA
Unesco Centro Regional en el Hemisfero Occidental,
Calle 5 No. 306 Vedado,
Apartado 1358,
HAVANA.

CYPRUS
M. E. Constantinides,
P.O. Box 473,
NICOSIA.

CZECHOSLOVAKIA
Artia Ltd.,
30 Ve Smečkách,
PRAGUE 2.

DENMARK
Ejnar Munksgaard Ltd.,
6 Norregade,
COPENHAGEN K.

ECUADOR
Libreria Cientifica,
Luque 233,
Casilla 362,
GUAYAQUIL.

EGYPT
La Renaissance d'Egypte,
9 Adly Pasha Street,
CAIRO.

ETHIOPHIA
International Press Agency,
P.O. Box 120.
ADDIS ABABA.

FINLAND
Akateeminen Kirjakauppa,
2 Keskuskatu,
HELSINKI.

FORMOSA
The World Book Co. Ltd.,
99 Chung King Rd.,
Section I,
TAIPEH.

FRANCE
Unesco Bookshop,
19 avenue Kléber,
PARIS-16e.

FRENCH WEST INDIES
J. Bocage,
Librairie,
rue Lavoir,
FORT DE FRANCE
(MARTINIQUE).

GERMANY
Unesco Vertrieb für Deutschland,
R. Oldenbourg,
MUNICH.

GREECE
Librairie H. Kauffmann,
28 rue du Stade,
ATHENS.

HAITI
Librairie 'A la Caravelle',
36 rue Roux,
Boîte postale III-B,
PORT-AU-PRINCE.

HONG KONG
Swindon Book Co.
25 Nathan Road,
KOWLOON.

HUNGARY
Kultura, P.O.B. 149,
BUDAPEST 62.

INDIA
Orient Longmans Ltd.,
Indian Mercantile Chamber,
Nicol Road,
BOMBAY.
17 Chittaranjan Ave.,
CALCUTTA.
36-A Mount Road,
MADRAS.
Sub-depots:
Oxford Book and Stationery Co.,
Scindia House,
NEW DELHI.
Rajkamal Publications Ltd.,
Himalaya House,
Hornby Road,
BOMBAY I.

INDONESIA
G.C.T. van Dorp and Co.,
Djalan Nusantara 22,
JAKARTA.

IRAN
Commission nationale iranienne pour l'Unesco,
Avenue du Musée,
TÉHÉRAN.

IRAQ
McKenzie's Bookshop,
BAGHDAD.

ISRAEL
Blumstein's Bookstores, Ltd.,
35 Allenby Road,
P.O.B. 5154,
TEL AVIV.

ITALY
Libreria Commissionaria G. C. Sansoni,
via Gino Capponi 26,
Casella postale 552,
FLORENCE.

JAMAICA
Sangster's Book Room,
99 Harbour Street,
KINGSTON.
Knox Educational Services,
SPALDINGS.

JAPAN
Maruzen Co. Inc.,
6 Tori-Nichome,
Nihonbashi,
TOKYO.

JORDAN
Joseph I. Bahous and Co.,
Dar-ul-Kutub,
Salt Road,
AMMAN.

KOREA
Korean National
Commission for Unesco,
Ministry of Education,
SEOUL.

LEBANON
Librairie Universelle,
Avenue des Français,
BEIRUT.

LIBERIA
J. Momolu Kamara,
69 Front and Gurley Streets,
MONROVIA.

LUXEMBOURG
Librairie Paul Bruck,
33 Grand-Rue.

MADAGASCAR
La Librairie de Madagascar,
TANANARIVE.

**MALAYAN FEDERATION
AND SINGAPORE**
Peter Chong and Co.,
P.O. Box 135,
SINGAPORE.

MALTA
Sapienza's Library,
26 Kingsway,
VALLETTA.

MEXICO
Difusora de las
publicaciones de la Unesco,
Artes 31, int. bajos,
MEXICO, D.F.

NETHERLANDS
N.V. Martinus Nijhoff,
Lange Voorhout 9,
THE HAGUE.

NEW ZEALAND
Unesco Publications Centre,
100 Hackthorne Rd.,
CHRISTCHURCH.

NIGERIA
C.M.S. Bookshop,
P.O. Box 174,
LAGOS.

NORWAY
A/S Bokhjornet,
Stortingsplass 7,
OSLO.

PAKISTAN
Ferozsons,
60 The Mall,
LAHORE.
Bunder Road,
KARACHI.
35 The Mall,
PESHAWAR.

PANAMA
Argencia Internacional
de Publicaciones,
Apartado 2052,
Plaza de Arango No. 3,
PANAMA, R.P.

PERU
Libreria Mejia Baca,
Azangaro 722,
LIMA.

PHILIPPINES
Philippine Education Co.,
1104 Castillejos,
Quiapo,
MANILA.

PORTUGAL
Publicaçoes
Európa-América, Ltda.,
Rua das Flores 45, 1°,
LISBON.

PUERTO RICO
Pan-American Book Co.,
SAN JUAN 12.

SENEGAL
Librairie 'Tous les Livres',
30 rue de Thiong,
DAKAR.

SPAIN
Aguilar, S.A. de Ediciones,
Juan Bravo 38,
MADRID.

SURINAM
Radhaskishun and Co., Ltd.,
(Book Dept.),
Watermolenstraat 36,
PARAMARIBO.

SWEDEN
A/B C.E. Fritzes Kungl.,
Hovbokhandel,
Fredsgatan 2,
STOCKHOLM 16.

SWITZERLAND
Librairie Antoine Dousse,
Ancienne Librairie de
l'Université,
Case postale 72,
FRIBOURG.
Europa Verlag,
5 Rämistrasse,

ZÜRICH.
Sub-depot:
Librairie Payot,
Place Molard,
GENEVA.

SYRIA
Librairie Universelle,
DAMASCUS.

TANGIER
Centre International
(Mr. Marcel Teisseire),
20 rue Molière.

THAILAND
Suksapan Panit,
Arkarn 9,
Rajdamnern Ave.,
BANGKOK.

TUNISIA
Victor Boukhors,
4 rue Nocard,
TUNIS.

TURKEY
Librairie Hachette,
469 Istiklal Caddesi,
Beyoglu,
ISTANBUL.

UNION OF BURMA
Burma Educational
Bookshop,
551-3 Merchant Street,
P.O. Box 222,
RANGOON.

UNION OF SOUTH AFRICA
Van Schaik's Bookstore (Pty)
Ltd.,
P.O. Box 724,
PRETORIA.

**UNITED KINGDOM AND
N. IRELAND**
H.M. Stationery Office,
P.O. Box 569,
LONDON, S.E.1.

**UNITED STATES OF
AMERICA**
Columbia University Press,
2960 Broadway,
NEW YORK 27, N.Y.

URUGUAY
Unesco,
Centro de Cooperación
Cientifica para América
Latina,
Bulevar Artigas 1320,
MONTEVIDEO.

VENEZUELA
Libreria Villegas
Venezolana,
Madrices a Marrón N. 35,
Pasaje Urdaneta,
Local B,
CARACAS.

YUGOSLAVIA
Jugoslovenska Knjiga,
Terazijc 27/II,
BELGRADE.

UNESCO BOOK COUPONS

Unesco Book Coupons can be used to purchase all books and periodicals of an educational, scientific or cultural character. For full information please write to: Unesco Coupon Office, 19 avenue Kléber, Paris-16e, France